ZEN MIND ZEN BRUSH

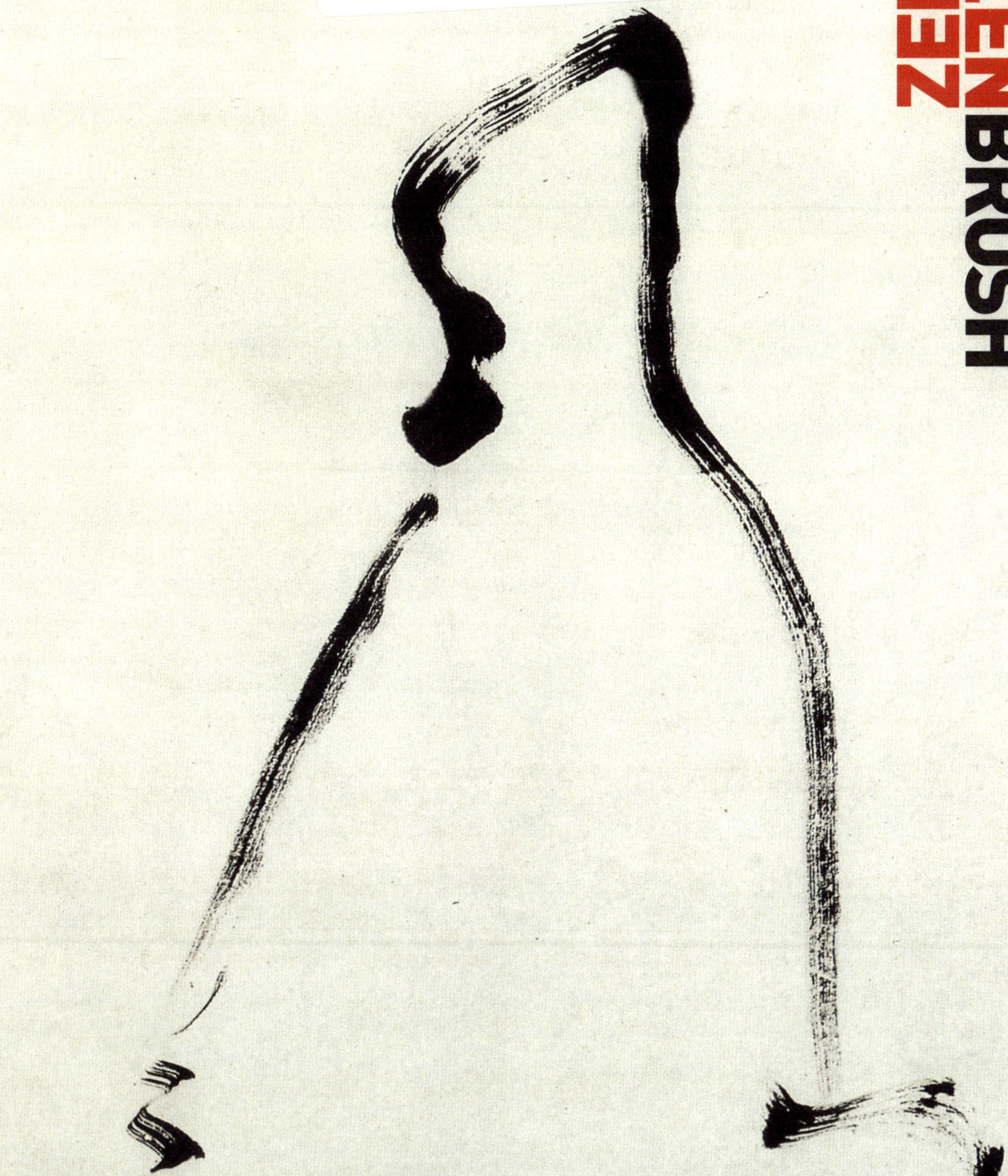

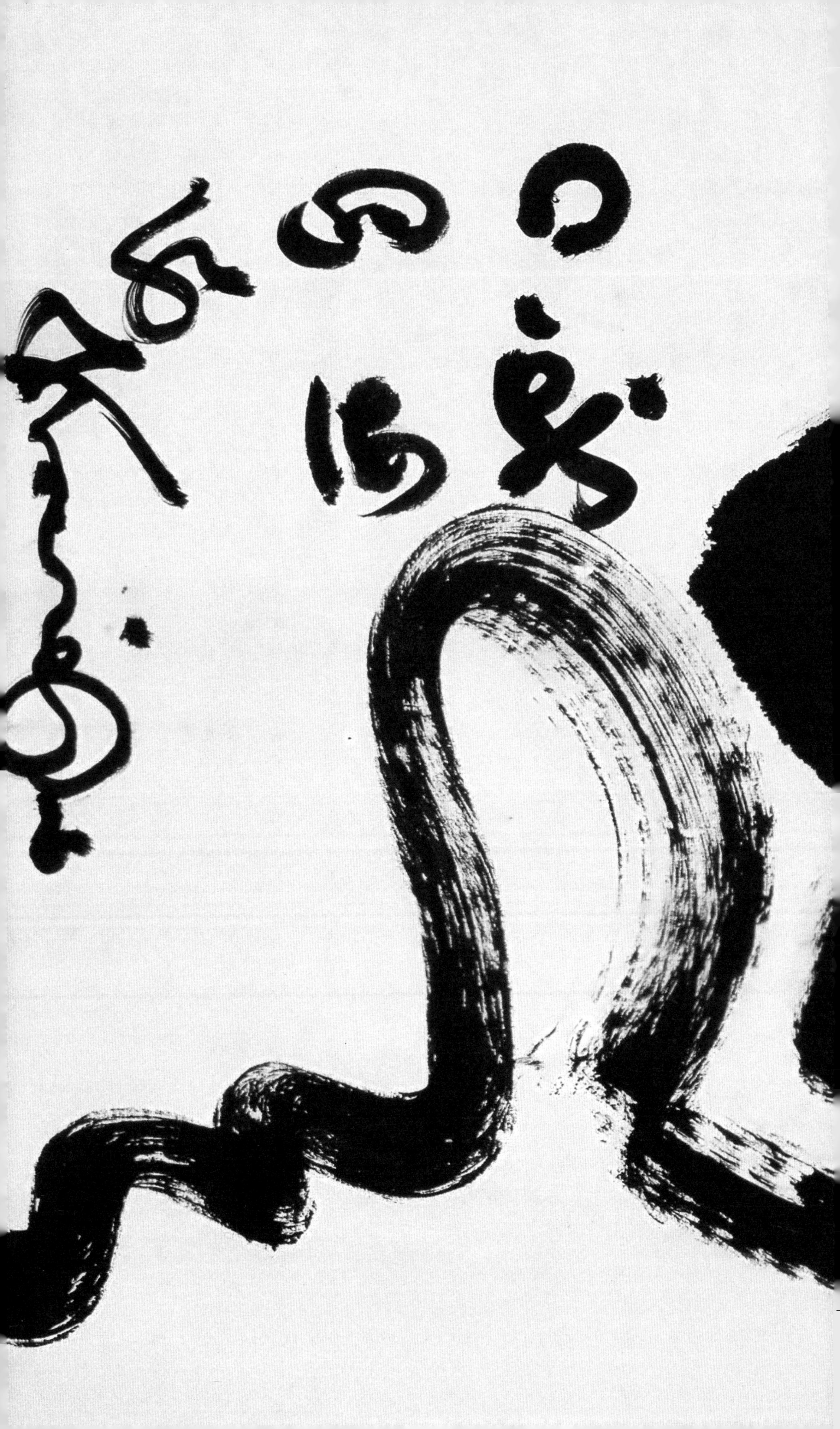

ZEN BRUSH
ZEN MIND

Japanese ink paintings from the Gitter-Yelen collection

禅心禅書

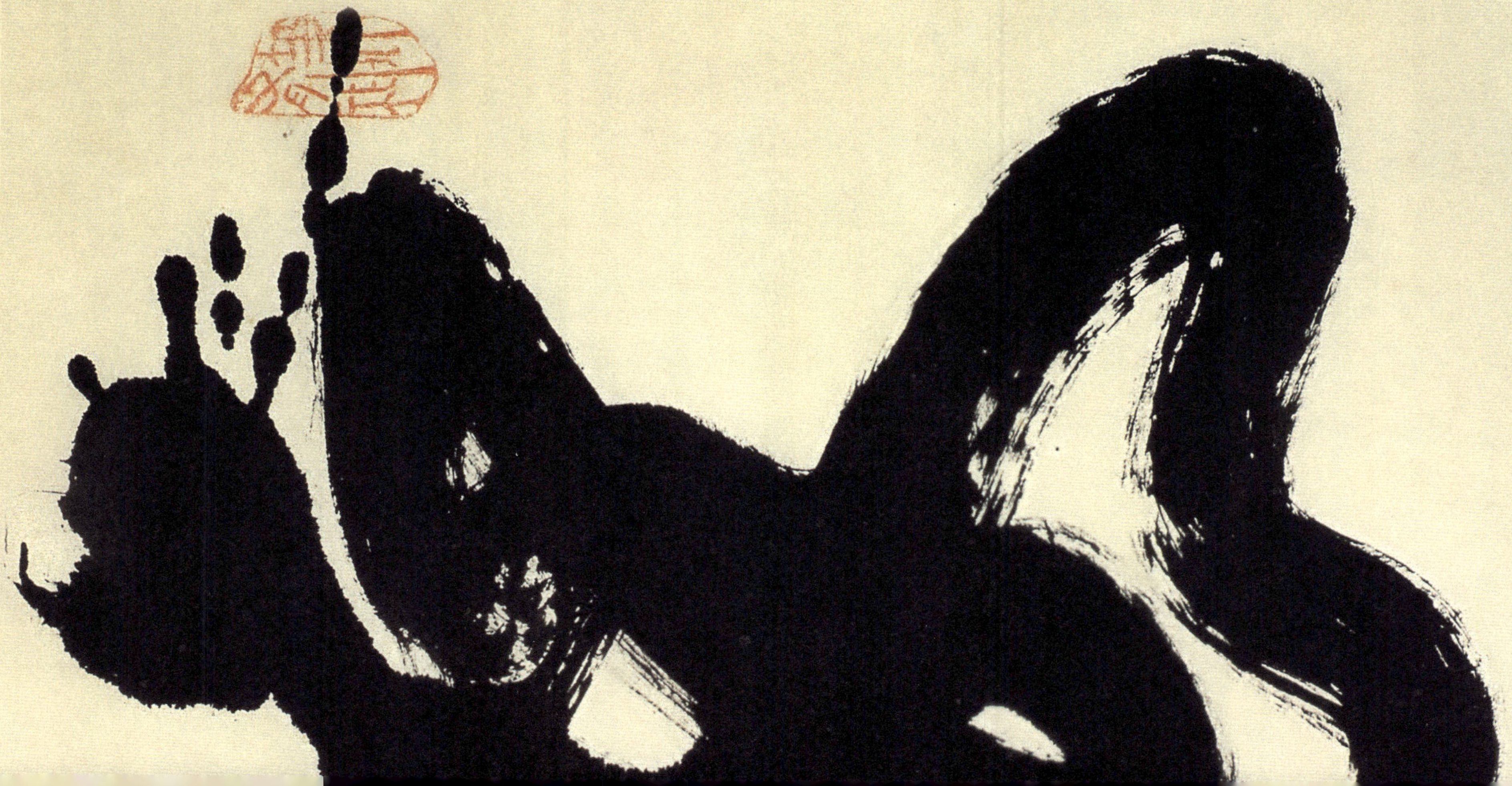

ART GALLERY NSW

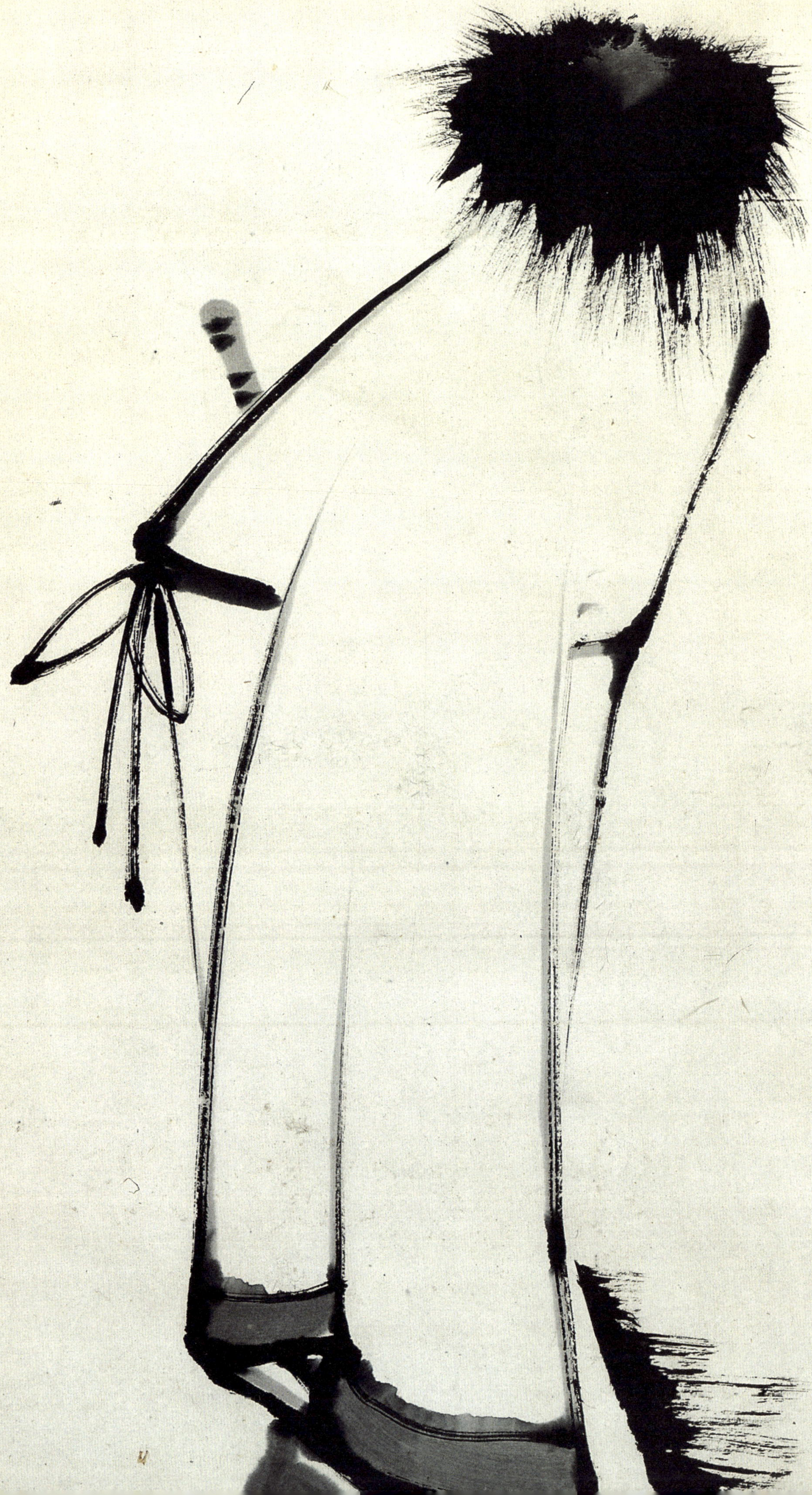

CONTENTS

FOREWORD

One of the most engaging and humorous scrolls in the Gallery's collection of Chinese paintings is Wang Zhen's (1867–1938) *Nine years facing the wall.* The subject is a characteristically grumpy Bodhidharma, the first patriarch of Zen (in China, Chan) Buddhism, who sat in meditation for nine years staring at a blank wall. He had, it could well be said, every reason to feel a little aggrieved at his extended predicament but what indeed is the price of true enlightenment? It is an image that not only richly captures the spirit of the gentle and often light-hearted anarchy of Zen but is also a reminder that whilst Zen as a philosophy, religion and attitude is firmly identified with Japan, its origins lie in China. There can be no surprise that the appealing and enigmatic image of Bodhidharma, Daruma in Japan, is a virtual emblem of Japanese Zen painting.

A glance through this catalogue of classic Zenga by masters of the art demonstrates the great paradox of Zen painting and calligraphy, for here we have expressions of the timeless and the limitless, yet they are at the same time succinct and complete. The sheer bravado and spontaneity of Zen is revealed in this art that is devoid of artifice, reality and knowledge but replete with truth, honesty and a wonderful sense of sheer experience.

At the heart of Zen thought and attitude is the quest to appeal directly to the human spirit; like poetry to avoid the strictures of process, such as mere words and specific imagery, in order to go directly to human nature and instinct. It is a quest that finds its purest expression in the notion of enlightenment, and especially in the peculiarly Zen idea of 'sudden' enlightenment, or *satori*, when the human mind is cleared of all impediments, details and information and relieved of all burdens and can thus lapse into unfettered harmony. It is the antithesis of 'wisdom' or intellectual conceptualisation. There is an air of whimsy in Zen, so manifest in these paintings and calligraphies, which has compelling appeal in our immensely material and accountable cultures of today.

Yet Zen painting and calligraphy has not always been thus. It may be argued that the tradition reached its finest moments in much earlier times, in the 14th and 15th centuries. The art of such masters of the Chinese Song dynasty landscape style as Soami (died 1525), Kenko Shokei (active late 15th century) and Sesshu Toyo (1420–1506) is indisputably more conventional and deferential to its Chinese heritage. It was this sophisticated Chinese-inspired style of monochrome Chan painting, so influentially patronised by the shogunates and, perhaps oddly, by the samurai class in medieval Japan, that laid the foundations for the emergence of the distinctive, abbreviated, populist and secular manner of later Zenga, the tradition which now virtually defines Zen and which is so richly represented in the Gitter-Yelen collection. It is here that those almost contradictory but typically Japanese characteristics of austerity and refinement are embraced with sublime aesthetic satisfaction and an uncanny instinct for the infinite.

Through its spirit of thoughtless spontaneity and its humorous brevity, 'modern' Zen as expressed in painting and calligraphy is easy to grasp, appreciate and instinctively comprehend. It is oddly down to earth and yet conveys, almost surreptitiously, the most profound sensibilities. The simple uncluttered directness of Zenga renders it anti-art. It is imagery that is not made in pursuit of beauty, verisimilitude or material reality but in pursuit of the kind of truth that only naturalness and instinct can inspire. The art of Zenga is the sublime child of the dictum so succinctly expressed by the great master Sengai: 'the true method is no method'.

We are indebted to Dr Kurt Gitter and Alice Rae Yelen and their Gitter-Yelen Art Study Center in New Orleans for their foresight and commitment in developing such a renowned and distinguished collection of Zenga, and for so generously lending these works to our exhibition. This is only the second exhibition devoted to the art of Zen to be held in this Gallery, the first being *Sengai, the Zen master* from the Idemitsu Museum of Art some 20 years ago. Sengai is of course also represented in this exhibition. Our special thanks to Prof John Stevens, who has been responsible for the translations and much of the catalogue material, and to the curatorial consultant Maiko Behr. Here at the Gallery the exhibition has been in the care of Clare Pollard, until recently our curator of Japanese art, and we express our thanks to her and our best wishes in her new role as curator of Japanese art at the Ashmolean Museum in Oxford. Also in the Gallery I express my thanks to our head curator of Asian art, Jackie Menzies; to members of the exhibitions team, Anne Flanagan, Erica Drew and Amanda Green; and for the catalogue design and production to Vivien Sung and Cara Hickman.

To our principal sponsor for this exhibition, Optimal Fund Management, its board of directors and managing director Warwick Johnson, we express our great appreciation for their continuing support of our Asian exhibition programs. Finally we acknowledge our VisAsia group, under the chairmanship of Dr John Yu, which supports the range of the Gallery's Asian programs.

Edmund Capon
Director, Art Gallery of New South Wales

FOREWORD

Zenga – paintings and calligraphy by Zen monks – is a special world with deep, spiritual meaning for practitioners of Zen Buddhism. The focus of my interest in Zenga, however, has always been on the aesthetics of this unique artform.

I grew up in New York and as a young doctor in training was intimately familiar with the avant-garde abstract expressionist movement of the late 1950s and 60s which was thriving there. My appreciation and understanding of the works of artists like de Kooning, Motherwell, Pollock and Kline, with their forceful imagery and dynamic abstraction, made the transition to understanding Zen imagery a natural one.

From 1963–65, I was stationed at Hakata air base on the Japanese island of Kyushu as a flight surgeon in the US air force. My family and I lived in a farming village facing the Sea of Japan. It was there that I learnt to value the rural Japanese way – a life lived in sharp contrast to the urban life I knew in New York City.

My first Zen painting, acquired in 1965, was by the artist Sengai, who had also lived in Kyushu (this painting was later given to the New Orleans Museum of Art, my first museum donation). I began collecting avidly in the 1970s and 80s and continue to do so to this day. Over the course of three decades, I educated myself about Zenga by going to dealers and galleries in Japan. In 1970 little if anything was published in English on the subject. I kept copious notes and photos of all objects and with time learnt to distinguish the visual characteristics of great masters of the Edo period like Hakuin, Sengai and others. Simultaneously, I became increasingly interested in the content of the paintings – the meaning of *koans* and the interpretation of the calligraphy.

Since 1987, my wife Alice and I have also formed a major collection of American folk artists. Our collection highlights the works of self-taught artists whose motivation is often a religious one. Much like the Zen masters, these folk artists create bold expressive works of great individual expression – works that are generally not influenced by the contemporary art world and are created without regard to an art market. Often their primary goal is to teach their students or disciples rather than to gain universal acceptance or financial reward.

On 29 August 2005 hurricane Katrina struck New Orleans with a horrific and unimaginable force. Like many in our community, we suffered severe losses, but ultimately those near and dear to us escaped safely. The survival of this collection, Zen Mind and Spirit, is truly miraculous. The floodwater rose over half a metre in our home and remained there for three weeks. But the water stopped centimetres below the *kura* (treasure house), where the majority of our collection was stored. The artworks (previously selected for this exhibition) remained undamaged, with one exception. A painting of Daruma, the first Zen patriarch, by Shaku Soen (who introduced Zen Buddhism to the West in the 19th century) lay twisted and soaked, unrecognisable on our living room floor. Torn from the wall by the force of the wind, it is included in this catalogue (below) so that its image can persist despite its loss.

These paintings reflect the visual sophistication, culture and beliefs of the individuals who created them from the early 1600s to the present. They have endured through generations in Japan, travelled safely across the seas to New Orleans in the 20th century and have now survived the worst that nature can conjure. Through their survival, their rich historical, religious and artistic context is conveyed to this generation. We are particularly moved and privileged to share these 78 paintings from our collection with the public.

Dr Kurt A Gitter

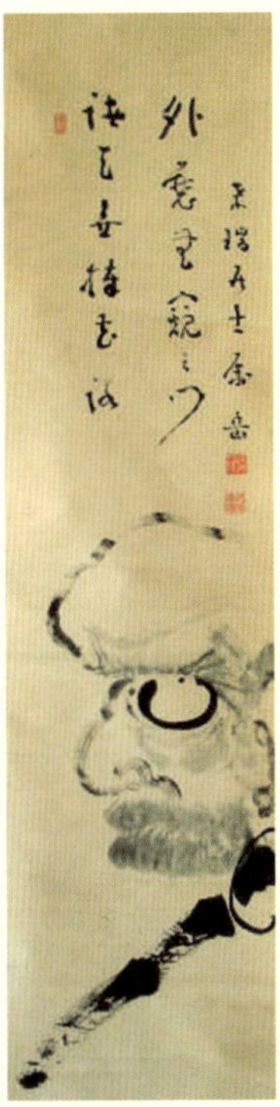

Shaku SOEN (1859–1919)
Daruma
hanging scroll, ink on paper,
201 x 46 cm

The gods have no way to offer flowers;
The demons have no way to peek inside.

The old auspicious philosopher Reigaku

The figure Daruma represents the absolute truth of Zen, a reality so big that neither the gods (who cannot offer flowers because Daruma is beyond sacred or profane) nor the demons (who cannot find a way to discern his essence so they can attack and weaken him) can define. Soen's Daruma is extraordinarily powerful. His eye, enclosed in an *enso*, is fixed directly on the viewer. The signature is intriguing as well – the character here translated as 'philosopher' is *koji,* a term used for a Buddhist layman, but Soen was a high-ranking abbot. Perhaps Soen is suggesting that he longs to be a simple layman again, living in harmony with nature, free of all the posturing and heavy duties required of an abbot.

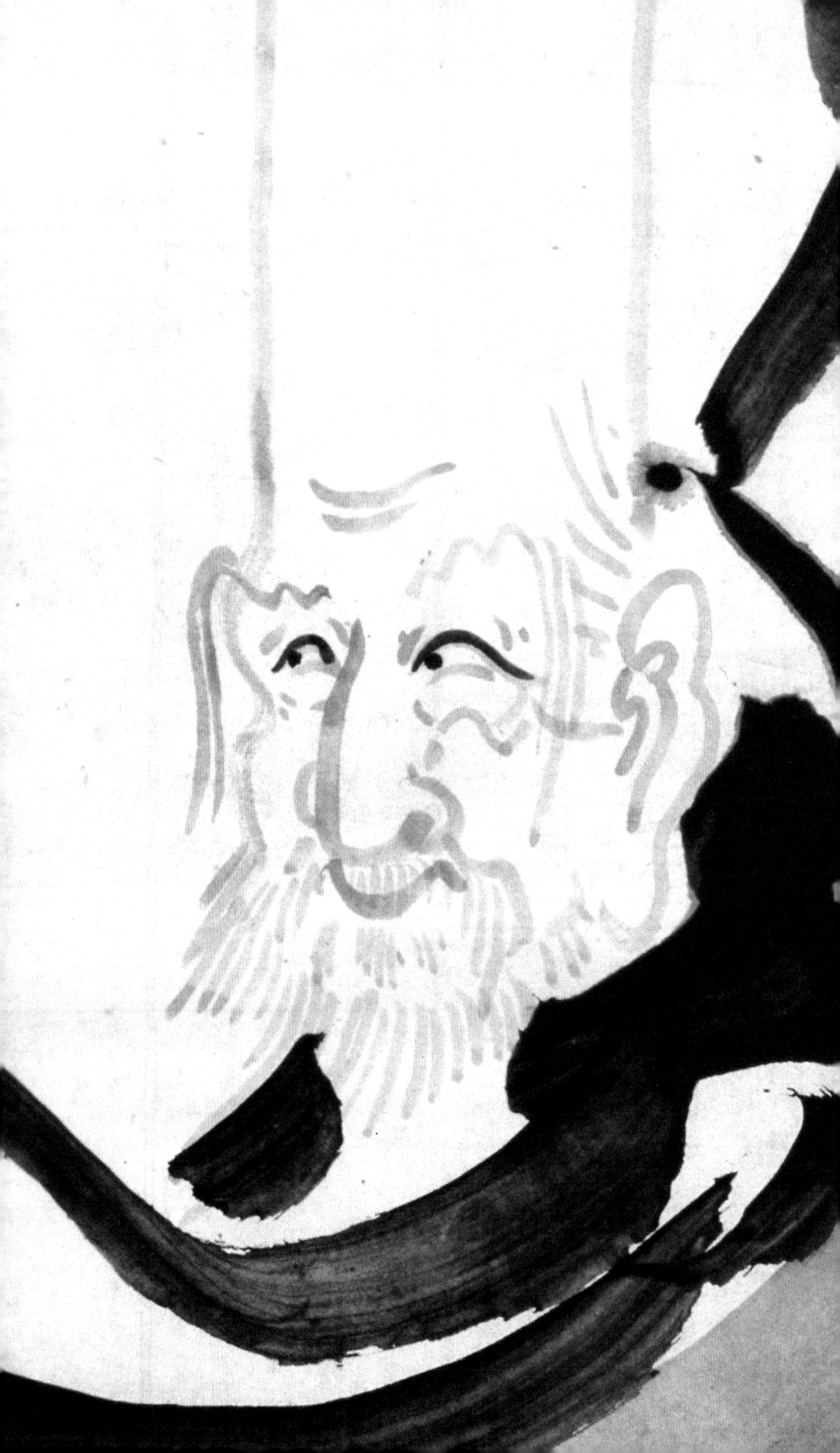

禅
心

ZENMIND

the development of Zen Buddhism

ZENMIND

the development of Zen Buddhism

CLARE POLLARD

There is a great interest in Zen Buddhism in the West, yet many people have only a hazy concept of its nature and origins. They may be familiar with elements of Zen practice such as *zazen* meditation, or with Zen conundrums such as 'the sound of one hand clapping'; they may have an awareness of haiku, the tea ceremony and other Zen-associated arts; or an appreciation of the Zen-influenced writings of the beat poets and the works of abstract expressionist artists such as Robert Motherwell or Franz Kline. But what is Zen Buddhism? Although Zen masters might say that it is something that cannot be described in words, since words themselves can be an obstacle to true understanding, Zen can be considered a religion, a philosophy or a way of life.[1] One way to define Zen is as the meditation school of East Asian Buddhism, whose teachings and practice are transmitted directly through the master-disciple relationship.

Like other schools of Buddhism, Zen is based on the teachings of the Buddha, the Indian nobleman who in the 6th century BCE taught that the way to salvation was through enlightenment – the state of eternal bliss from which one escapes the suffering of existence ('Buddha' simply means 'enlightened' or 'awakened' one). He taught that by clearing our minds of distracting thoughts and material concerns we will awaken to the true 'Buddha-nature' hidden within us. Although words can never adequately capture this state of enlightenment, it has been described as a deep awareness of truth or a joyous feeling of becoming one with the universe.

Unlike many other Buddhist traditions, however, Zen teaches that enlightenment is not to be found in sacred texts or rituals, but through strict meditation. Indeed, Zen is a translation of the Sanskrit term *dhyana*, meaning 'meditation'. Zen is said to have originated with the Buddha, who himself achieved enlightenment after many hours of sitting quietly in meditation. According to legend, the Buddha once gathered his followers around him and instead of giving his usual verbal sermon simply held up a flower in his hand. Only one disciple, Kasyapa, understood this silent message, realising that no words could be a substitute for a living flower. The Buddha then gave Kasyapa the flower, signifying the first Zen transmission. The ideas encapsulated in this 'flower sermon' were handed down from teacher to pupil for 1000 years until the time of the semi-legendary Persian or Indian monk Bodhidharma (known in Japanese as Daruma).

Zen teachings and practice

Accounts of Bodhidharma's life vary, and indeed his very existence is still a subject of debate, but according to Zen tradition he travelled to China in the early years of the 6th century to spread his Zen message. By this time Buddhism was well established in China alongside the indigenous Daoism and Confucianism, and Bodhidharma eventually settled at a Buddhist monastery in Shaolin in northern China. Here he sat in meditation for nine years facing a wall. After this he began to accept pupils and so established the school of Buddhism that would later become known in China as 'Chan' (the Chinese translation of *dhyana*).[2]

Buddhism in 6th-century China was dominated by devotional schools of the Mahayana Buddhist tradition. These schools emphasised sacred scriptures and rituals and offered a host of divine beings to help the faithful achieve enlightenment or rebirth in paradise. Although Bodhidharma's teachings also stemmed from the Mahayana tradition, they differed substantially from those of other sects of doctrinal Buddhism. For he stressed personal enlightenment, rather than the promise of heaven, and taught that awakening can only be the result of one's own efforts – deities and sutras offer only limited assistance. The essential nature of Bodhidharma's message is often summarised in these lines:

A special transmission outside the scriptures
No dependence on words or letters
Zen is a direct pointing to the human heart
See into your nature and become Buddha

The Zen experience of 'becoming Buddha' is known in Japanese as *satori*.[3] It is often described as 'sudden enlightenment', but a Zen practitioner needs to undergo a long and strict training before it can occur. The two primary methods of Zen practice are a form of seated meditation known as *zazen* and the study of paradoxical riddles called *koans*. In *zazen*, which is adapted from the pre-Buddhist Indian tradition of yoga and inspired by the example of the Buddha, the Zen practitioner sits in the lotus posture and uses slow, rhythmic breathing to calm the mind and free it from ideas and chatter until the world can be seen exactly as it is, without being filtered through cloudy thoughts or feelings.[4]

The second key Zen practice is the study of *koans*. The term denotes the bizarre scenes and enigmatic questions that have been used since the early period of Chinese Zen as tools to trigger enlightenment by forcing the mind beyond conventional ways of logical thinking until a breakthrough occurs. One of the best-known *koans* was created by the 17th-century master Hakuin Ekaku: 'Two hands clap and there is a sound. What is the sound of one hand?' *Koans* cannot be solved rationally and the practitioner is obliged to hold the *koan* constantly in mind, day and night, concentrating until the intellectual process gives way under the pressure and reality can be experienced directly.

The development of Zen

Zen (Chan) Buddhism flourished in China, especially with the literati class of officials, scholars, poets and painters. By the 8th century a number of different sects had developed, all sharing a basic approach to meditation and personal instruction but with variations in practice and emphasis. Zen gradually absorbed elements of Daoism and Confucianism, and survived a major persecution of Buddhism in the 9th century that destroyed several other forms of Chinese Buddhism. Only with the success of Neo-Confucianism in the 14th and 15th centuries did it finally lose momentum.

Soon after its establishment in China, Zen began to spread through East Asia to Vietnam, Korea and Japan. Although Buddhism was introduced to Japan in the first great cultural borrowing from China in the 6th century, Zen was largely obscured by other more dramatic and powerful aspects of the new religion. Zen as a distinct Buddhist sect did not emerge in Japan until the late 12th century. At this time, formal contact resumed with China after a break of about three centuries and Japanese Buddhist priests began to travel to China on pilgrimage, where they trained in various Zen centres before returning to Japan to spread the teachings of their respective schools. Two sects of Zen became established in Japan. The larger of these was the Soto sect, which particularly stressed the importance of *zazen*; the second was the Rinzai sect, known for its emphasis on sudden enlightenment and the use of methods such as the *koan* to achieve this end (a third major sect, the Obaku school, was established by émigré Chinese monks in the 17th century).

Zen quickly became a favourite of the samurai warriors, who had recently seized power from the nobility to establish a military government in Kamakura. Zen's simplicity and its emphasis on inner strength and self-discipline were hugely appealing to the samurai, who readily became its champions. The new form of Buddhism also offered the warrior class a way of asserting their cultural independence from the aristocracy, and Zen flourished quietly under the Kamakura shoguns. Then in 1392 the military government at Kamakura was overthrown and another clan of warrior lords, the Ashikaga, established a new military government with its headquarters in Kyoto. The Ashikaga shoguns actively supported Zen Buddhism, and during the two centuries of their rule Zen became the principal religious and cultural force of country. *Daimyo* (feudal lords) and their leading followers were educated in Zen precepts, large monastic complexes were constructed and Zen monks fulfilled not only general priestly duties but also advised the government on matters ranging from governmental policy to foreign relations, trade, scholarship and art. The result was a great flowering of Zen culture – from poetry, theatre, architecture and landscape gardening to calligraphy and painting.

Zen and the arts

Zen is a way of life and for Zen devotees all activity is a form of meditation – whether cleaning, gardening, painting or practising formal *zazen*. Equally, art can be used as a method of visual instruction, to communicate the profundity of Zen enlightenment. For this reason, the arts have often been used as part of Zen training. Perhaps the most direct and important artistic expressions of the Zen spirit are ink painting and calligraphy: in Asia brush-work is considered a direct expression of personal character and it is therefore an ideal vehicle for conveying a Zen master's enlightened vision. However

Zen, with its hallmarks of simplicity, naturalness, harmony and precision, has also had a great influence on many other aspects of Japanese culture.

For instance, many of the finest Japanese landscape gardens, especially dry gardens created from sand and stone, were designed by leading Zen masters. The extreme sparseness of the gardens and their symbolic depiction of nature and the universe within a small area aimed to create an awareness of the meaning of hidden essentials behind outward appearances. Again, in No drama, another Zen-inspired art, all gestures are abstracted by simplification. No does not attempt the illusion of reality: rather, it suggests reality in its essence. Haiku too, a condensed poetic form (17 syllables) that became popular in the 17th century, is particularly Zen – perfectly formed to give the reader momentary flashes of intense awareness or enlightenment.

The tea ceremony, a new way of drinking powdered tea introduced by the Zen monk Eisai in the 12th century, can also be a profound meditative experience. The mind is stilled by simple, harmonious surroundings and precise actions so that one's entire being is totally involved in each moment. Similarly in the martial arts, whether archery, kendo or karate, the student must cultivate an inner balance of mind and an outer mastery of the body so that all movements arise without the intervention of thought. While they can be used for self-defence, the real aim of these martial arts is self-knowledge, leading to enlightenment. All these artforms combine discipline, extreme simplicity and the elimination of all that is unnecessary, so that nothing stands in the way of the intuitive grasp of reality.

'People's Zen'

By the end of the 16th century, the role of Zen Buddhism in Japan – and also the course of Zen art – changed significantly. During this century, civil wars raged between rival clans until the military strongman Tokugawa Ieyasu finally reunited Japan under a central government. The Tokugawa (Edo) period, which was to last until Japan was forced to open to the West in the mid 19th century, marked the end of the official sponsorship of Zen, for the Tokugawa shoguns fostered the strongly hierarchical Neo-Confucianism as the philosophical and ethical basis of their rule. Now Confucian scholars rather than Zen monks educated the ruling elite and advised the government on matters of state. Zen art no longer enjoyed the same degree of official patronage; shoguns, *daimyo* and wealthy samurai who had once turned to Zen artist-monks to decorate their palaces and homes now commissioned flamboyant screens from the professional ateliers of secular painters.

Yet despite the loss of official favour, Buddhism – including the Zen schools – retained an important administrative and social role under the Tokugawa regime, which required all Japanese to register at Buddhist temples. As part of the legally established religious structure of the new age, Zen sects led a peaceful, well-regulated existence. Indeed, Zen gained spiritual strength by being separated from government sponsorship: without high-powered support, Zen's only practitioners were those genuinely committed to its precepts and Zen flourished as a counterculture. Moreover, the Edo period produced some outstanding Zen masters who changed the course of Zen Buddhism. Perhaps the best known is Hakuin Ekaku, represented in this exhibition by 14 works.[5] These extraordinary individuals succeeded in popularising Zen as never before, by travelling through rural Japan among people of all social and economic classes. The major teaching tool and expression of this later 'people's Zen' was the ink painting known as Zenga, the subject of this exhibition.

1. Zen denies all attempts to rationalise it, make sense of it or turn it into a philosophy and compares our desire to grasp it intellectually to a finger pointing at the moon – the finger continually being mistaken for the moon itself

2. The earliest historical record of Bodhidharma (in which he was said to be Persian) was the *Record of the Buddhist monasteries of Luoyang* (*Luoyang qielan ji*), compiled in 547 by Yang Xuanzhi. A later text, the *Continued biographies of eminent monks* (*Xu gaoseng zhuan*), was written in 645 by Dao Xuan. For further information, see *The Zen teachings of Bodhidharma* translated by Red Pine, North Point Press, San Francisco 1989

3. *Satori* literally means 'removing distinctions', for example between this and that, self and others, self and Buddha. It is a sense of oneness with Buddha-nature, a state of being beyond all (mental) discrimination, and a condition with no separation of body and mind

4. The lotus posture is the external sign of enlightenment and Buddhas are most often depicted sitting in this posture

5. Other important early Edo period masters to popularise Zen were Takuan Soho (1572–1645), Munan Shido (1603–1676) and Bankei Yotaku (1622–1693). Although Takuan was a teacher to the Tokugawa Shoguns, he had a wide popular following as well. Munan and Bankei taught a simple form of Zen, based around the concept that we all have Buddha-mind but are unaware of it, and they attracted thousands of followers

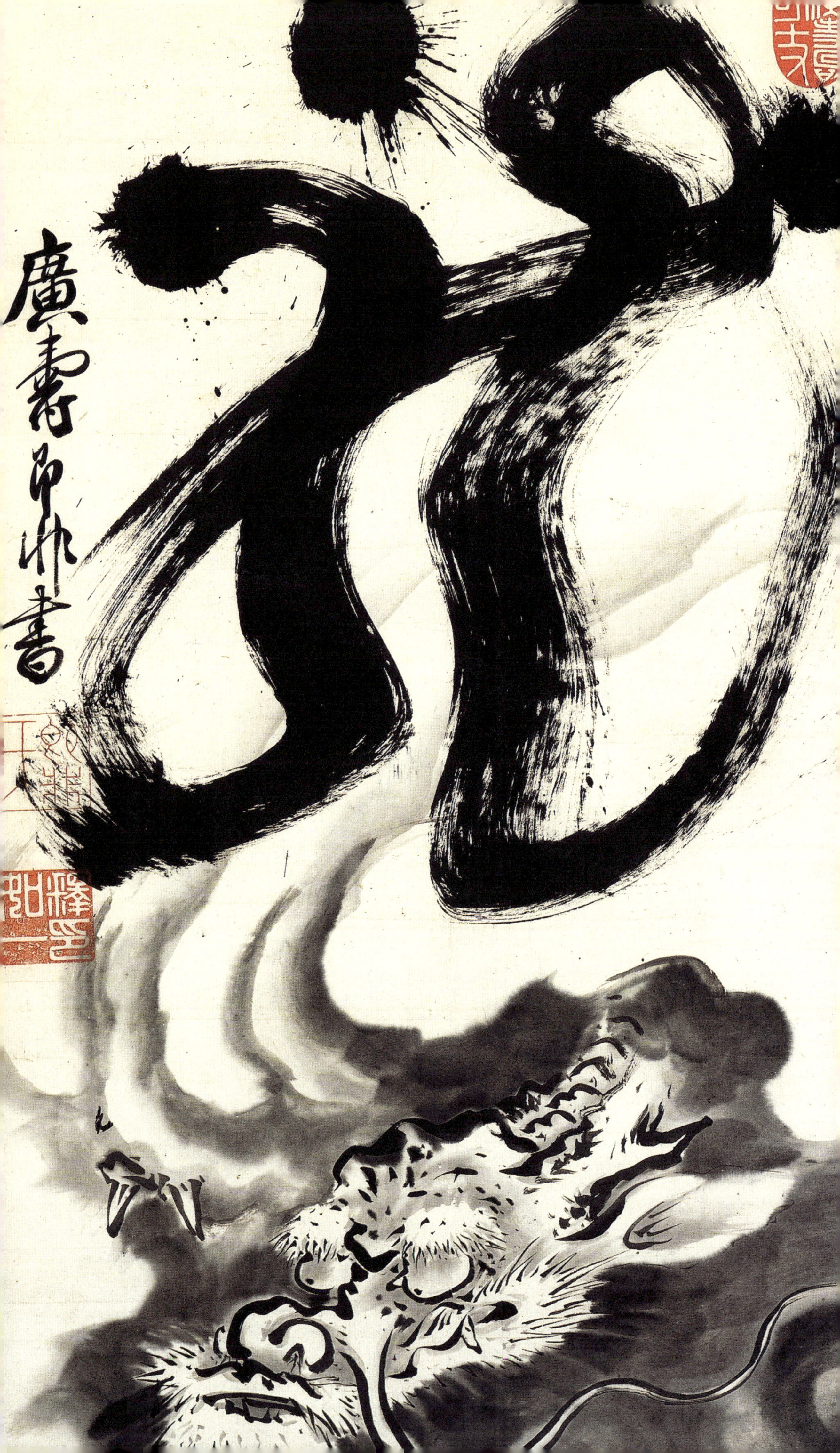
廣壽即非書

禅書

ZEN BRUSH

the development of Zen art

ZEN BRUSH

the development of Zen art

JOHN STEVENS

Zen is the meditation tradition of Buddhism. It began with the profound meditation of Buddha himself and thereafter every practitioner of Zen hoped to experience, at least in part, the same enlightenment that transformed Prince Siddhartha into Buddha more than 2500 years ago in India.

Zen art – the visual manifestation of the Zen mind – first appeared in China. Originally, Buddhist art in China was highly structured and strictly detailed; an image was thought to lose its spiritual efficacy if it deviated in the slightest from the iconographically dictated form. This type of formal art reflected the complex cannons of Buddhist scholasticism.

Bodhidharma, first patriarch and legendary founder of Zen, came from India to China in the 6th century, it is said, to overturn the elaborate superstructure of doctrinal Buddhism. Bodhidharma symbolised the abandonment of all things external and the demand for personal and immediate realisation of the Buddha-mind in the here and now. This is summarised in Zen lore as 'Direct pointing to the human heart; see your nature, become Buddha!' In a celebrated dialogue with the Chinese Emperor Wu (502–49 CE), Bodhidharma expressed the futility of the external manifestations of Buddhism:

> *Emperor Wu:* 'I have built numerous temples, commissioned many sutras, and supported hundreds of monks and nuns. How great is my merit?'
> *Bodhidharma:* 'No merit!'
> *Emperor Wu:* 'What is the first principle of Buddhism?'
> *Bodhidharma:* 'Vast emptiness, nothing holy!'
> *Emperor Wu:* 'Who are you?'
> *Bodhidharma:* 'Don't know!'[1]

Since the emperor could not grasp his (Zen) meaning, Bodhidharma abandoned the palace, miraculously crossed the Yangtze River on a reed and settled in a cave at Shaolin, where he sat facing the wall in meditation for nine years. Paintings based on this legend of Bodhidharma (Daruma in Japanese) eventually became the principal theme of Zen artists, and their inscriptions often reproduce answers taken from his dialogue with the Emperor Wu.

Combined with the ancient Daoist principles of spontaneity, harmony and non-action, Zen teachings inspired Chinese Zen artists to break confining rules, allowing them dynamically to portray the 'heart of things' with only a few vital strokes, using nothing more than a brush, black ink, water and paper or silk. The first recorded Zen painting is an *enso* (circle), brushed in 9th-century China (see the chapter on *enso*, p 126). Portraits of Bodhidharma began to appear a little later. Chanyue (832–912) is considered the first artist to have painted Daruma in the 'Zen style'.

Although the seeds of Zen painting and calligraphy were sown in China, the genre attained full flower in Japan, where it was introduced along with Zen Buddhism in the 12th century. Masterpieces of Zen ink painting were enthusiastically imported to Japan during the 12th and 13th centuries, with the early 13th-century Chinese Zen artists Liang Kai, Muqi and Yintolo becoming particular favourites, and a number of Japanese artists travelled to China to study. The new style of ink monochrome painting became known as *suibokuga.*[2] Calligraphy also became an important Zen tool in Japan, used by masters such as the famous and influential monk Ikkyu Sojun (1394–1481) to convey their teachings.

Here is an example of how Ikkyu used calligraphy as a Zen tool, an example that was followed by countless Zen masters over the centuries. A simple but sincere farmer came to Ikkyu with this question: 'Some priests tell us at death we will go to the paradise of the Pure Land. Others say we will be reborn, becoming a god, human or beast depending on the good and evil we did in life. What is the truth'? Ikkyu brushed this poem in easy-to-read script for the farmer to contemplate.

If there is no one
before your
birth
then there is nowhere
to go at death.

The farmer had the calligraphy mounted as a hanging scroll, and every morning he would meditate before the scroll. One day, he suddenly understood the message: 'Live here and now and don't worry about the rest'.

The early Zen artists in Japan were mainly painter-priests who were associated with the cultural establishments of Kyoto and Kamakura. Receiving their commissions from major temples, important lords and wealthy aristocrats, they painted traditional Buddhist, Zen and Daoist subjects: portraits of Chinese and Japanese patriarchs, figures from the Buddhist pantheon, depictions of nature, calligraphy of sacred texts or profound sayings. Sesshu Toyo (1420–1506), the most famous of the early Japanese Zen painters, entered a Zen monastery at the age of 11. His primary subject was landscape, and he travelled to China more to improve his brushwork than to study Zen. It is said that he would begin a painting session by contemplating the sea and mountains beneath his studio window. After a cup of rice wine, he would play his bamboo flute until his mind was properly composed. Only then would he put his brush and ink to paper.

During the first three centuries of its existence in Japan, Zen was primarily a creed for aristocrats, samurai and the cultured literati. However by the 16th century, Zen monks began to take an active interest in the physical and spiritual welfare of ordinary folk, the 'people's Zen' movement. This shift saw a corresponding shift in Zen art, from an emphasis on art for a select few – as *bokuseki* (ink traces) displayed ostentatiously in major temples or in the rarefied atmosphere of the tea ceremony – to an art for everyone, and marked the real beginning of Zenga, 'brushstrokes of enlightenment'.

Zenga in Japan

Fittingly, this exhibition opens with the work of Fugai Ekun (1568–1654), the first and perhaps greatest of all Zenga artists in terms of artistic quality, spiritual refinement and manifestation of the Zen mind. Not much is known about Fugai's life, other than he was a monk of the Soto sect of Zen Buddhism who spent most of his life wandering the countryside or living in caves, much like Daruma himself and the Chinese patriarchs of old. According to legend, Fugai died on the road at the age of 86. After using his last remaining coins to pay a workman to dig his grave, he entered it and died standing up. Fugai left no temples, no students, no recorded lectures – only some sublime Zenga.

It is not known where he learnt to paint, but Fugai was technically very skilled. His paintings are well composed and remarkably powerful; but they were also an essential part of his Zen life. It is said that when he needed more provisions, Fugai would hang a painting of Daruma outside his cave, which the villagers would take in exchange for rice and vegetables. Although some of Fugai's Zenga were painted for temples and *daimyo* castles, most were given to local farmers, villagers and children.

Although Fugai's life was unconventional, his subject matter was traditional: Daruma portraits, depictions of the jolly Zen monk Hotei and other Zen heroes, self-portraits, scenes from nature and religious calligraphy (*myogo*). Almost all of his paintings were brushed in monochrome, and his poetry was composed and brushed in classical Chinese. It was Hakuin and Sengai (pp 37–55 and pp 56–61) who dramatically expanded the scope of Zenga.

Hakuin Ekaku (1685–1768), considered the greatest religious teacher of the last 500 years, is prominent in Japanese history. One famous story of this virtuous priest tells how the daughter of one of his temple members became pregnant after a secret love affair with a neighbourhood boy. To protect the identity of her lover, the girl blamed the child on Hakuin (Japanese Buddhist priests were notoriously promiscuous; it was easy to make such a charge stick). As soon as the baby was born, the girl's irate father took the infant to Hakuin, bitterly denounced him in public, and demanded that Hakuin raise the child. After the outburst, Hakuin replied calmly, 'Is that so?' and readily accepted the newborn. For several years, Hakuin gently cared for the baby, took him to a wet nurse and carried him on his back during begging rounds, silently enduring the scorn of the local populace. Unable to bear the injustice further, the girl finally confessed the truth to her father, who ran to beg Hakuin's forgiveness. Hakuin simply said, 'Is that so?' and handed the child back without ever mentioning the incident again.

Much of the interest in Hakuin is centred on his attempted reform of the Rinzai sect of Zen Buddhism and his voluminous written works (one of which, the *Hebi ichigo*, was banned by the authorities because it was so critical of the powers that be). However his paintings and calligraphy have always attracted the most attention. Recently there has been an increasing international awareness that Hakuin's paintings and calligraphy are as important to world cultural history as the art of Rembrandt or William Blake. The real treasure Hakuin bequeathed to humankind was his enormous corpus of Zenga.

In his youth Hakuin was adept at brushwork, yet after viewing a piece of calligraphy by a Zen master he is said to have burnt his brushes and painting manuals in the belief that 'the only way to create such profound brushwork is to be enlightened'. It was not until his mid 50s that Hakuin felt confident of his own state of 'Zen mind' to paint seriously again. In the last three decades of his life, Hakuin produced a vast number of pieces on an extraordinary variety of subjects. He brushed traditional themes – sometimes in colour – in a strikingly fresh, highly personalised manner, drawing inspiration from other schools of Buddhism, Confucianism, Shintoism, Daoism, Chinese and Japanese folklore and scenes from everyday life. Hakuin's subjects included Buddha, Daruma, Hotei and Kannon and the Chinese and Japanese patriarchs, as well as courtesans, farmers, fishermen and children. In his compositions he used many kinds of plants, animals, birds, fish and insects, producing keen and careful observations of (Buddha) nature in all its manifestations. Like Ikkyu, Hakuin's works often contained veiled criticism of social injustice brought about by the excessive and ostentatious spending of the ruling classes. As well as quotations from Buddhist texts, his calligraphy embraced nursery rhymes, popular ballads, comic verse and bawdy songs from the geisha quarters.

In a sense, Hakuin's work was 'anti-art', not something consciously created to be 'beautiful'. Hakuin never corrected mistakes or omissions in his calligraphy and if the pieces had drips, splashes or cat's paw tracks on them, so much the better. Many of his finest works were created with semi-congealed ink that most other artists would have thrown away. Paper was precious in those days so Hakuin used practice sheets for finished pieces, nonchalantly painting right on top of brief sketches and outlines, creating a kind of three-dimensional effect on many of his works (pp 44–45).

In addition, Hakuin expanded the realm of Zen practice among the general public. Buddhism has always emphasised renunciation of the world so until Hakuin's time, Zen training was largely restricted to monks. Of course Hakuin had hundreds of monastic disciples but he also had many lay students, ranging from young girls to grandmothers, from samurai lords to farmers, craftspeople and merchants, even pleasure girls from the nearby red-light district. It seems that he sanctioned some 80 of his monastic and lay disciples to spread Hakuin-style Zen throughout the country.

Sengai Gibon (1750–1837) was abbot of Shofukuji in Kyushu. Like Hakuin, many anecdotes have been handed down about him, although perhaps the best known is this: Sengai had a brilliant but wayward disciple named Tangen. Almost every evening after the day's final meditation, Tangen secretly scaled the temple wall and headed straight for the red-light district. One night as Tangen climbed back over the wall at the customary spot, he stepped on something soft and warm instead of the usual propped up rocks.

It was too dark to see what is was, but the next morning when Tangen was told that Sengai was indisposed due to a terrible headache, Tangen realised that the master had been his human ladder. Full of remorse, Tangen mended his ways.

Founded in 1195, Shofukuji was the oldest Zen temple in Japan but over the centuries, its fortunes had declined. During his time as abbot Sengai gradually restored most of the temple's buildings. His work largely complete, Sengai resigned at the age of 61 and spent the next quarter of a century leading a happy-go-lucky life, freely associating with all manner of people – lords and vagrants, aristocratic ladies and prostitutes – and instructing everybody through the medium of Zen art with a delightful combination of worldly and transcendental wisdom. Although he once complained that 'people must think my hermitage is a toilet because they bring so much paper here', Sengai rarely turned down a request for a sample of his visual Zen teachings. Sengai's motto: 'Worldly painting has a method; Sengai's paintings have no method. As Buddha said, "The true Law is no Law"'.

Like Hakuin, Sengai painted a huge number of pieces on every imaginable subject. When parishioners came to ask for counsel (and typically for a specimen of his brushwork as well) Sengai often used the people themselves as his subject matter. Once Sengai drew a painting of a woman thrashing her three children with the inscription, 'You are not only abusing your children. Sengai too is oppressed by your excessive demands. I have brushed this to put an end to both'. On another, he painted the figure of a man with this inscription, 'This is Mr Iwane bringing me some boiled beets to exchange for a painting'. A haughty samurai named Kenyu refused to leave Sengai's hermitage without a painting. Sengai brushed two big round circles. When the samurai asked the significance, Sengai added this inscription, 'Kenyu [really has a lot of] balls'. Sengai expanded the realm of Zenga by including the erotic aspects of life. While there is an erotic undercurrent in many of Hakuin's paintings (which for some reason many Japanese researchers refuse to acknowledge), in Sengai's art sex was out in the open. Sengai insisted that (Buddha) nature has a physical side that cannot be ignored or explained away, and his cartoons show people (and gods) passing gas, answering the calls of nature and warming their testicles. A self-portrait depicts Abbot Sengai squatting in a field defecating, while the inscription jokes, 'I hope no one comes!' Sengai painted Monju Bosatsu, the bodhisattva of wisdom, with an erection, adding this verse, 'A treasure to be fully activated!' Another of his paintings depicts a man thoughtfully offering his giant penis to a lovely Shinto goddess marooned on a lonely island. Sengai put this inscription on a painting of a beauty: 'A face lovely as a peach blossom, A heart full of passion, A seductive perfumed body worth its weight in gold, She is an incarnation of the Goddess of Compassion'. Sengai even did a painting of a couple making love, on which he inscribed, 'This is the original form of interpenetration with the cosmos: a Buddhist practice to harmonise the two roots; naked, climb the opposite peak and achieve non-dual union'. Sengai composed this Zen poem: 'Falling in love is dangerous, for passion is the source of illusion; yet being in love gives life flavour and passions themselves can bring one to enlightenment'.

To this day, many Japanese families that have had such Hakuin and Sengai scrolls handed down as heirlooms display them reverently on special occasions, and the scrolls continue to inspire and instruct. Sengai's Zenga are perhaps better known in the Western world than Hakuin's, thanks to the Idemitsu Museum of Art, which has exhibited its large Sengai collection outside Japan on many occasions – for example, in the USA in 1956 and at the Art Gallery of New South Wales in 1985. There are also several books in English on Sengai. His *Circle, triangle, square* is the most famous and widely reproduced Zenga in history.

Zenga as a teaching vehicle

Fugai, Hakuin and Sengai firmly established painting and calligraphy as a medium for teaching Zen. Hakuin had a seal that read 'paintings to liberate beings' (*hojo-e*); another term used to describe such paintings is *e-seppo*, 'visual sermons' (Tibetan Buddhists say the same thing about their *thangka* paintings; that they are for 'liberation through beholding', serving as a visual guide and help in meditation). As a Zen priest and scholar I have dutifully read (and translated a few of) the hundreds of Buddhist sutras and Zen textbooks that exist, but by far I have gained most from my study, contemplation and enjoyment of Zenga. It is my contention that after Fugai, Zenga became the primary teaching vehicle of Japanese Zen Buddhism. Zenga as visual sermons have much greater accessibility than dry, largely incomprehensible texts, and their impact is immediate and long lasting, even if the meaning is not at first clear. Zenga can be studied generation after generation, the inspiration remaining fresh; we can, in a real sense, still encounter masters like Fugai, Hakuin and Sengai 'face-to-face' in their art, which was the intention when they created their Zenga. Today people all over the globe have access to Zenga and refreshingly, unlike much Asian art that was, and is, in fact 'loot', Zenga was meant to be exported to the far corners of the world. The 19th-century master Yamaoka Tesshu, for example, wanted to produce a Zenga for each human being.

Following the example of Hakuin and Sengai, it became de rigueur for Zen meditation masters to do most of their teaching through the medium of brush and ink, and this exhibition includes works from successive generations of several Zen traditions, notably Rinzai, Soto and Obaku Zen. Works in the Hakuin monastic line show clearly the master's artistic influence on each painting; yet the brushwork, tonality and line quality of each artist are quite distinct, demonstrating that Zenga reflects the inner vision of each Zen master. Other Rinzai lines differed in style to the Hakuin line. The Soto tradition is different again, and there is one work by a Chinese émigré monk Sokuhi (pp 74–77) of the Obaku sect, which was founded by Chinese émigré monks in the 17th century and maintained a distinctly Chinese style. There are also scrolls by Zen laymen Konoe Nobutada, Ito Jakuchu and the greatest Zenga artist of modern times, the lay Zen master Yamaoka Tesshu.

It is important to note that Zenga means 'Zen-inspired calligraphy and painting'. It is not limited to art produced by monastic or lay practitioners of the three Zen sects in Japan mentioned above. Zenga has little to do with sectarian affiliation. Two of the greatest Zenga artists were from different schools of esoteric Buddhism: Jiun Sonja Onko (1718–1804), a Shingon monk, and Gocho Kankai (1749–1835), a Tendai abbot and miracle worker. In this exhibition we also have a painting by a Pure Land sect nun, Otagaki Rengetsu, and calligraphy by the modern folk artist Munakata Shiko.

Interpreting and appreciating Zenga

There is one framed Zenga in this exhibition (*Daruma*, by Nakahara Nantenbo, no 60) but the other works are mounted as hanging scrolls, called *kakejiku* in Japanese. Scroll-making in Japan is a fine art, and much care is taken in selecting the right fabric and background colours to bring out the best in the work of art. Some of the mountings in this exhibition are very simple and inexpensive, some are elaborate and costly; some are over a hundred years old, some are brand new. All are different. The scroll would be hung in the temple or home alcove (*tokonoma*) to be contemplated. Smaller scrolls like the *Lotus pond Kannon* (no 7) by Hakuin, would be placed in a home altar (*butsudan*) as objects of veneration, to be prayed to every morning and evening. Certain calligraphies, such as the name of a Buddha or Shinto god (see no 28 by Torei Enji), or a calligraphic dragon (no 58 by Tesshu), served as good-luck charms and talismans. Other forms of Zenga were usually rotated in the alcove, depending on the owner's mood or the season, or for visitors to enjoy. Tea ceremony instructors needed a large stock of scrolls, preferably Zenga from Daitokuji monks, for their different venues.

In *Zen and the fine arts* (1971), the philosopher and Zen calligrapher Hisamatsu Shin'ichi distinguished seven characteristics of Zen art: asymmetry, simplicity, lofty dryness, naturalness, subtle profundity, detachment and tranquillity. Other scholars, such as Terayama Tanchu, feel that *bokki*, 'the degree of *ki* [vital energy] in the ink' is most important. This vital energy can be studied in terms of clarity, liveliness, intensity, substance, sensitivity, suppleness, extension, and, lastly, technical competence. I like to savour Zenga in terms of the artist's state of mind and his or her manifestation of enlightenment through the vehicles of brush, ink and paper. Zenga is an expression of the Buddha-mind, a form of Zen activity. A master's Zen mind permeates, and radiates from, the work of art. There is something timeless about Zen art: it is difficult to tell if a Zen circle was brushed yesterday or hundreds of years ago, and it does not really matter. Another example: a depiction of a train on a railroad line in the midst of a traditional Chinese or Japanese landscape painting would be jarring, but in Zenga even modern inventions can easily be incorporated. I once organised a Zenga exhibition with about 40 scrolls, including a painting by Tesshu of a steamboat, a modern contraption that caused a sensation when it first appeared in Japan in the 19th century. Yet that Zen steamboat, certainly not a traditional theme in most Buddhist art, complemented the other Zenga and did not seem at all out of place. The message of a Zenga is universal, transcending cultural borders.

All of these characteristics are factors in appreciating Zenga, but above all it is an individual and personal process. Every Zenga has something to teach us; the first and best approach is to take in the whole work of art: the flow of energy in the brushstrokes, the dynamic shape of the characters or painting, the thrill of encountering this particular master heart-to-heart. From the earliest days of brush art in China, it was felt that the best paintings were 'seals of the mind' that created an environment where viewer and viewed became one. Eventually, we need to try to understand the meaning of the painting, its Zen Mind, and decipher the words written there as best we can. But this too is a full body experience. The heart of a Zenga, its inner meaning, lies beyond words; like Zen itself, a Zenga must be contemplated, enjoyed and comprehended with one's entire being.

1. Unless otherwise cited, the various Zen stories referred to in this catalogue exist in numerous versions and can be found commonly within the literature on Zen and Zen painting. Note also that Zen masters were often extraordinarily well-read scholars with an impressive command of thousands of Chinese characters, including many obsure Buddhist terms, so their calligraphy and inscriptions can be very difficult to read. Most masters also had their own idiosyncratic calligraphic style, again difficult to decipher. This is coupled with the fact that Zen artists are recalling texts from memory when they are doing brushwork, and that occasionally leads to mistakes in order or the wrong characters; errors that Zen artists are loathe to correct since mistakes are part of the creative process! In short, while the readings given here are based on the best and most recent scholarship, it is impossible to be 100% accurate in all cases

2. Early Japanese pioneers of Zen art were Kao (d1345), Mokuan (d1345), Tesshu Tokusai (d1366), Jakushitsu Genko (1290–1367), Josetsu (1386–1428), Gyokuen Bonpo (1349–1420), Kichizan Mincho (1350–1431) and Tensho Shubun (d1463)

Lineages of Zenga artists represented in the exhibition

RINZAI ZEN

RINZAI: HAKUIN LINE
HAKUIN Ekaku
(1685–1768)

SUIO Genro 遂翁元盧
(1716–1789)

TOREI Enji 東嶺円慈
(1721–1792)

REIGEN Eto 霊源慧桃
(1721–1785)

KOGAN Gengei 弘巌玄猊
(1748–1821)

SHUNSO Joshu 春叢紹珠
(1750–1839)

SOZAN Genkyo 蘇山玄喬
(1799–1888)

KOKAI Jiko 臣海慈航
(1800–1874)

Yamaoka TESSHU 山岡鉄舟
(1836–1888)

Nakahara NANTENBO 中原南天棒
(1839–1925)

SHOUN, Sohan Genpo 松雲、宗般玄芳
(1848–1918)

DEIRYU Kutsu 泥龍窟
(1895– 1954)

ROZAN Eko 盧山恵行
(1865–1944)

Yamamoto GENPO 山本玄峰
(1886–1961)

RINZAI KOGETSU SCHOOL
SENGAI Gibon 仙厓義梵
(1750–1837)

SEISETSU Shucho 誠拙周樗
(1745–1820)

RINZAI OTHER
DAISHIN Gito 大心義統
(1656–1730)

DAIDO Bunka 大道文可
(1680–1752)

Ashizu SEKIREN
(1850–1924) 蘆津石蓮

Hashimoto DOKUSAN 橋本獨独山
(1869–1938))

Seki SEISETSU 関精拙
(1877–1945)

SOTO ZEN

FUGAI Ekun 風外慧薫
(1568–1654)

GESSHU Soko 月舟宗胡
(1618–1696)

CHINGYU Zuiko 珍牛瑞岡
(1743–1822)

RYOKAN Daigu 良寛大愚
(1758–1831)

MOTSUGAI Fusen 物外不遷
(1794–1867)

OBAKU ZEN

Obaku SOKUHI 黄檗即非
(1616–1671)

ZEN LAYMEN

Konoe NOBUTADA 近衛信伊
(1565–1614)

Ito JAKUCHU 伊藤若冲
(1716–1800)

SHINGON BUDDHISM

JIUN Sonja Onko 慈雲飲光
(1718–1804)

TENDAI BUDDHISM

GOCHO Kankai 豪潮寛海
(1749–1835)

PURE LAND BUDDHISM

Otagaki RENGETSU 太田垣蓮月
(1791–1875)

FOLK ART

MUNAKATA Shiko 宗像志功
(1903–1975)

Daruma (Bodhidharma), the legendary first patriarch, is Zenga's most important icon. Daruma may have been an actual historical figure who travelled from India to China in the 6th century, but in Zenga he represents penetrating insight and realisation – the mind of Buddha. Daruma is almost always depicted as a half-body: according to a Zen saying 'Daruma [Truth] is so big that he can only be portrayed in a half-body'. In many Daruma portraits, his half-body is formed out of the character *kokoro* (mind), and that is how we are to look at a portrait of the patriarch: we must enter into the heart of the painting and grab Daruma's essence.

Often Daruma looks directly at the viewer but here he gazes intensely into the distance. His field of vision seems very wide, taking everything in, missing nothing: the eyes of enlightenment (the eyes are the last element to be brushed into a Daruma painting).

It is a fine painting by any standard, but it is the Zen energy projected in this work that makes us feel that this really is a portrait of Daruma, a visual expression of the Zen mind. As with most Fugai paintings, which were drawn on coarse paper and hung in smoky farm-houses for centuries, the condition is poor but the ink tones remain rich and bright. There is no inscription, unusual for Fugai, since most of his paintings carry his inscription or one by another Zen master. However, there is plenty of space for an inscription, and it is not impossible that someone bold and enlightened will come along and add one!

The true value of Zenga was not recognised until recently. At some time in the past, a misguided art dealer effaced Fugai's original seal on the upper right side and added a false 'Nobutada' seal in the lower right corner, no doubt in the hope of getting a better price. [1]

1. The courtier Konoe Nobutada (1565–1614) was a celebrated calligrapher, painter and poet. See p 78

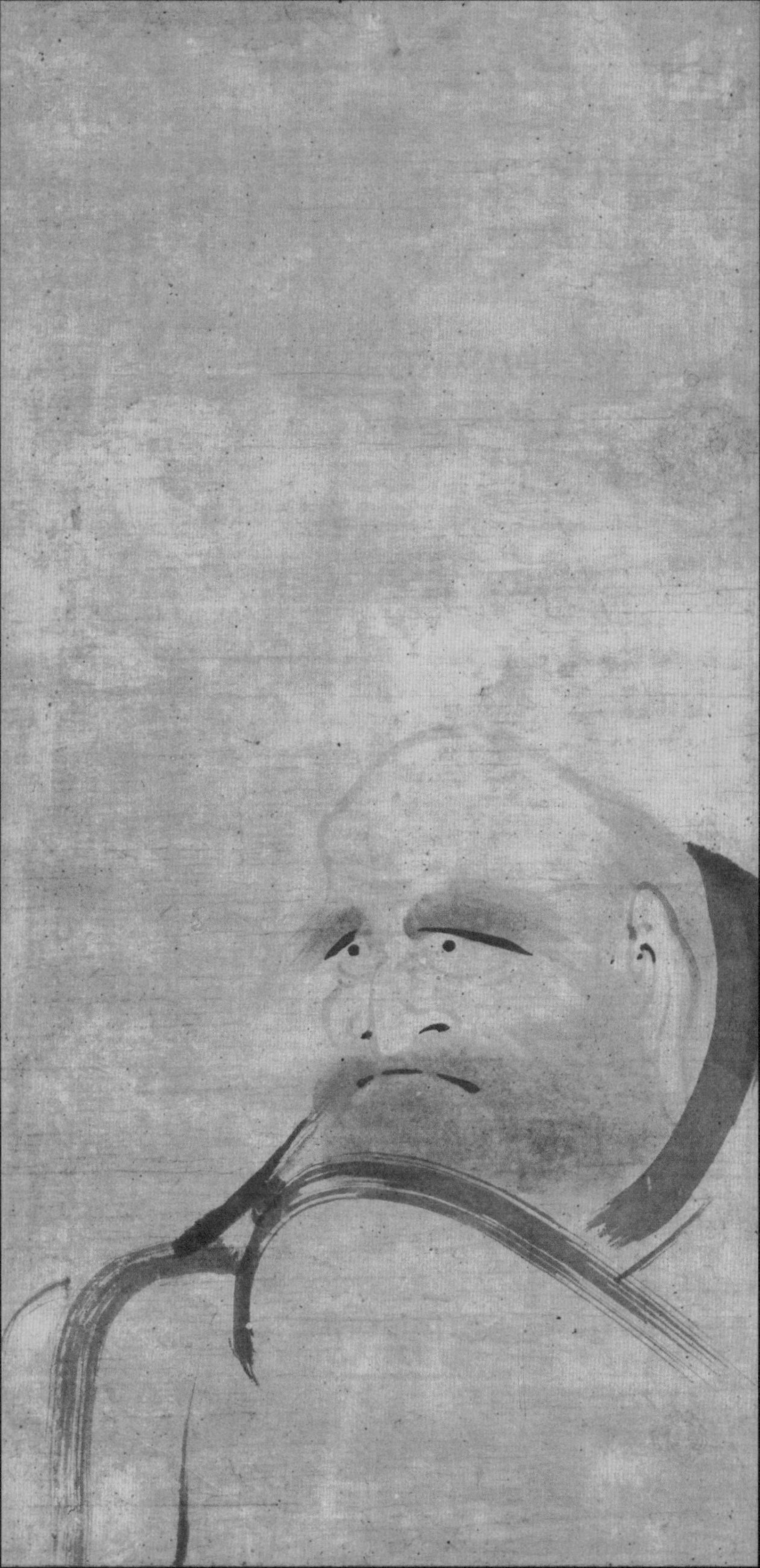

1
FUGAI Ekun (1568–1654)
Half-body Daruma
hanging scroll, ink on paper,
63.5 x 30.5 cm

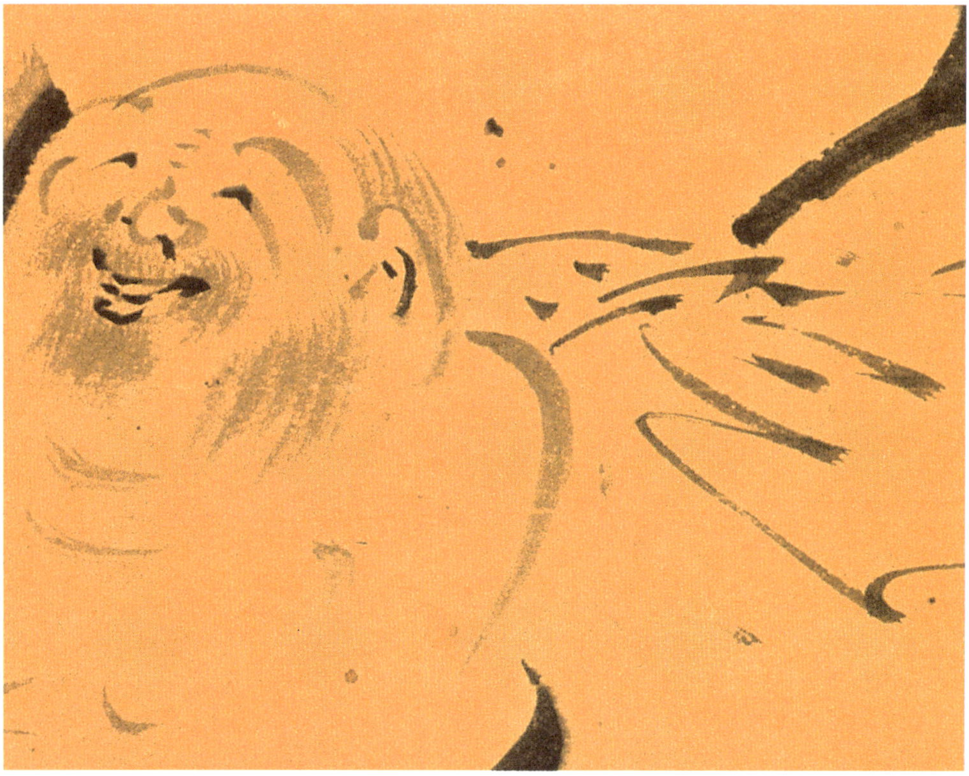

In addition to his Daruma portraits, Fugai is best known for his paintings of Hotei, the Zen vagabond who symbolises freedom from worldly cares and enlightenment in the midst of everyday life. Like Daruma, Hotei is a partly historical, partly legendary figure. Historically, Hotei was a good-natured, fat-bellied 10th-century Chinese hobo monk. Despite his appearance, he was believed by some to be an incarnation of Maitreya, the Buddha of the Future. Hotei eventually became a popular folk god of good luck in China and Japan.

Here Fugai has depicted Hotei resting on his sack of goodies, with his staff nearby, gaily pointing to the moon. 'The moon represents our mind, but do not mistake the finger [methods] for the reality of the moon [enlightenment]', Hotei is telling us. His big smile seems to say, 'and do not forget to enjoy yourself!' The moon is not shown but it is present; one needs to see it with a Zen mind.

The composition is technically outstanding. With minimum strokes, Fugai has deftly brought Hotei to life. Every brushstroke has a purpose, and this is characteristic of good Zenga in general. Like Fugai's *Half-body Daruma* (no 1), there is no inscription, but that is perhaps because it would obstruct our search for the moon.

風
外

Fugai

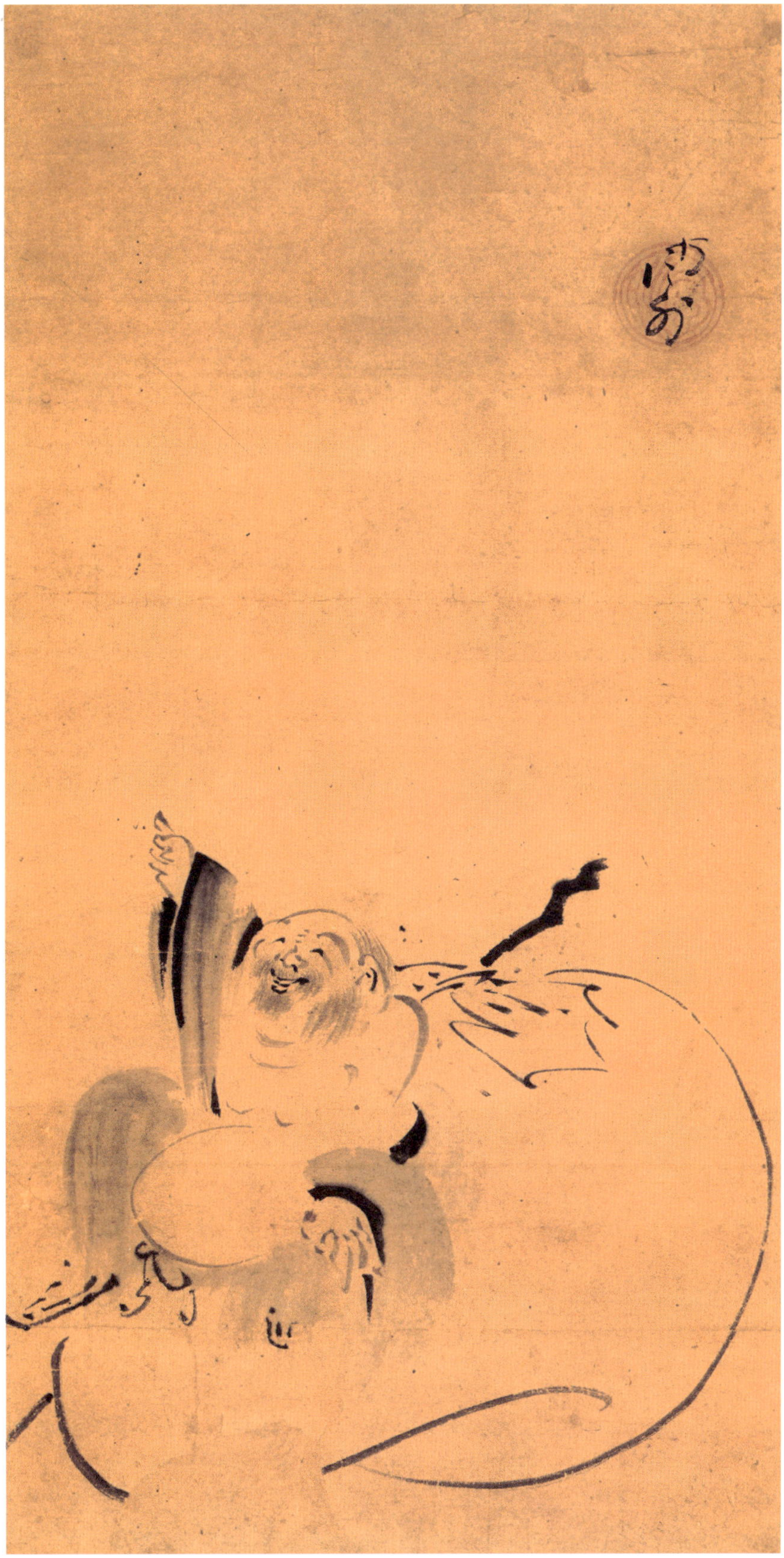

2
FUGAI Ekun (1568–1654)
Smiling Hotei
hanging scroll, ink on paper,
47.3 x 23.9 cm
(left) detail

讃共風外図之
吾生涯是沈吟
那月白又風高

Yes, the moon is bright and the wind splendid,
But here I am bemoaning my fate.

Inscription and painting brushed by Fugai

Hotei represents enlightenment within everyday life, and, as taught in Buddhism's first principle, everyday life is unavoidably incomplete, imperfect, suffering. The famous Zen saying, 'Every day is a good day', also means 'Every day is a bad day'. Even mirthful Hotei sometimes feels down, and it is the genius of Zen to be able to paint him in both moods. This frowning Hotei also points to the moon, but a moon that is behind him, as if to say, 'true enlightenment has passed me by'. The moon remains bright and the winds refreshing no matter how we feel, so the problem is in our minds and not in the realm of Buddha-nature, which is eternal and pure.

The brushwork here is even finer than in the *Smiling Hotei* (no 2); the frown is deep, just as the smile on the other painting is wide. Taken together these two aspects of Hotei teach an important Zen lesson: 'Accept equally the good with the bad, just avoid clinging to one or the other state'.

3
FUGAI Ekun (1568–1654)
Frowning Hotei
hanging scroll, ink on paper,
52.2 x 21.6 cm

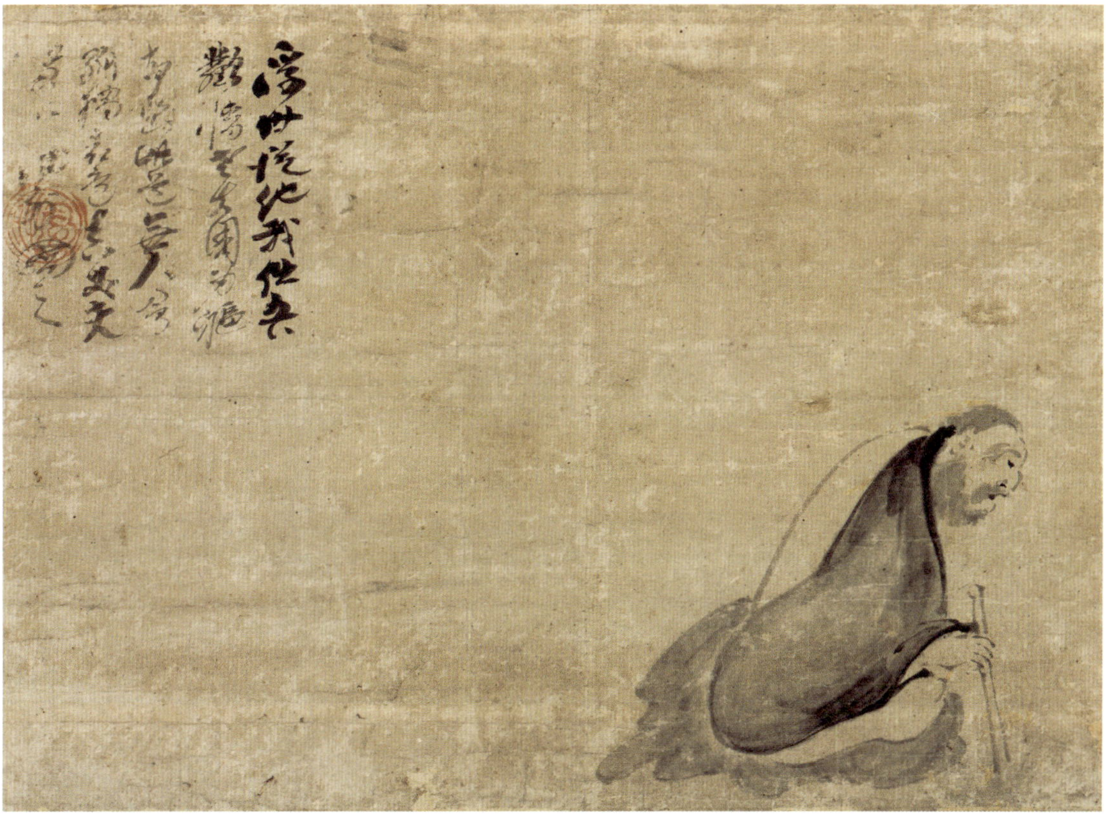

浮世従他我仕吾
歓情老去因身軀
却悲此道無人会
弧獨岩辺真丈夫
讃共風外図之

Others may be captivated by the floating world, but I am just me;
Enjoying myself to the very end in this body.
That is the way I show my compassion, and meet with no one;
I live alone in a cave and everything is just fine!

Inscription and painting brushed by Fugai

This delightful portrayal of the eccentric 8th-century Chinese monk Myosan (Mingzan), known as Lazy San, is one of Fugai's most important and impressive pieces. Lazy San lived in a cave and did not read the sutras, pray to the Buddhas, give sermons or take disciples – much like Fugai himself. He survived on potatoes cooked with smelly cow dung. Despite this strange behaviour, Lazy San's virtue came to the attention of the Chinese emperor, who sent an emissary to summon him to the palace. In this painting, Lazy San is shown responding to the emissary's command: 'Reverend, please receive this message from the emperor. Stand up and show your respect'. Lazy San kept his back turned, tending the fire and cooking a potato. 'Well, if you want to cook potatoes that is all right' said the messenger, bemused by his behaviour, 'but can't you at least wipe your nose?' (The fire was very smoky and made Lazy San's nose run.) When Lazy San replied 'What! Wipe my nose for the likes of you!', the emissary gave up, returned to the palace and reported to the emperor. 'That monk is the real thing', the emperor exclaimed, and respected Lazy San even more.

The story of Lazy San was a favourite among Zen artists (Hakuin and Sengai also painted versions of the tale). Fugai especially identified with Lazy San because his own way of life was so similar. By painting Lazy San in a corner, turning his back on common affairs, Fugai conveys a sense of his isolation from the world. Cooking potatoes is a humble act, but Lazy San performs it with full concentration. Again, the painting is in poor condition and some of the inscription has disintegrated, yet it retains a powerful, indeed almost mysterious quality.

4
FUGAI Ekun (1568–1654)
Lazy San, the potato monk
hanging scroll, ink on paper,
32.7 x 44 cm

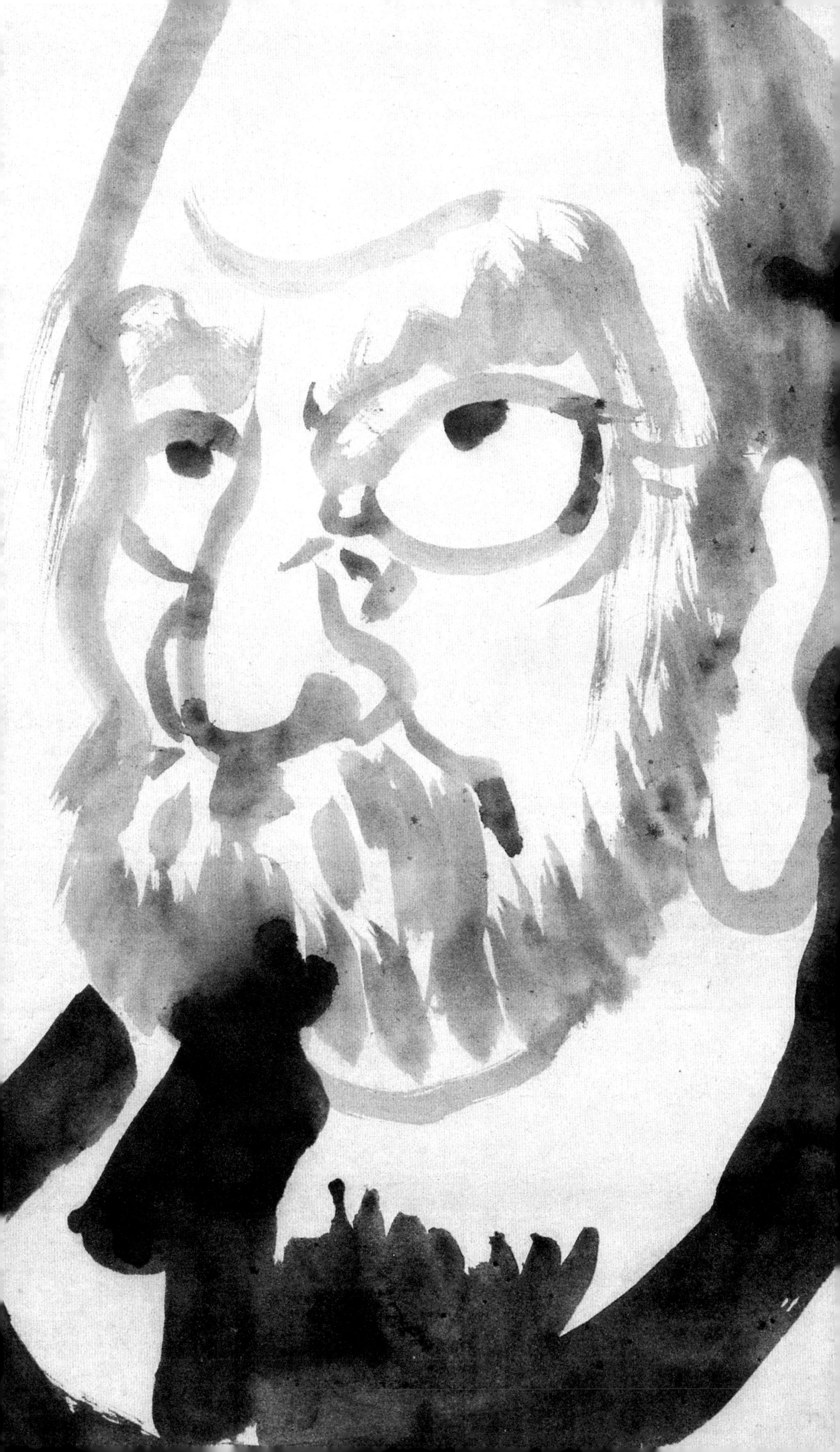

直人見成
指心性佛

Direct pointing
To the human heart
See your nature
Become Buddha!

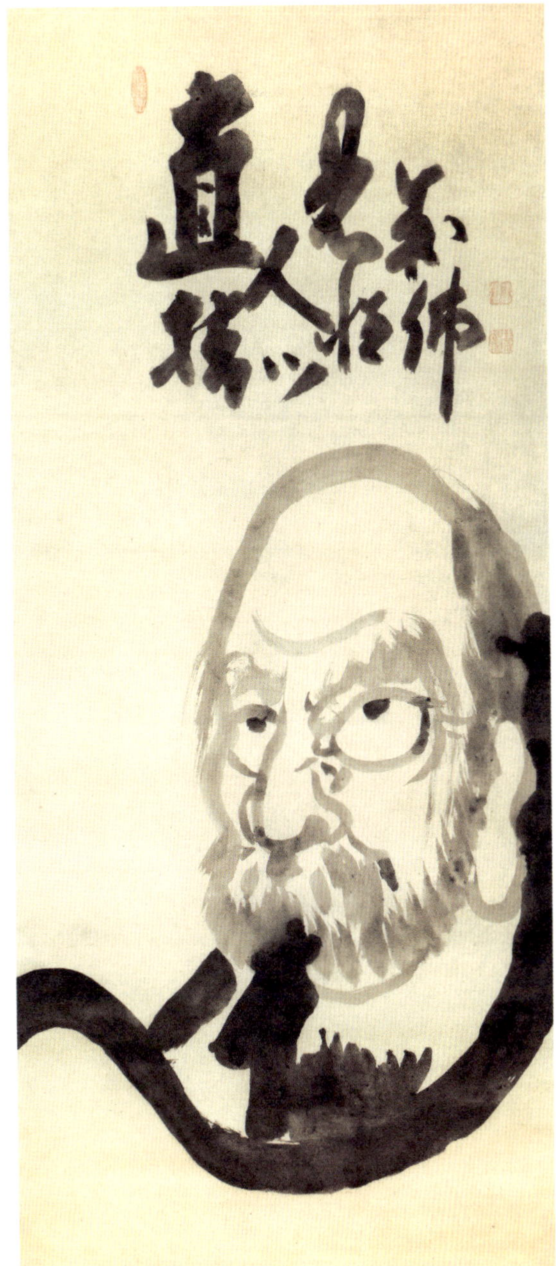

Representing Zen, this giant Daruma points directly to the human heart and does not depend on sutras, temples or prayers. 'Look inside, see your own nature, and you will realise you are no different from Buddha.' This was Hakuin's battle cry and he inscribed it on hundreds of his Daruma paintings. Hakuin was adept at painting huge Darumas, some almost 3 metres high, and this is one of his signature pieces: brushed quickly with tremendous confidence, in big strokes with wet ink. Hakuin's technical approach contrasts with the fine, detailed brushstrokes Fugai used to compose the hair, beard and eyebrows of his Darumas.

Once asked how long it took to paint a Daruma, Hakuin replied, 'ten minutes and eighty years'. Each Zenga in this exhibition embodies many years of Zen practice.

5
HAKUIN Ekaku (1685–1768)
Giant Daruma
hanging scroll, ink on paper,
130.8 x 55.2 cm
(left) detail

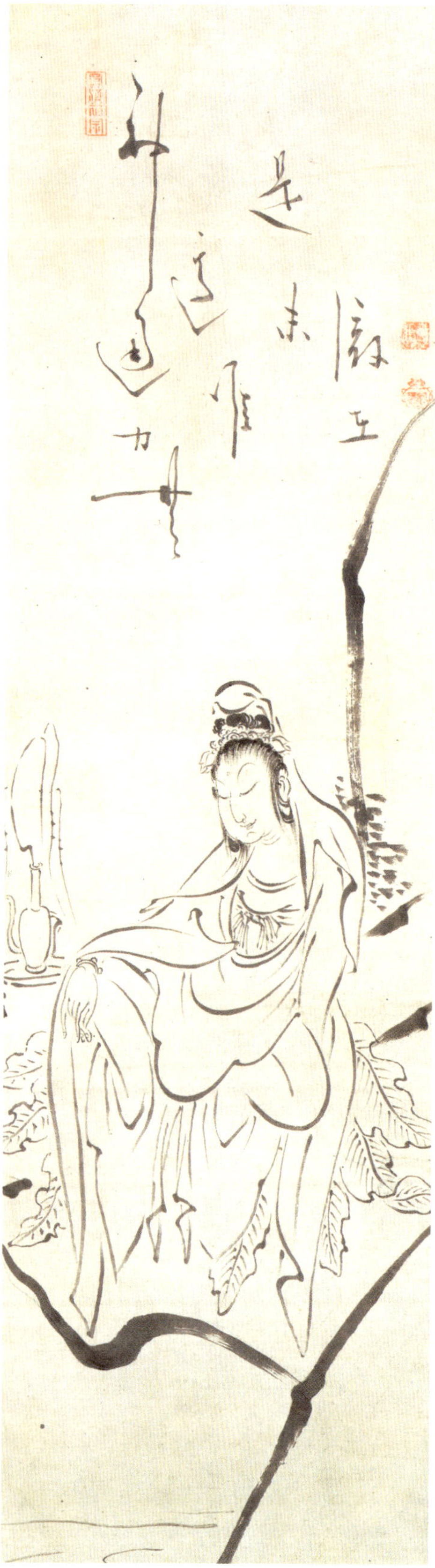

神　　是
通邊
力　唯末依
無　　　在

[Kannon's] miraculous spiritual power is unlimited;
She is always there for us to the end.

Buddhism's two pillars are insight, symbolised by Daruma, and compassion, represented by the bodhisattva (potential Buddha) Kannon. Kannon is said to be able to manifest herself in any form to save sentient beings. This is Kannon in a classic iconographical form: in white flowing robes and veil, adorned with jewels, and with a willow branch in a water jar, symbolising her powers of healing.

As far as we know Fugai did not paint Kannon, but Hakuin did hundreds of portraits of the female bodhisattva of compassion, painted as a lovely queen as we see here, as well as many of Otafuku, considered to be an incarnation of Kannon. Otafuku is a plump, homely folk goddess of good luck, often portrayed by Hakuin as a country courtesan. The mark of a good Zen master is the ability to identify with both male and female aspects of Buddha-nature; Hakuin could brush tough, masculine Darumas and delicate, feminine Kannons like this one equally well. In his 70s, Hakuin was busy with his many disciples, conducting teaching tours all over the country. This painting dates from Hakuin's 60s, when he had more time to brush such detailed portraits. The painting may have been intended for a high-ranking samurai family since it was expensively mounted and well preserved.

6
HAKUIN Ekaku (1685–1768)
White-robed Kannon
hanging scroll, ink on paper,
93.5 x 26.3 cm

無量
福聚海
衆生
慈眼視

She looks upon all sentient beings with eyes of compassion,
[She is] an unlimited ocean of good fortune and succour.

In near perfect condition, this exquisite little painting of Kannon at the water's edge gazing at the reflection of the moon was probably done for the home altar of a high-ranking samurai family, for morning and evening prayer. While the previous *White-robed Kannon* (no 6) was shown in a relaxed, almost languid posture created by Hakuin's soft, monochromatic brushstrokes, this depiction of Kannon in what is known as the 'water moon' (or 'lotus pond') is much sharper and shows her in the formal *zazen* posture. The painting is in colour and is more detailed than *White-robed canon*. Iconographic elements are added too: the moon, the scrolls, and different coloured lotus flowers in the pond. Hakuin was fond of doing such complex paintings in colour and was clearly a talented creative artist as well as a great Zen master.

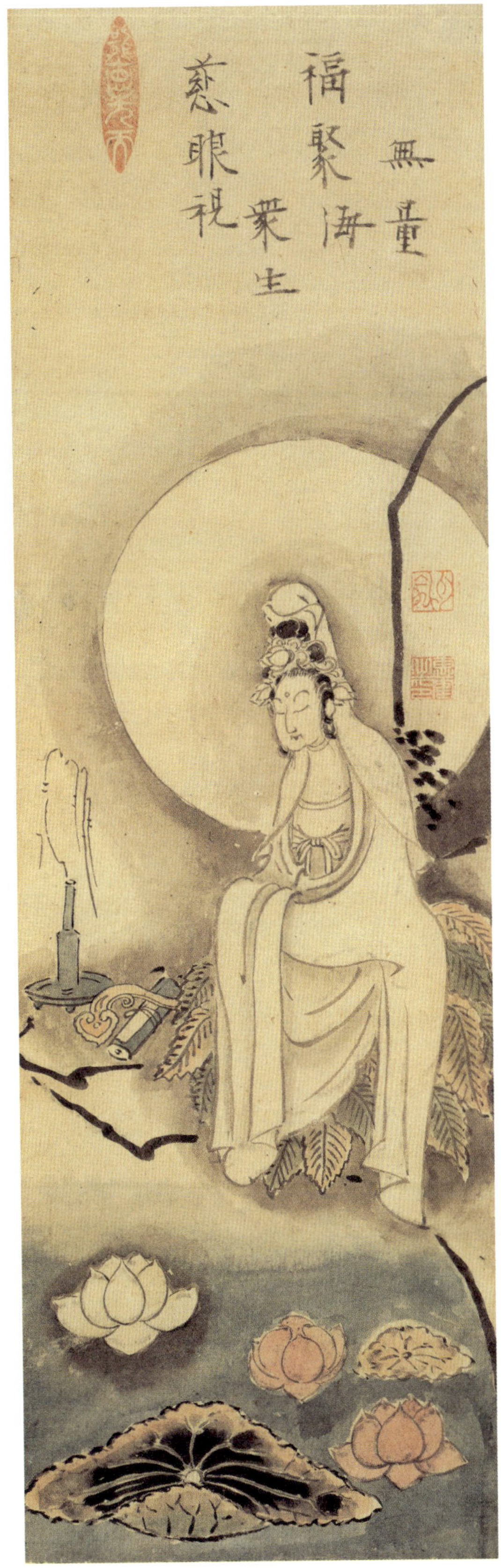

7
HAKUIN Ekaku (1685–1768)
Lotus pond Kannon
hanging scroll, ink on paper,
44.2 x 13.9 cm

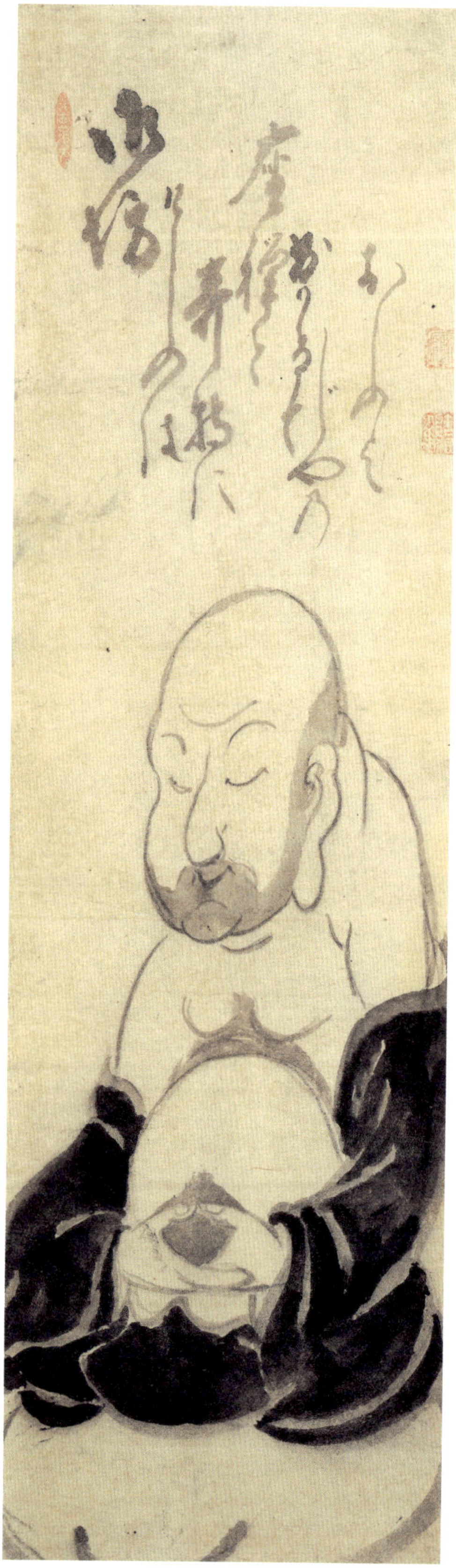

おふよ
じやの
出可奇て
座禅と
奇特に
けふは
御坊

Mr Monk,
How unusual! Today you are actually doing zazen.

Yeah, so what!

Paintings of Hotei were another speciality of Hakuin. We have seen *Smiling Hotei* and *Frowning Hotei* by Fugai, and this may be called 'Serious Hotei' by Hakuin. *Zazen* is formal meditation in the posture assumed by Hotei here in this painting. Hotei is usually shown making merry while moving about and that is why the inscription expresses surprise at Hotei's repose. Hotei – here a self-portrait of Hakuin as well – sits serenely on his big bag, taking time out to connect to his inner nature: from the Zen perspective *zazen* is as natural as smiling and frowning. Thus this Hotei says, 'I just feel like doing *zazen* today. Got a problem with that?' Even after one is enlightened, it is fitting to practice formally from time to time.

Hakuin did a number of versions of *zazen* Hotei but the sense of Hotei in meditation is particularly deep here. The painting's 'centre of gravity', so to speak, is quite low, and we feel drawn into Hotei's core.

8
HAKUIN Ekaku (1685–1768)
Zazen Hotei
hanging scroll, ink on paper,
88.9 x 26.7 cm

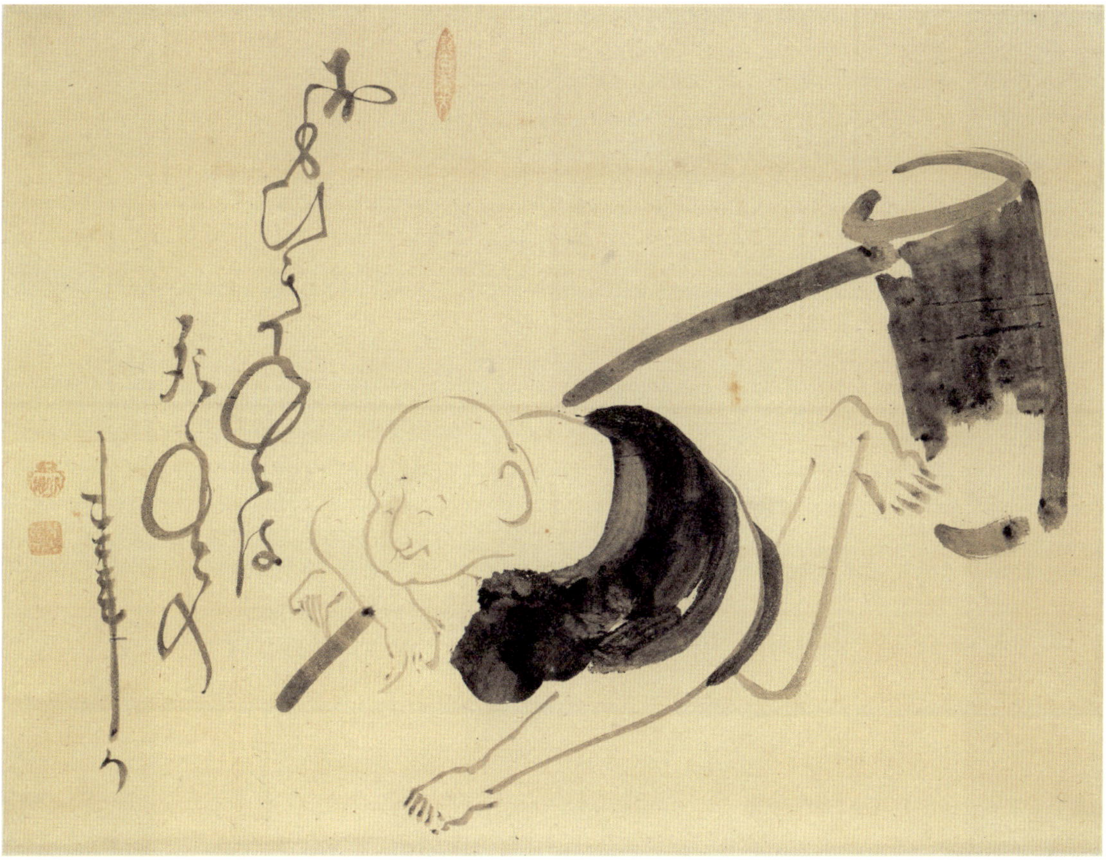

おもひきねとは
死ねとの
事可

This heavy mallet –
Will it be the death of me?

Although this figure looks like Hotei, it represents humankind in general. The massive mallet, used to pound rice, symbolises the heavy burdens of fame, fortune and status that can weigh us down as we hurry to-and-fro in this world, and if we work too hard to attain them may cause our early demise. 'Put the mallet down', Hakuin seems to be saying, 'and you will feel so much lighter'.

The brushwork of this inscription is particularly animated. The *kana* characters of the first two lines are skilfully drawn together in long, single brushstrokes, appearing to dance across the paper.

9
HAKUIN Ekaku (1685–1768)
Running Hotei
hanging scroll, ink on paper,
40.9 x 52.4 cm

The folk god Fukurokuju (sometimes called Jurojin) is the god of longevity, good fortune, wealth and, as the phallic shape of his head makes abundantly clear, fertility. Although people want long life, good fortune and wealth, from the Zen perspective the greatest treasure is enlightenment – it will never rust or be lost or stolen, and it will allow us to overcome anything. In this inscription, Hakuin suggests that the quality of one's life is far more important than one's material possessions.

We must not overlook the erotic element of this painting. Fukurokuju has a sly smile on his venerable face, and we could interpret the inscription to mean, 'If it stays long and hard like this that will be a real treasure, and you will have a pleasant and productive life'.

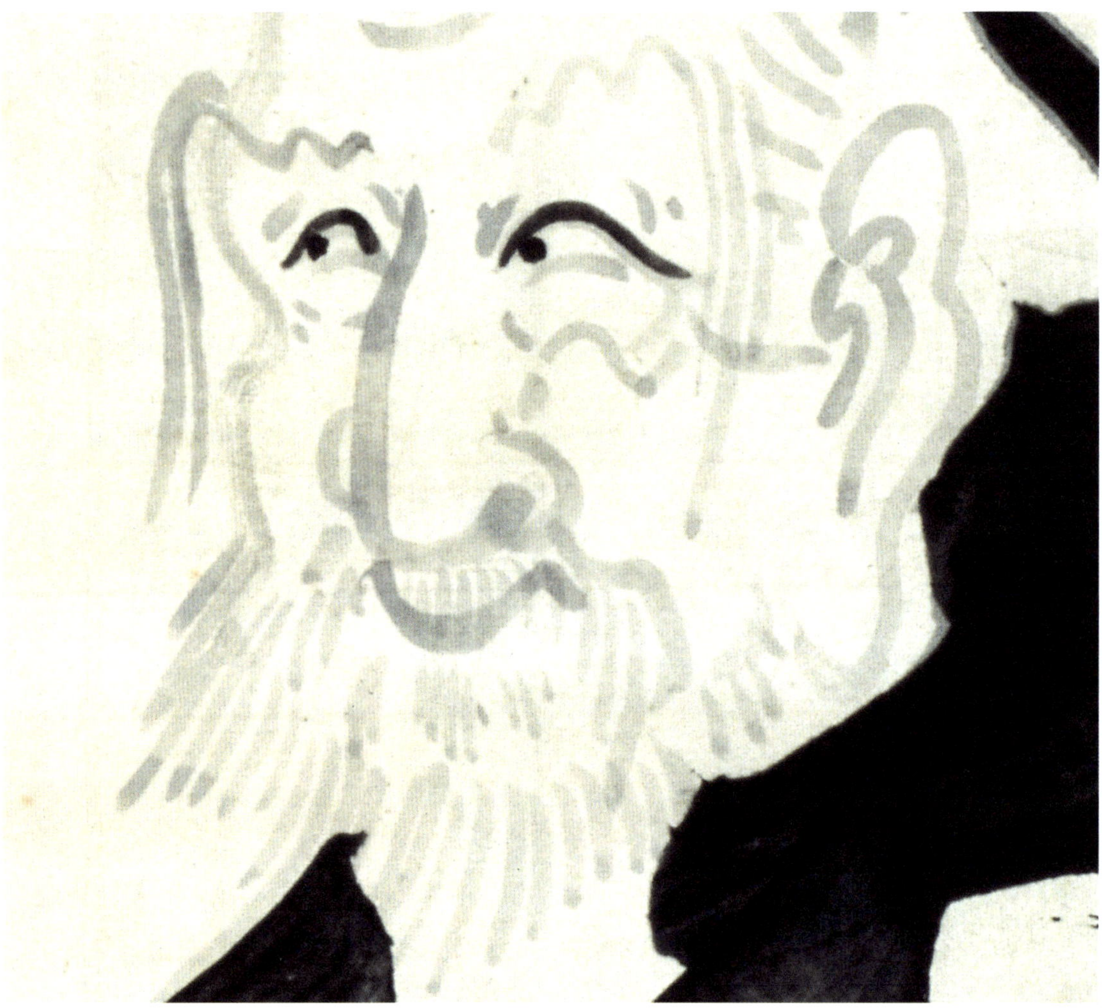

ともかくも
ならば
ナガイキ
壽　なひが
及びも
福と禄とは

LONGEVITY,
Good fortune and wealth
We want to be long lasting,
But life itself will be long enough
In the long run.

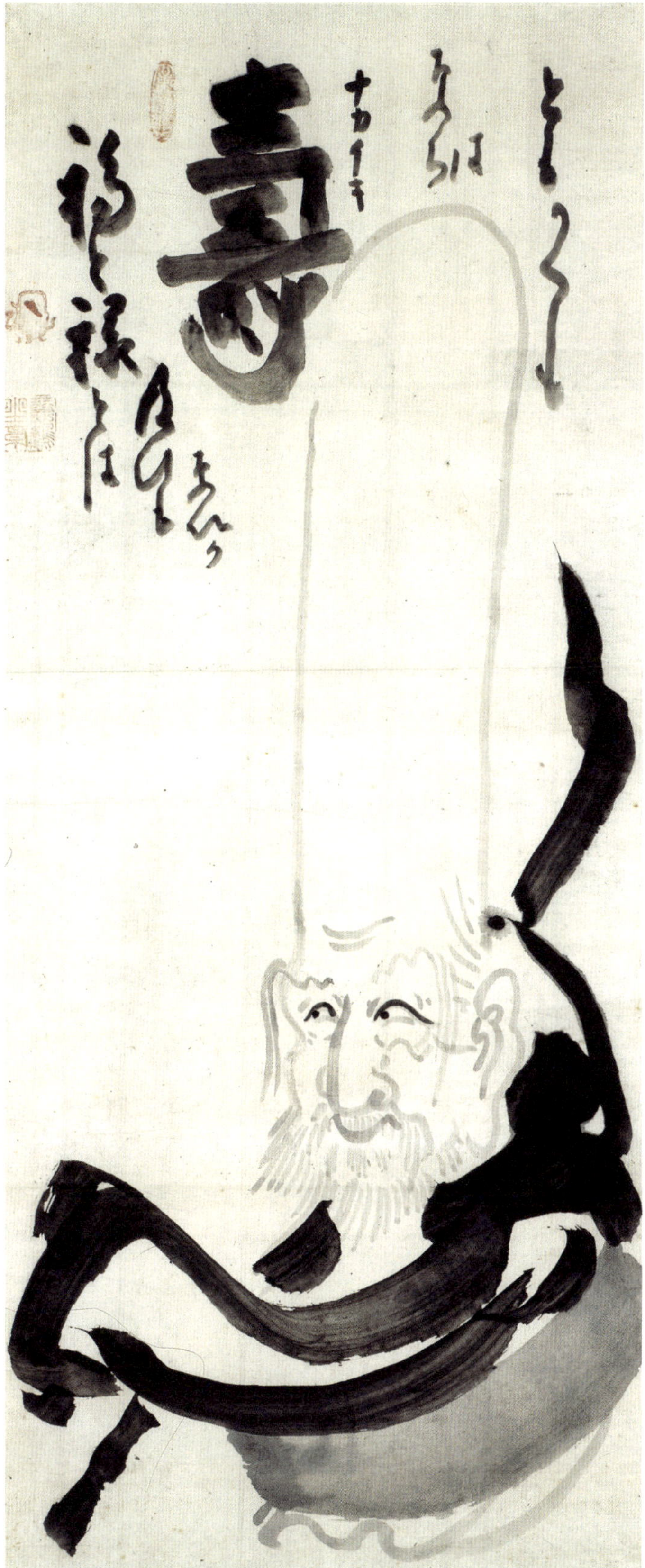

10
HAKUIN Ekaku (1685–1768)
Fukurokuju
hanging scroll, ink on paper,
173.5 x 38 cm
(left) detail

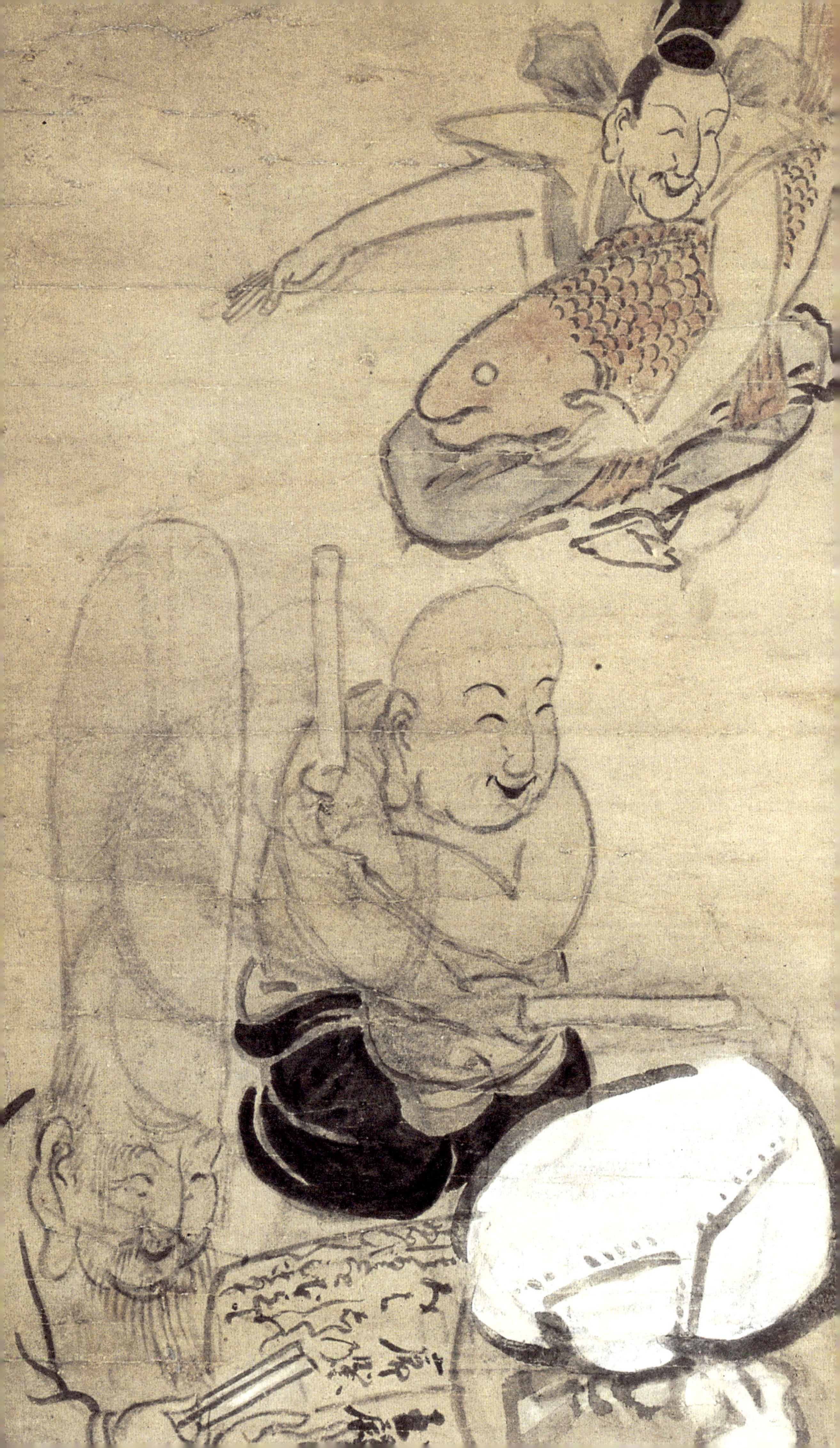

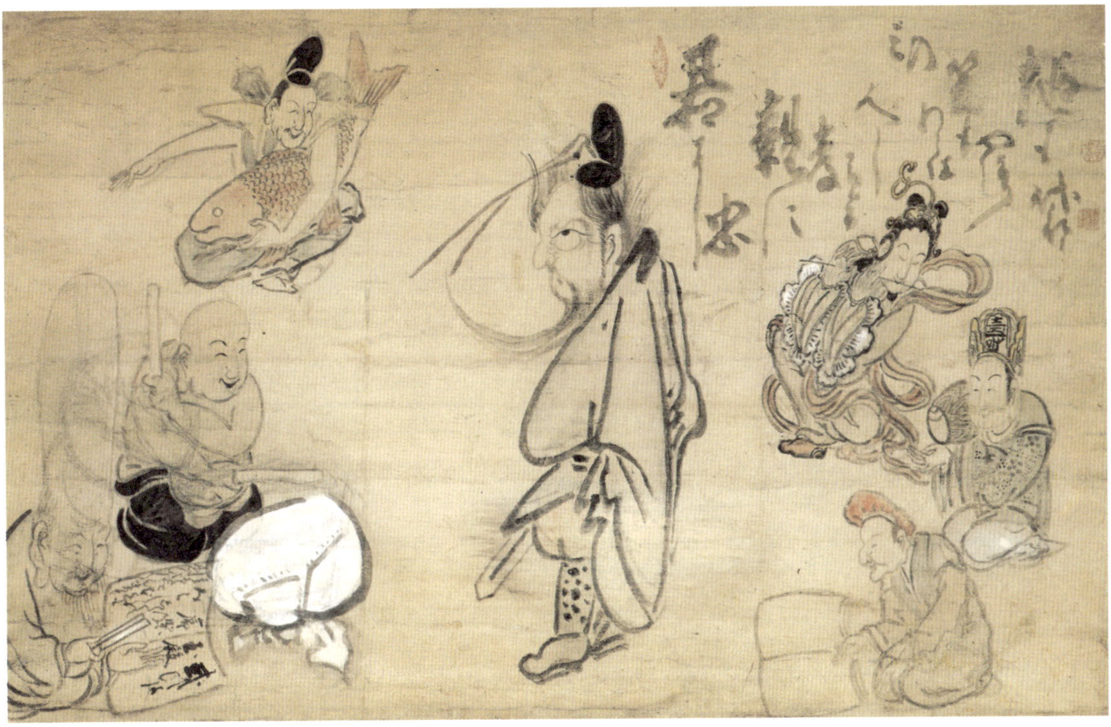

槌も袋も
やろ
も
笠
の
ミ
あらば
人しる
有
孝
親に忠
君に

One who is loyal to his lord and filial to his parents
Will receive my straw raincoat, straw hat, magic mallet
and bag.

びにぶ忍
そめて忍
るぎをひ
までも津
はしの本
のしたみ
廊架
玉殿
或いは

[on Fukurokuju's book]
Under the eaves of the palace [Shoki] *conceals his sword,*
and stealthily guards the imperial household.

A complex and intriguing painting, this work depicts the Seven Gods of Good Fortune performing the No play *Shoki*. Clockwise from bottom left we see: Fukurokuju, god of good fortune, reading the score and keeping time with his fan; Hotei, god of contentment, using his white bag for a drum; Ebisu, god of fishing, dancing and chanting; Benzaiten, goddess of art, music and love playing her flute; Daikoku, god of prosperity, beating his magic mallet; and Jurojin, god of longevity, reading from a text. In the middle is the central character Shoki, the demon queller (Shoki has replaced the more commonly included warrior god Bishamonten).The painting appears to have been composed in at least two separate sessions, something very rare for a Zenga. Shoki, the three gods and the inscription on the right side were done first, but it seems that for some reason Hakuin did not have time to finish this detailed painting in one sitting and did only a preliminary sketch of the left side. When he completed the painting later, he left the preliminary sketch underneath, giving the painting a three-dimensional effect. This is a common feature of Hakuin's Zenga.

Paintings such as this were displayed during the festive New Year season to bring good luck to a family in the coming year. Hakuin's inscription reminds viewers that the Confucian virtues of loyalty and filial piety must be cultivated first and then true wealth will follow. All seven gods are playing harmoniously, suggesting that good fortune is based on a combination of factors and an integrated approach to all aspects of life.

11
HAKUIN Ekaku (1685–1768)
Seven Gods of Good Fortune
hanging scroll, ink on paper,
57.8 x 89.4 cm
(left) detail

養生(も)世も
浮頭の
座木はし
丸
ワたる
心が
よき手ひき
なり

In both spiritual training and dealing with the world
Keep in mind the example of blind men
crossing a log bridge.

This is one of the masterpieces in the Gitter-Yelen collection of Zenga. The blue ink tones here are extraordinarily rich and lucid, and the painting appears so fresh and bright it could have been painted yesterday. The delicately animated blind men appear agile and lively.

A gorge like this existed near Hakuin's temple so it is a painting of a real place. In Buddhism, crossing from this shore of illusion to that shore of enlightenment over the raging river of *samsara* (the endless cycle of birth, death and rebirth to which all living creatures are condemned) is a common metaphor. Usually the vehicle used to cross over is described as a boat, a symbol representing Buddhist teachings, but it can also be a log bridge as shown here. In dealing with matters of the spirit and matters of the world, Hakuin tells us, be as circumspect and careful as a blind man inching his way across a slippery pole bridge, and you will make it safely though life.

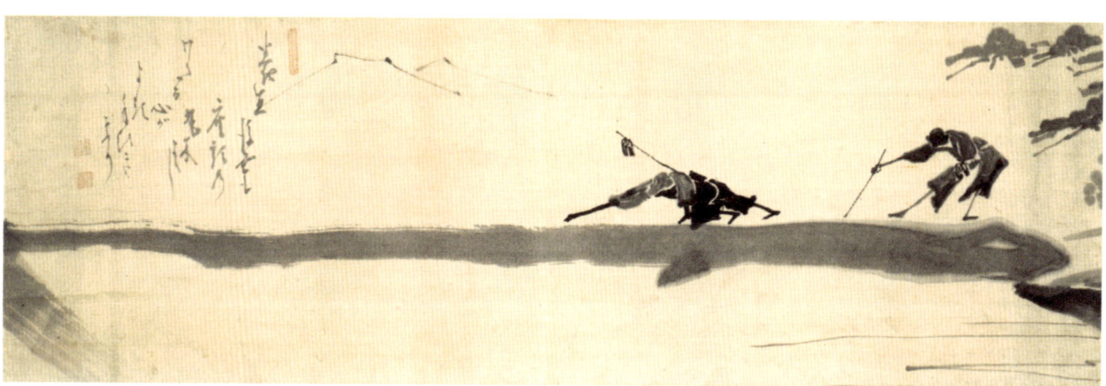

12
HAKUIN Ekaku (1685–1768)
Blind men crossing a log bridge
hanging scroll, ink on paper,
28 x 83.8 cm

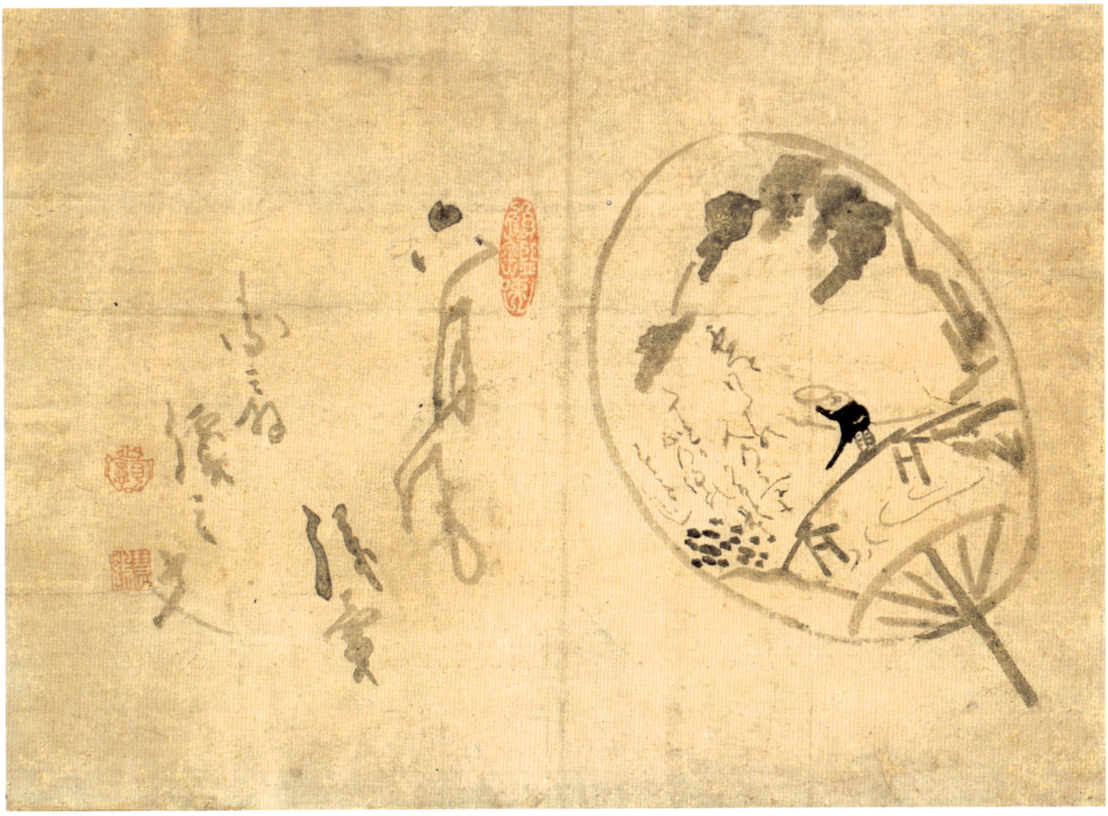

世をワたる
人乃うへにも
かけて見よ
これが
心乃まま
の
すぎ
はし

六月風
賎売
団扇
価三
文

In June wind costs
Three cents for a fan.

[on the fan]
For people passing above through this world
How about making a plank bridge with your mind?

This is a visual *koan*, a Zen puzzle. One interpretation of the inscription would be that although a fan is quite inexpensive, the refreshing breeze it provides in the hottest time of the year is priceless. In other words, a seeming trifle can be very valuable at certain times, both in life and in Zen training. On the fan itself we have a bridge, this time the famous plank bridge of Mama, an actual place often referred to in Japanese poetry. The solitary monk is a self-portrait of Hakuin and also represents human beings in general, moving from one shore to the other buffeted by a strong wind from behind (notice his robe). The inscription includes several clever puns, but the main meaning is, 'Use your mind to build bridges among different kinds of people'.

There is a sense of playfulness in the brushwork here, and although the painting is more light-hearted than other works by Hakuin in this exhibition, the meaning is no less profound.

13
HAKUIN Ekaku (1685–1768)
Fan
hanging scroll, ink on paper,
32.7 x 44.7 cm

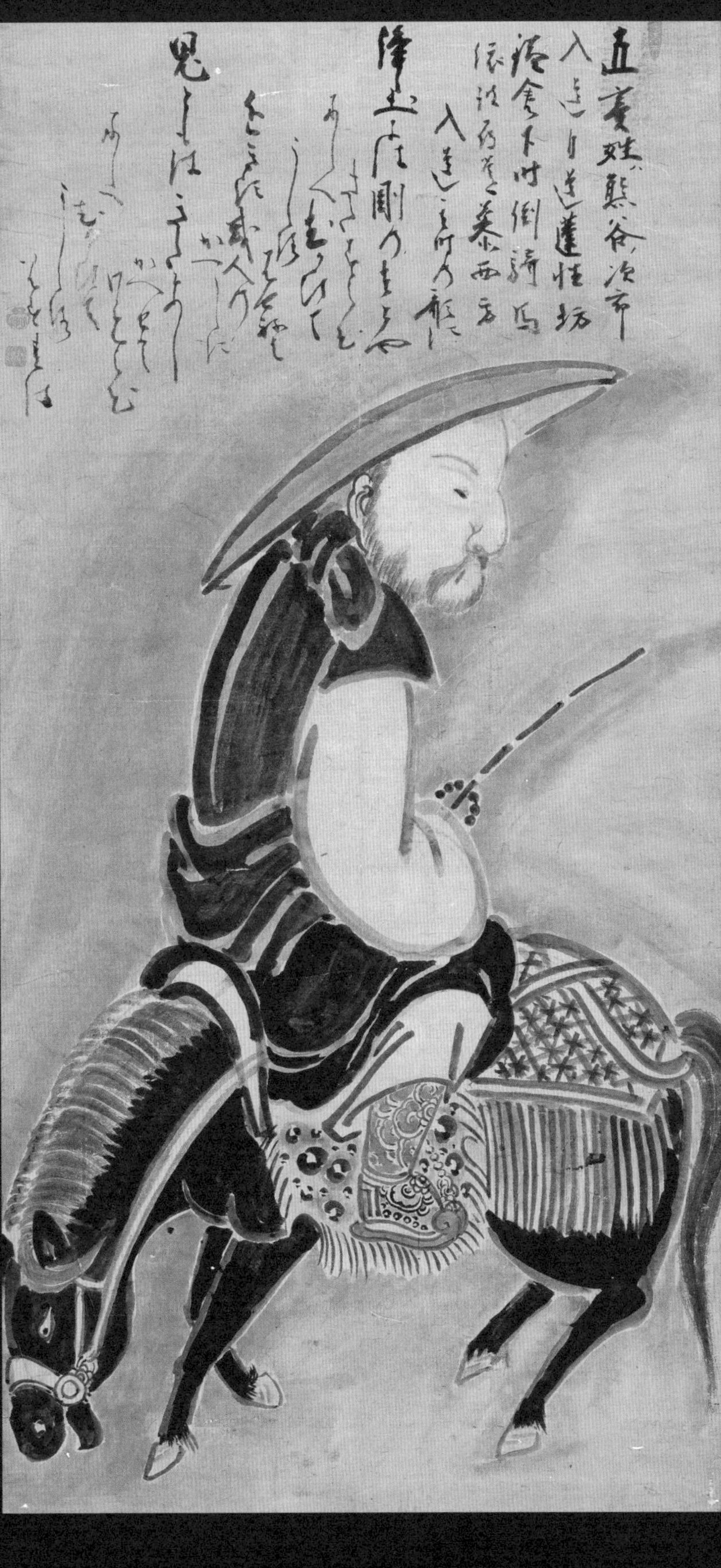

14
HAKUIN Ekaku (1685–1768)
Renshobo on his horse
hanging scroll, ink on paper,
118 x 56 cm

直實姓熊谷次郎
入道自道蓮性坊
鎌倉下時倒騎馬
依彼尋常慕西方
入道其時乃歌に
浄土には剛乃者とや
さたすらむ
にしへむかひて
うしろ
見せねは
近き頃或人乃に
かへし
鬼ともはきたなし
かへせと
ワめくらむ
にしへ
むかひて
うしろ
見すれは

His original name was Kumagai Jiro.
After be became a Buddhist monk he called himself Renshobo.
When he visited Kamakura he rode backwards on his horse.
He wanted always to be facing the west.
The monk at that time composed this verse:

Those brave souls[1]
in the Pure Land
are impressed
that he always faces the west,
never turning his back to that direction.
Recently,
someone [Hakuin] *said,*
the devils
would cry out, 'come back',
if turned his back [on the Pure Land].

Hakuin was fond of this story of Kumagai Jiro Naozane, a Minamoto general of the 12th century, and brushed it often, usually in a much smaller format. During a famous battle at Ichinotani, Kumagai killed the warrior Taira no Atsumori. Atsumori looked so much like Kumagai's own son that the general was stricken with remorse and became a monk called Renshobo. Renshobo was a fervent believer in the Pure Land sect of Buddhism established by the patriarch Honen (1133–1212). Honen taught that even the worst sinner could be reborn in the Pure Land (also known as the Western Paradise) if he believed in Amida Buddha, the Buddha of the Pure Land, and continually chanted his name. Out of respect for Amida, Renshobo vowed never to turn his back to the Pure Land and when he had to travel east from Kyoto to Kamakura, he rode his horse backwards to keep facing west. Kumagai's last battle with the Taira army had taken place in the west, so the inscription on the painting also means that Renshobo was not afraid to face the ghosts of his former enemies.

This is an unusual and outstanding work. Near life-size, the portrait emphasises the monk holding his staff and rosary. Although the horse is well executed, it is much too small to bear the weight of the rider, who appears giant-like. Hakuin admired Kumagai/Renshobo's single-mindedness and deep devotion, and praised his example. Because of its large size and detailed composition, the painting was probably intended to be hung in the spacious alcove of a samurai household that belonged to the Pure Land sect of Buddhism or had some warrior link with Kumagai.

1. The ghosts of slain warriors of the Taira clan

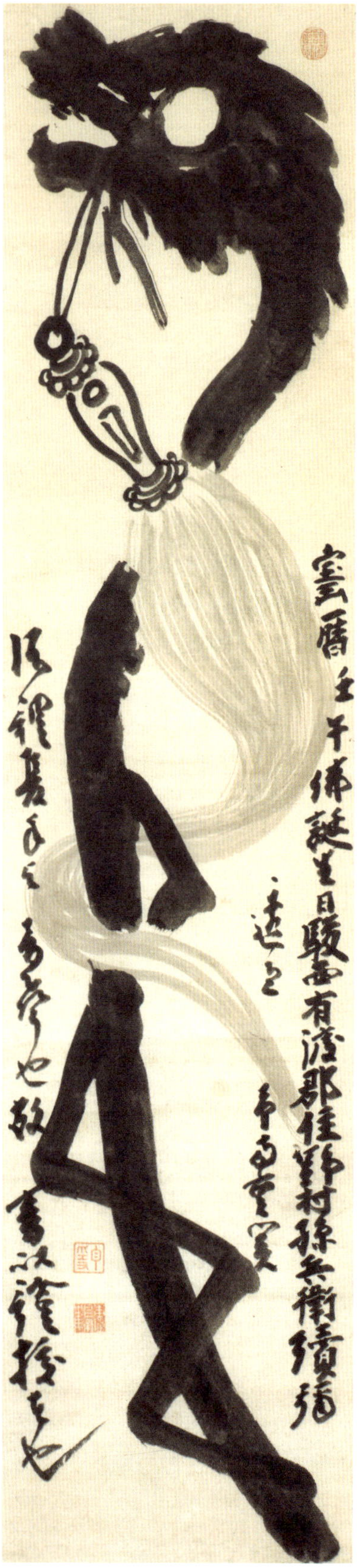

宝暦壬午佛誕生日駿西有渡郡住野村孫兵衛續彌
透過予両量関
所謂隻手之音聲也故書以證拠者也

On Buddha's Birthday [April 8] *in 1762, Nomura Magobe from a county in Suru* [Shizuoka] *penetrated my two massive barriers and heard the sound of one hand. I therefore brush this as a certificate for this heroic person.*

Hakuin gave certificates like this to dozens of his students. Judging from the name and location, the original recipient for this certificate was a layman who lived near Hakuin's temple. The staff and fly whisk (*hossu*) are symbols of the authority and majesty of Buddhist Law, and the ability to understand and teach Zen. In case 60 of the *Hekiganroku* collection of *koans* (Zen riddles), 10th-century Zen master Unmon held up his staff and declared: 'This staff has transformed itself into a dragon and swallowed up the universe!' Interestingly, in Hakuin's early versions of this theme the staff looked like an ordinary staff. It later become more dragon-like, but it was not until a few years after this one (painted when Hakuin was 78), and just before his death, that Hakuin painted it as a complete dragon with eyes. The famous *koan* 'What is the sound of one hand clapping?' was invented by Hakuin to test his students, and 'two massive barriers' may mean 'doubly difficult'.

15
HAKUIN Ekaku (1685–1768)
Dragon staff with fly whisk
(enlightenment certificate)
1762
hanging scroll, ink on paper,
127.1 x 28.8 cm

常念
観世音菩薩

ALWAYS REMEMBER
Kanzeon Bosatsu!

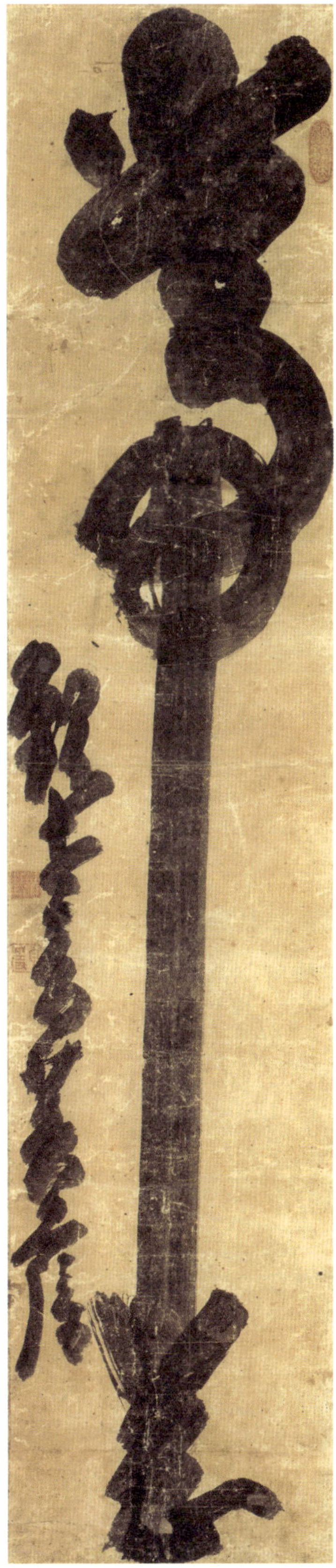

This is another of Hakuin's signature pieces, dating from his final years. As we have seen, Hakuin was quite capable of painting finely detailed pieces, but at the end of his long and productive life, the brushstrokes in both his paintings and calligraphy became big and expansive. The first two characters here, 'always remember', are run together with tremendous zip. The large character 'always' swirls round and round and then is elongated to emphasise sense of time; 'remember' connotes 'set in mind', 'firmly keep in focus' and 'continually invoke', and this character is grounded at its base. Kanzeon is the longer, more formal name of Kannon, bodhisattva of compassion, and *bosatsu* is the Japanese pronunciation of the Sanskrit word bodhisattva. In short, the calligraphy means 'Always strive to be as compassionate as Kannon herself'.

16
HAKUIN Ekaku (1685–1768)
Always remember Kanzeon
hanging scroll, ink on paper,
132.7 x 27.9 cm

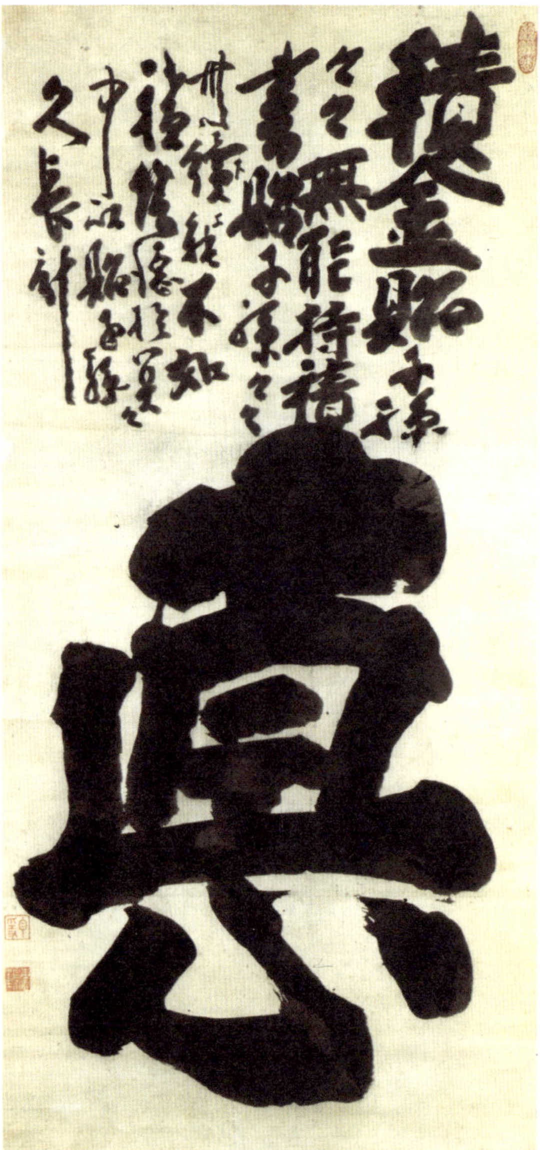

積金胎子孫
々々無能持積
書胎子孫々々
無讀能不如
積陰徳於冥々
中以胎子孫
久長計

徳

If you pile up money for your descendants,
they will be sure to waste it;
If you collect books for them,
they will probably not read a word.
It is better to pile up secret virtue –
such a legacy will last a long, long time.
VIRTUE [TOKU]

Another masterpiece from the Gitter-Yelen collection, this ranks among Hakuin's best calligraphic works. The huge character at the bottom (*toku* in Japanese) is a 'one-word barrier' (a giant character set off for emphasis). In Zenga such a character, either alone or with an accompanying inscription, is used as a visual puzzle, or *koan*. 'Be virtuous in all your actions!' the *toku* character seems to shout. The character *toku* in a general sense means 'virtue', but it refers more specifically to a good deed done inconspicuously, a good act that goes unrewarded, a good thought that attracts no praise; in other words, 'secret virtue'. In East Asia, such *toku* is believed to pass from generation to generation, increasing (or decreasing) depending on how it is used.

Hakuin brushed the character with semi-congealed ink, one of his trademarks, and it has plenty of splotches and drips. The accompanying inscription, delightfully brushed with characters of different shapes and sizes, is universally applicable advice from the Chinese sage Sima (1018–86).

17
HAKUIN Ekaku (1685–1768)
Virtue
hanging scroll, ink on paper,
117.3 x 55.2 cm
(right) detail

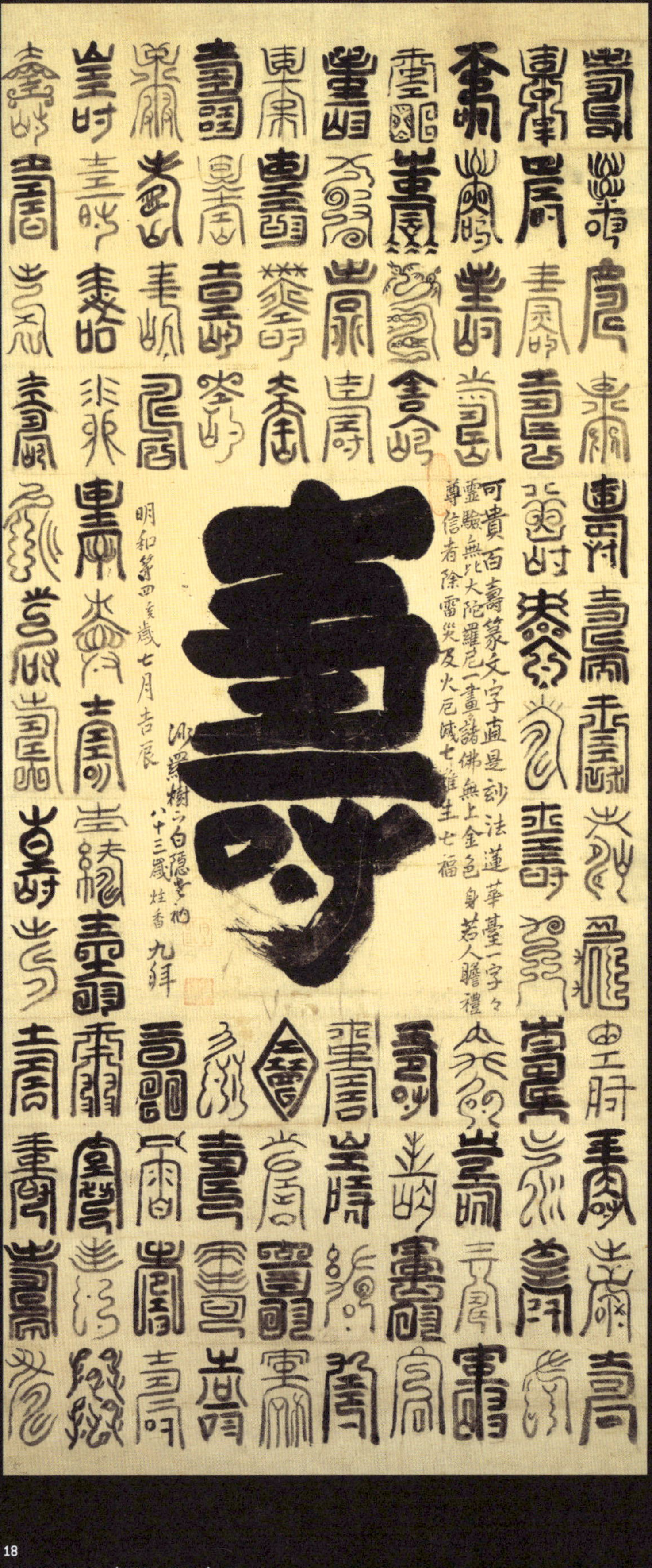

18
HAKUIN Ekaku (1685–1768)
One hundred times 'longevity'
1767
hanging scroll, ink on paper,
124.1 x 54.3 cm

可貴百壽篆文字直是妙法蓮華臺一字々
霊驗無比大陀羅尼一画々諸佛無上金色身若人瞻禮
尊信者除雷災及火危滅七難生七福

壽

沙羅樹下白陰老衲
八十三歳　炷香　九拝

明和第四亥歳七月吉辰

Venerate the 100 seal script characters for longevity [kotobuki]*; each one is a lotus pedestal of the marvellous law, a source of miraculous, unsurpassed magic and a picture of the golden body of a Buddha. Those who bow, respect and believe in them will avoid thunder and fires, be safe from the seven disasters, and bring forth sevenfold good fortune.*

LONGEVITY [KOTOBUKI]

The old monk Hakuin, under the trees of nirvana [ie, near death]
83 years old, burns incense and prostrates nine times
1767, seventh month, an auspicious day

This wonderful scroll is a recent addition to the Gitter-Yelen collection. With the exception of his enlightenment certificates, Hakuin rarely signed his calligraphy and paintings, instead putting only his seals on them until he was in his 80s (this scroll, and the enlightenment certificate no 15, are the only signed Hakuin pieces in this exhibition). In the last few years of his life, Hakuin brushed this very difficult and demanding 100 *kotobuki* theme a number of times. On one such painting, he wrote, 'It took half a day to brush this'. (On a giant Daruma brushed the same year, Hakuin proudly wrote, 'I painted this without my spectacles' so his eyesight in his last years must have been poor, making creation of such difficult calligraphy even more impressive.) For a calligrapher, the ability to brush 100 *kotobuki* characters is considered the supreme test of artistic ability and scholarship. As indicated in the inscription and his signature, Hakuin's entire life is in each brushstroke here. It is clear that by taking up this challenging theme, he wanted to provide his students (and future generations) with a powerful visual image to be remembered by. Even though he was dying, 'longevity' – life lived to its fullest – was his final statement.

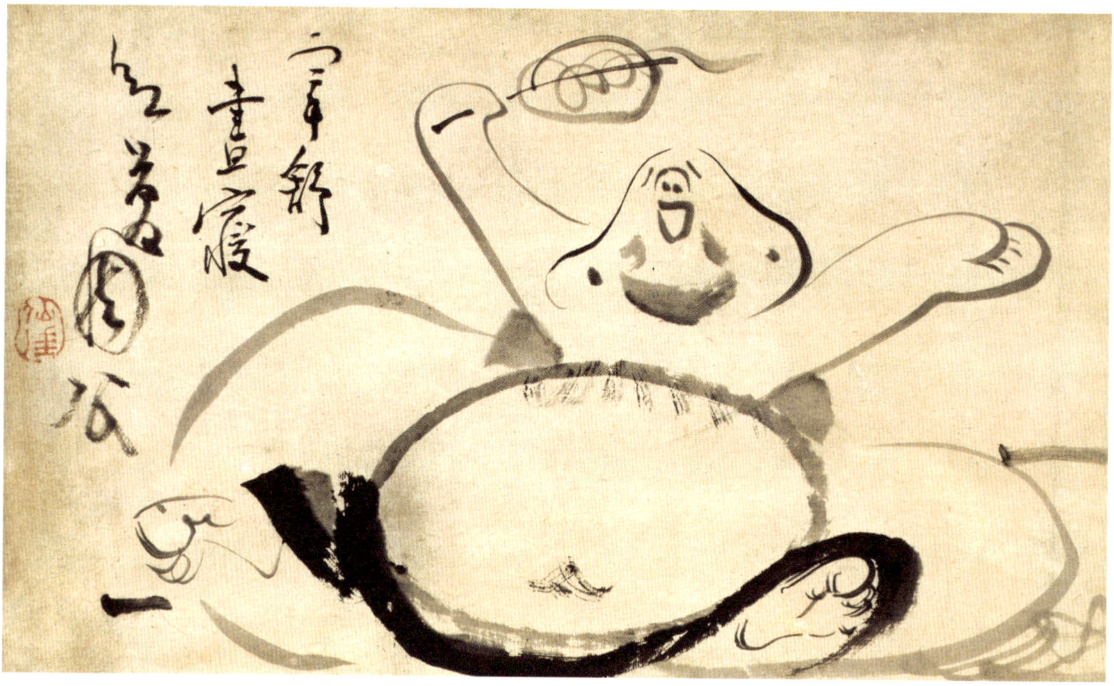

宰舒
晝寢
欲夢周公

What a pleasant nap! I dreamed I was Zhougong![1]

Although Sengai was probably a more prolific Zen artist than Hakuin, with a wider range of subjects, paintings by him of Daruma are comparatively rare (and those he painted tend to feature humorous inscriptions, such as 'Nine straight years of meditation – what a drag!'). Sengai's favourite was Hotei, and his depictions of the portly Zen hero are characterised by wild abandon and irreverent inscriptions: on another Hotei painting Sengai wrote, 'Oh, I am taking this philosophy far too seriously – I actually dreamed I was Buddha!' Sengai could paint detail accurately, but he preferred creating rough, cartoon-like sketches such as this, which is the kind of Zenga Sengai is known for throughout the world. On the surface, Sengai's work appears more light-hearted in execution than Hakuin's, but it is just as serious in intent, with an important message to teach. Hotei's big stomach here doubles as an *enso* (Zen circle), symbolising Hotei's embrace of all aspects of life.

19
SENGAI Gibon (1750–1837)
Hotei wakes from a nap
hanging scroll, ink on paper,
29.5 x 48.4 cm

1. Zhougong, the Duke of Zhou, was a famous sage and ideal statesman in Chinese history. Confucius admired Zhougong and often dreamt of him. One day, however, Confucius felt that he had become Zhougong and no longer needed to dream about him

常の道蹈み
迷ふなと
朧月
仙厓

This is the Way I always tread
but I am completely lost just the same
under the hazy moon.

Sengai

Zen and Daoism have much in common, and here Sengai portrays the Daoist founder Laozi riding out of China. The emperors of China had ignored Laozi's teachings and the country had fallen into ruin. As Laozi heads for the border on his ox, a border guard pleads with the master to write his teachings down. The result is the Daoist classic, the *Daodejing*, contained in the scroll Laozi is holding. Sengai playfully shows Laozi as being somewhat confused in the haze of the moon, even though he knows well the Way – all of us, even the wisest philosophers, can sometimes get lost.

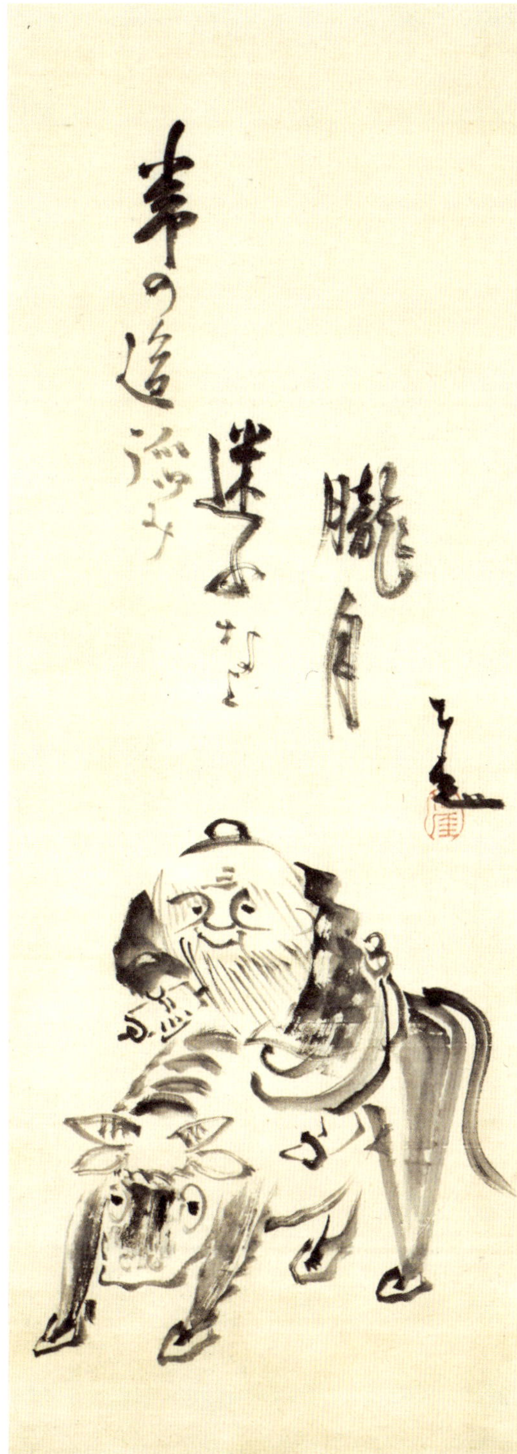

20
SENGAI Gibon (1750–1837)
Laozi riding an ox
hanging scroll, ink on paper,
78.4 x 27.9 cm

露に泣(く)千艸の色も
秋深て月に
吟よふ
松風の音
仙厓

[Jittoku]
Dew soaks a thousand grasses one shade that reflects the autumn moon;
Like a song, the sound of the wind in the pines.

Sengai

泣露千般草
吟風一様松
仙厓

[Kanzan]
A thousand grasses weep with dew,
The wind sings in the pines.

Sengai

Apart from Daruma and Hotei, the most popular figures in Zenga are Kanzan (Hanshan in Chinese) and Jittoku (Shide), two eccentrics who were said to have resided on a mountain in China around the 8th century. Kanzan lived in a cave and wrote poems, while his friend Jittoku brought scraps for them to eat. The two carefree ragamuffins are typically portrayed laughing uproariously at some Zen joke. Neither monks nor laymen, Kanzan and Jittoku symbolise creative, enlightened living that is untroubled by petty concerns and unfettered by social conventions.

Here Kanzan is shown reading a line from one his poems (from a blank scroll!). Jittoku listens, leaning on his ever-present broom. The inscription on the Kanzan is written in Chinese and on the Jittoku helpfully gives a Japanese translation, which stresses the universal nature of Kanzan and Jittoku's Zen message and the different ways different people experience nature.

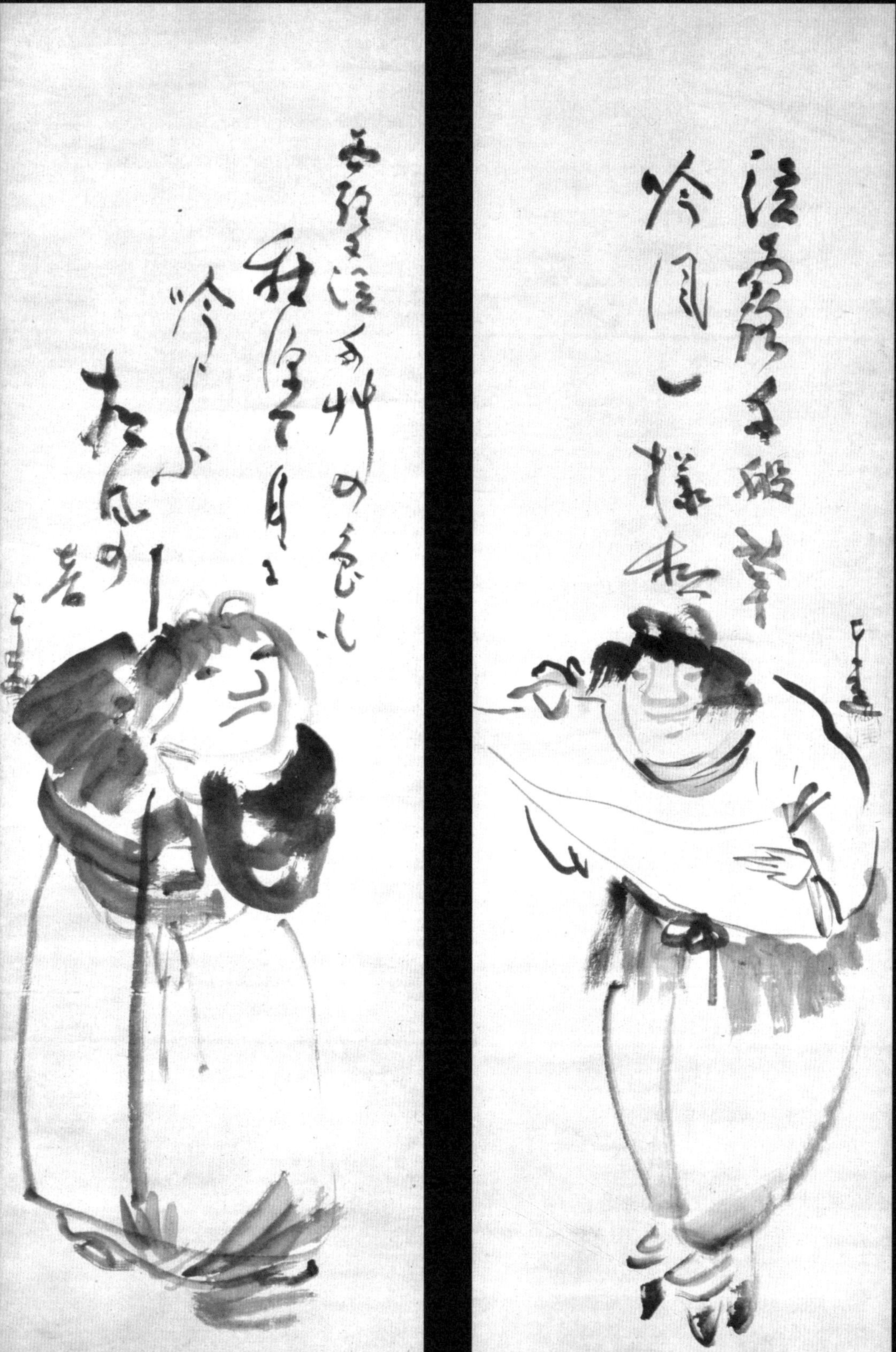

21
SENGAI Gibon (1750–1837)
Kanzan and Jittoku
pair of hanging scrolls,
ink on paper,
each 94 x 29 cm

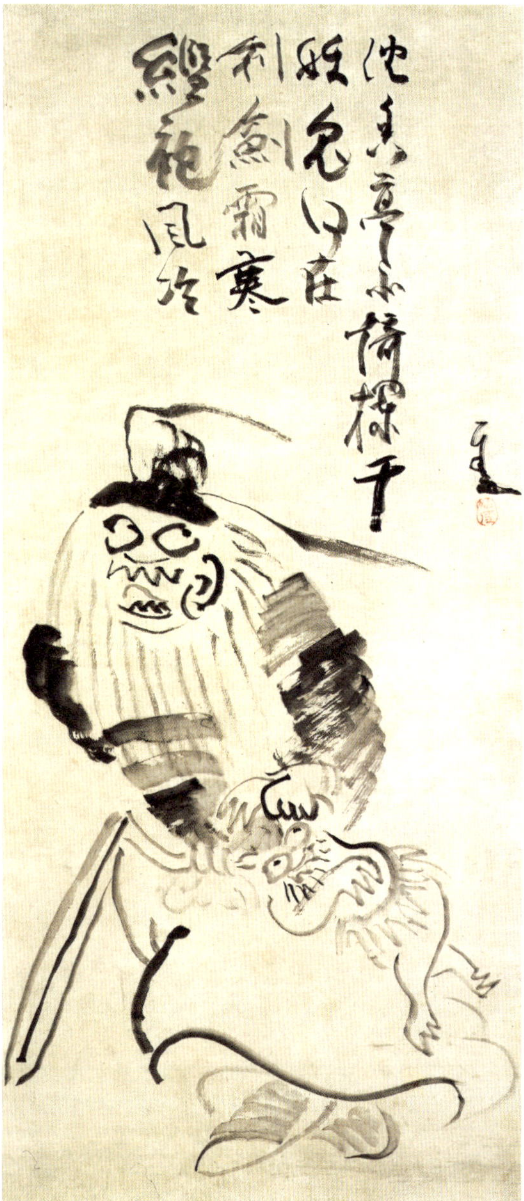

仙厓

沈香亭北倚欄干
妖鬼何在
利劍霜寒
縕袍風冷

His flowing robes chill the air;
His sword is as cold as frost.
He will find demons wherever they hide,
Even under the eaves of the Fragrant Palace!

Sengai

This is Shoki (Zhong Kui), the mythical hero of a Chinese legend. Ill with a high fever, the emperor dreamt that a spirit named Shoki had quelled the fever demon and cured his illness. The emperor commissioned a painting of Shoki subduing the demon, and had copies distributed throughout the land. Although the Chinese lost interest in Shoki, he became a favourite Japanese guardian deity, especially for protecting male children from smallpox. Nearly every family had a painting of Shoki, armed with a double-edged sword and wearing his special winged cap, to serve as a talisman.

Sengai and Hakuin loved the subject of Shoki; Hakuin painted him dark and severe, while Sengai brushed him as the cartoon-style madcap military man we see here, with a perfect expression of surprise and befuddlement on the little demon's face.

22
SENGAI Gibon (1750–1837)
Shoki, the demon-queller
hanging scroll, ink on paper,
123 x 53.4 cm

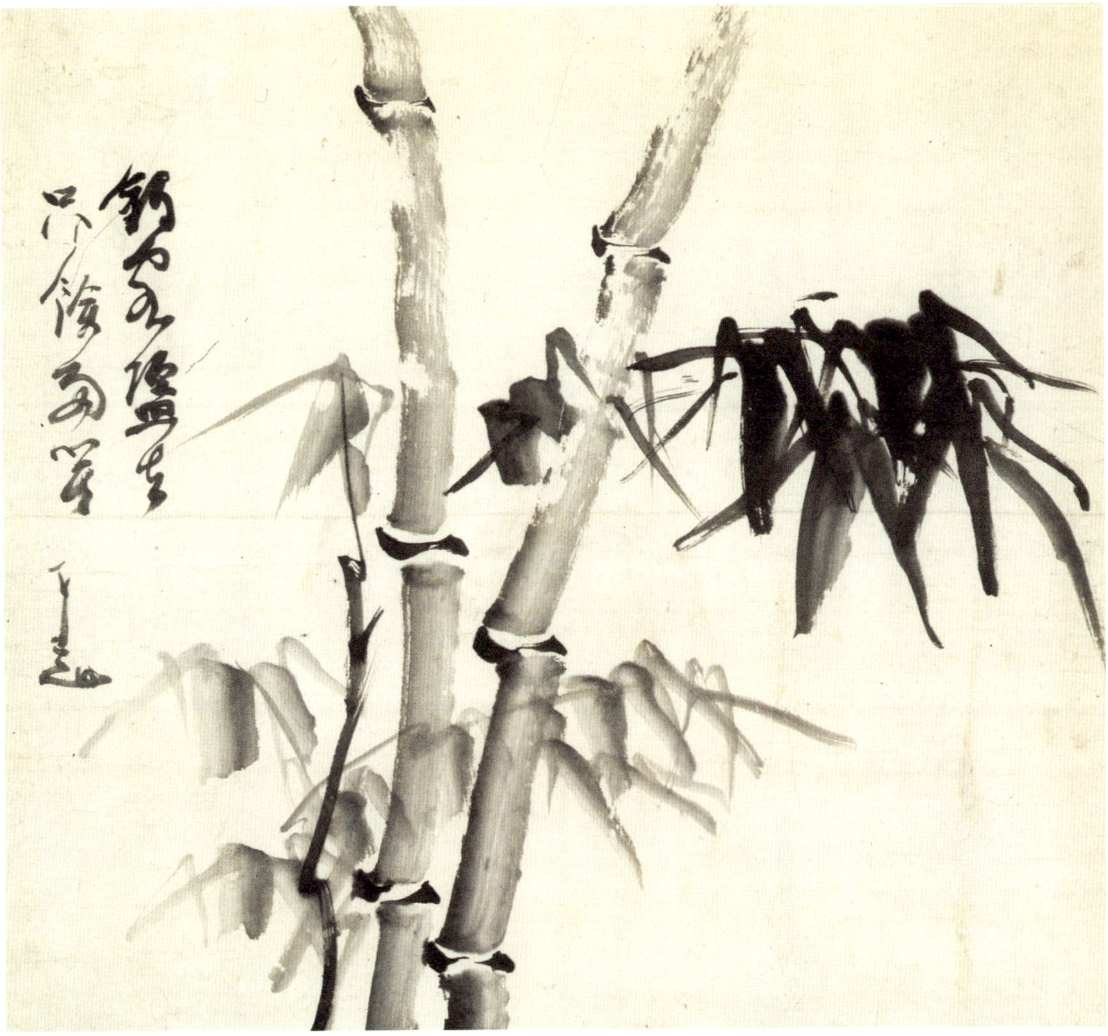

釣客盗去
只餘兩竿
厓

After the fisherman has stolen what he wants,
All that is left are a couple of poles.

Gai

In old Japan, fishermen fashioned their poles from bamboo. The noble bamboo surrenders to so many purposes without complaint, but the sturdy plant renews itself and continues to flourish despite adversity. The bamboo is beautiful under all conditions. On similar paintings of bamboo Sengai wrote, 'After the fisherman has stolen what he wants, all that remains is the pure wind' and 'This will serve as a fishing pole for the four seas'.

In Asian art, bamboo is considered the most difficult natural object to paint correctly (there is a saying among Chinese artists, 'When angry paint the bamboo; when happy paint the orchid'). There is nothing rigid or artificial about Sengai's bamboo. The brushstrokes are pliant, but like bamboo, they have a strong core.

23
SENGAI Gibon (1750–1837)
Bamboo
hanging scroll, ink on paper,
59.2 x 63.7 cm

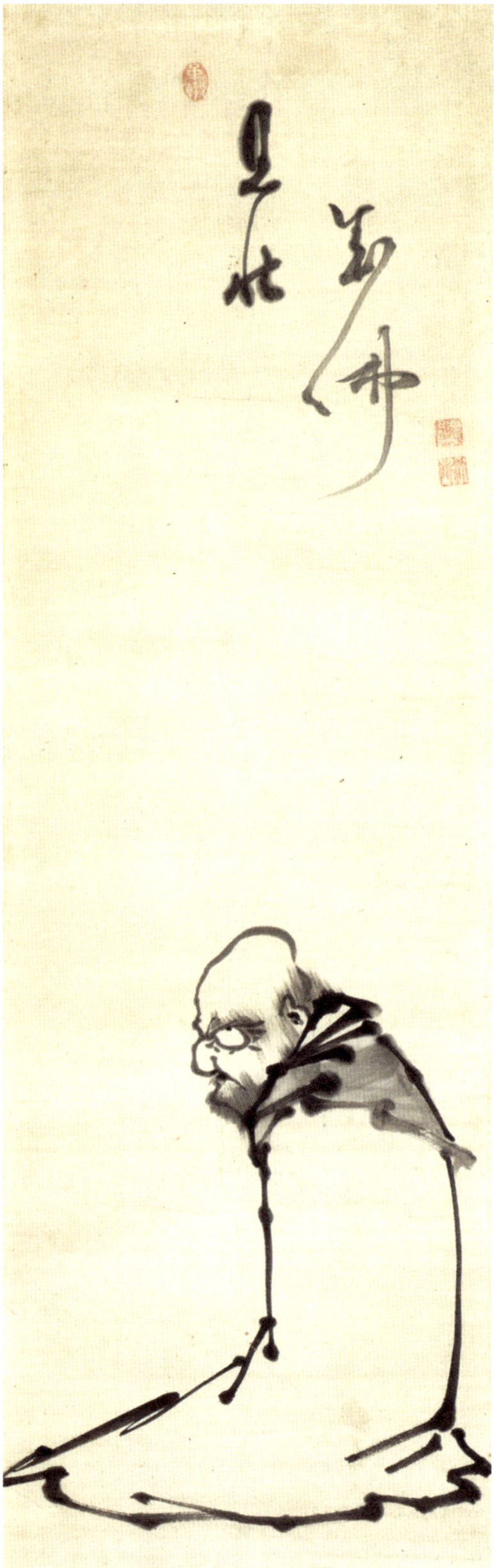

見
性
成
佛

See your nature
Become Buddha.

Hakuin's long-time disciple Suio succeeded his master as abbot of Shoinji.

The two had a rather complicated relationship, with Suio keeping his distance, literally and figuratively, from Hakuin. Suio disliked chanting sutras and doing *zazen* – in public at least (some say he did *zazen* at night when no one was around) – but he loved to drink sake, dally with geisha, play the board game *go*, and paint. Suio was essentially homeless, wandering to-and-fro as the mood struck him. He and Hakuin had several disagreements over the years, but were reconciled by the time of Hakuin's death. Although Hakuin entrusted him with the affairs of Shoinji, Suio did not change much as an abbot. When people asked to study with him, he would say, 'I know nothing about Zen. Go and see Torei at Ryutakuji'. Yet students still clamoured to see him, and hundreds of people came when he gave a public talk.

As we can see here, Suio was a talented artist, perhaps in the pantheon of Zen painters the most technically able after Fugai. Suio's brushstrokes are supple and bright. The patriarch's robes are particularly well formed, and in this side-view portrait Suio has captured well Daruma's fierce meditation.

24
SUIO Genro (1716–1789)
Side-view Daruma
hanging scroll, ink on paper,
96.5 x 29.2 cm

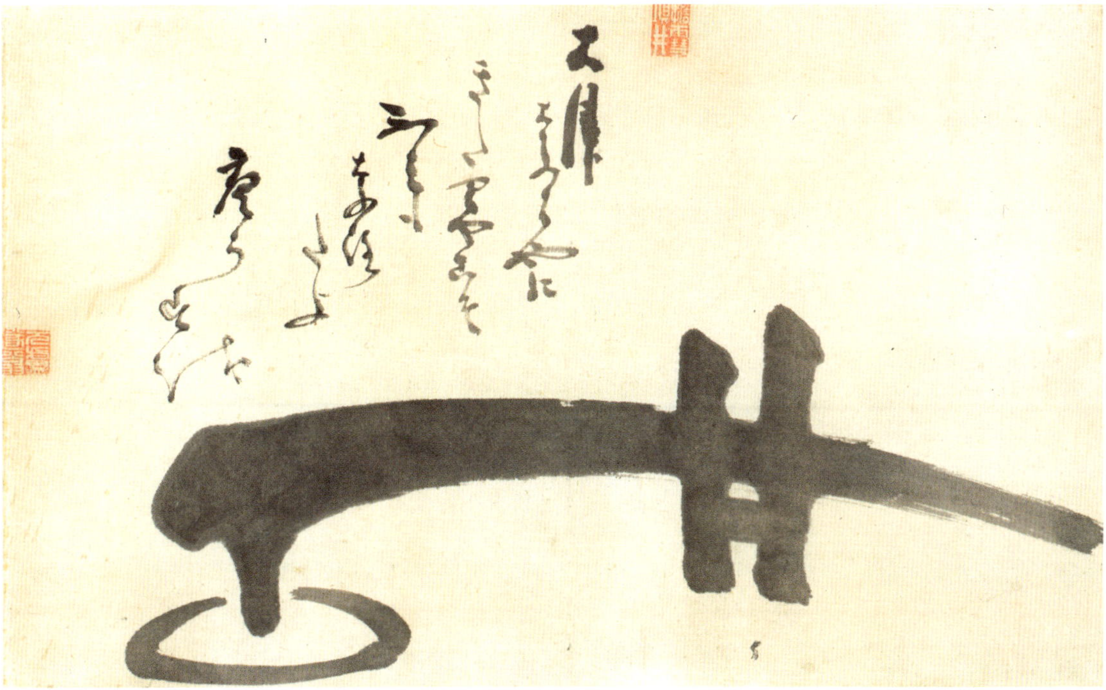

大津
奈らやに
き多里や古そ
ふミも
習憂
多よ
唐う
春越

When you come to the Naraya in Otsu
You also learn
To pound a mortar.

This simple painting has several levels of meaning. It shows a *karausu*, a cantilever device pushed up and down to hull rice in a mortar. In Zen tradition the sixth Chinese patriarch Eno (Huineng, 638–713) was believed to have been an illiterate lay monk who laboured in the rice-threshing room of a monastery until he was discovered to be a person of superior insight. In Zen lore, this story is very important – as Sengai wrote in one of his poems, acts like gathering firewood and hulling rice can also transform one into a Buddha – and in Zenga, the rice-pounder is an immediately recognisable symbol of the sixth patriarch.

On another level however, the inscription refers to a brothel called Naraya in Otsu, a pilgrimage city about a day out of Kyoto. That is to say, when you visit Otsu on a pilgrimage for your spirit, you can also enjoy physical pleasure ('pound the mortar up and down'). This combination of images may be shocking at first, but the painting is a wry comment on human nature and makes the point that everyday acts of life – pounding rice, having sex – can all be vehicles for Zen training (some researchers reject this interpretation, and insist the inscription is mere word play despite the obvious sexual connotations of 'pound the mortar').

Suio has employed a wet brush to create the rice-pounder in a few strokes. The inscription dances impishly across the paper, and the lush imagery makes this work a subtle *shunga* (erotic painting) as well as a Zenga.

25
SUIO Genro (1716–1789)
The sixth patriarch's rice-pounder
hanging scroll, ink on paper, 32 x 50.6 cm

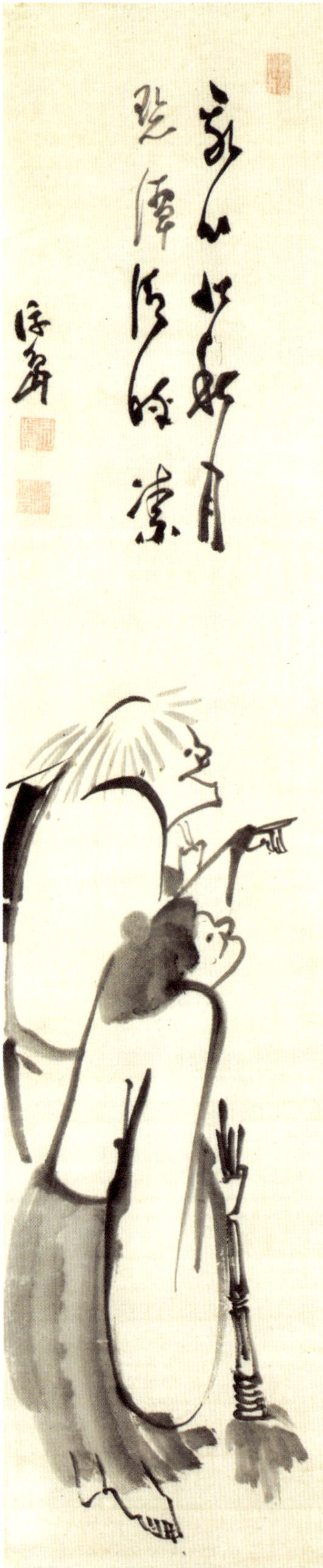

我心似秋月
碧潭清皎潔
浮島

My heart is like the autumn moon,
Shining pure and clear upon the blue pond.

Futo[1]

Kanzan and Jittoku are usually painted on separate scrolls which hang together as a pair, but sometimes they are painted together on a single sheet. Here they are pointing to the autumn moon, and the inscription is the most famous couplet from Kanzan's poems. The composition of the two figures and the placement of the calligraphy are perfectly integrated; the painting refreshes the viewer both visually and spiritually.

26
SUIO Genro (1716–1789)
Kanzan and Jittoku
hanging scroll, ink on paper,
113.5 x 24 cm

1. One of Suio's pen names

浮島翁画

東輝庵禅慧敬讃

阿弥陀佛一咲開
随時々々
和臺古鏡摧
萬徳不將來

All the virtue [of the Buddha] *is not in the future.*
The old mirror and the stable platform are shattered.
[Bukan says] *'Whenever! Whenever!'*
And makes Amida Buddha blossom all at once in this world.
Respectfully inscribed by Zenne

Painted by the old monk Futo[1]

Sidekick to the crazed pair of beggars Kanzan and Jittoku, the monk Bukan (Fengkan) was just as eccentric. Bukan had a pet tiger, alluded to here by the footprints, and would answer any question about Buddhism with 'Whenever! Whenever!' He was believed by some to be an incarnation of Amida Buddha, the Buddha of the Pure Land. The inscription means, 'you do not have to wait until you die to see the Pure Land of Amida, Bukan is showing it to you here right now'.

Although Bukan is alone here, sometimes Kanzan, Jittoku, Bukan and the tiger are painted harmoniously napping together as the Four Sleepers. The inscription is by Gessen, one of Sengai's teachers and a monk of the Kogetsu line (one of the two main streams of Rinzai Zen along with the Hakuin line). Kogetsu (1667– 1751) was its spiritual founder and its artists tended to be more low-key than those of the Hakuin line. The collaboration of the two artists here is unusual and intriguing.

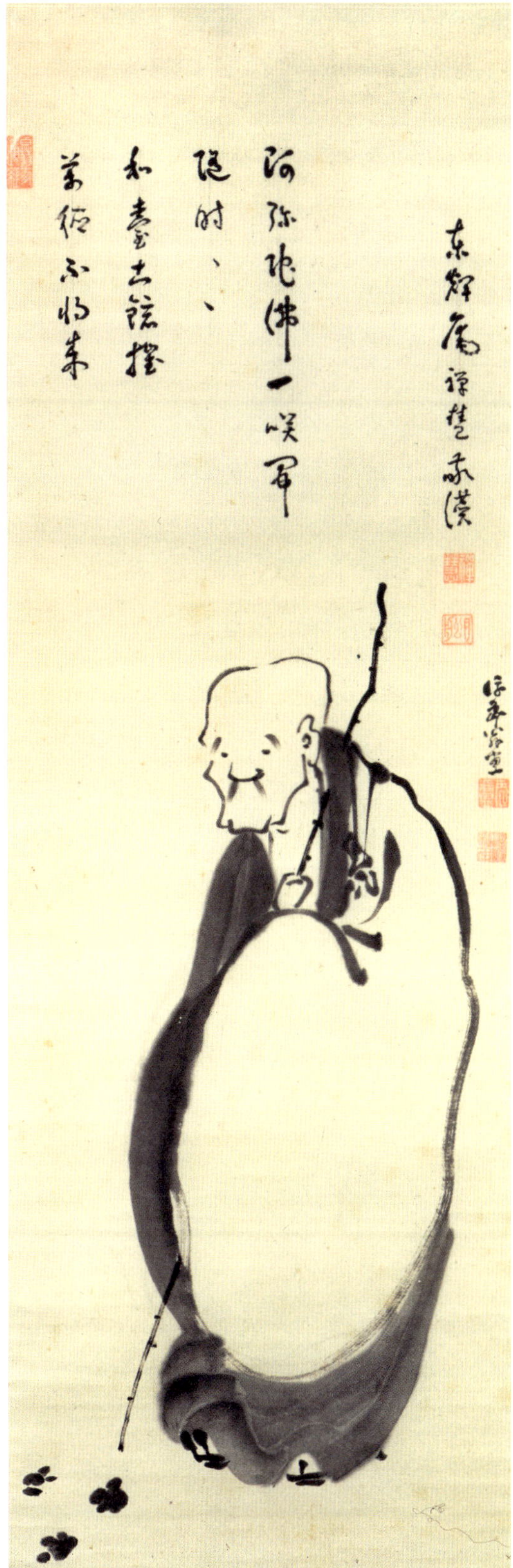

27
SUIO Genro (1716–1789), painting
GESSEN Zenne (1701–1781), inscription
Bukan and the tiger
hanging scroll, ink on paper,
129.3 x 41.9 cm

1. One of Suio's pen names

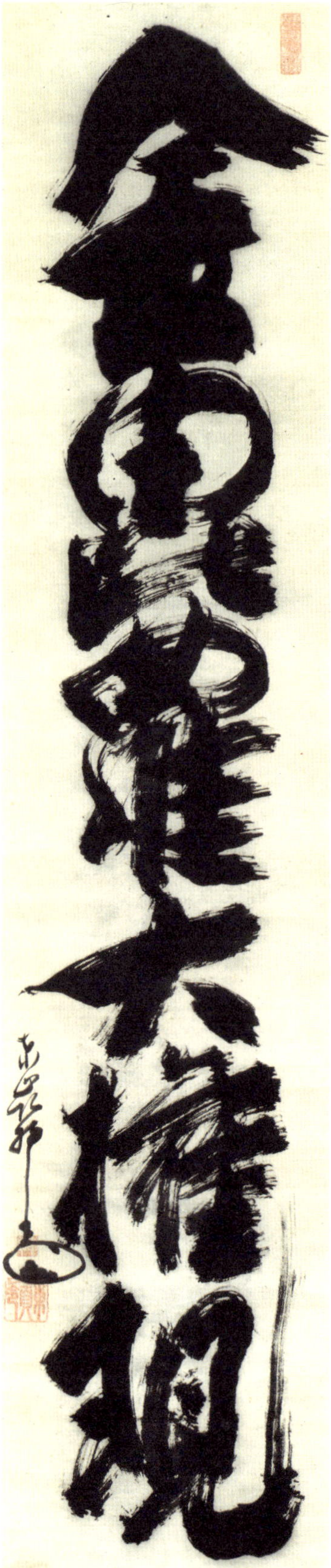

28
TOREI Enji (1721–1792)
Calligraphic talisman
hanging scroll, ink on paper,
128.9 x 27.6 cm

金毘羅大権現
東嶺書 [花押]

Konpira Daigongen

Torei kao[1]

Konpira is the patron deity of sailors, fishermen and travellers; *daigongen* means 'avatar', a universal Buddhist principle manifesting itself as a local Shinto deity. This kind of talismanic calligraphy is an important aspect of Zenga, since virtuous Zen masters were constantly being called upon to create such scrolls for their followers, patrons and friends. As Hakuin wrote in his book *Yaemugura* (goose grass):

> *Rather than hanging pretty pictures in your home alcove, mount a piece of calligraphy reading 'Konpira' or 'Akiba' [another avatar] and put it there. Pray to it, offer incense and it will ward off fire and theft, prevent disasters, foster the martial spirit, bring happiness and long life and secure peace for one's home and the entire world.*

Suio and Torei were Hakuin's key disciples, but the two could not have been more different. A child prodigy, Torei became a monastic acolyte at age five. Strict, meticulous and an outstanding scholar, he brushed many calligraphies and paintings enthusiastically. But if Suio was one of the most technically gifted Zen artists, Torei was one of the worst, or at least genuinely did not care how the finished product looked. The calligraphy here is not too bad, and the ink tones are almost electric, but the comparatively good brushwork displayed here is the exception rather than the rule. While Suio's personal life was free spirited, his brushwork is tight and controlled; on the other hand, Torei was known for his serious character but is often totally abandoned in his brushwork.

1. A *kao* is a special calligraphic cipher added to a signature for authenticity. It was used by samurai lords on their documents, and sometimes also by Zen monks. The clam-shaped *kao* was used with most of Torei's signatures

因甚麼
暗渡江
何處是
生荊棘
雲叟拝讃［花押］

Fate brought Daruma
across the river;
Where is he?
Among the thorns.

Respectfully inscribed by Old Cloud[1]

This work shows Daruma's miraculous crossing of the Yangtze River atop a single rush leaf after his enigmatic interview with the Chinese emperor (see p 21) – an important legend in Zen history. It signifies Daruma (symbolising Zen) approaching the world of entanglements (the thorns of the inscription) to teach human beings.

Not much is known about Reigen, a mysterious, reclusive figure, who lived as a hermit much of his life. He was the third great Zenga artist among Hakuin's direct students and it is said he would travel many miles in the walking meditation posture; he would bow politely if he met someone along the way but would never say a word. Reigen was the first of Hakuin's disciples to serve as an abbot at a major temple (Rokuoin, on the grounds of Tenryuji) in Kyoto. Suio and Torei almost always signed their work and Hakuin began to sign his paintings late in life, but there is no known work with a Reigen signature, rather than a seal. Thus Reigen's pieces are often mistaken for the work of Hakuin or Suio. Ishin was also a student of Hakuin, but did very few Zenga. A teacher, Ishin was said to keep an unsheathed sword in his interview room to chase away students who gave unacceptable answers to his Zen questions.

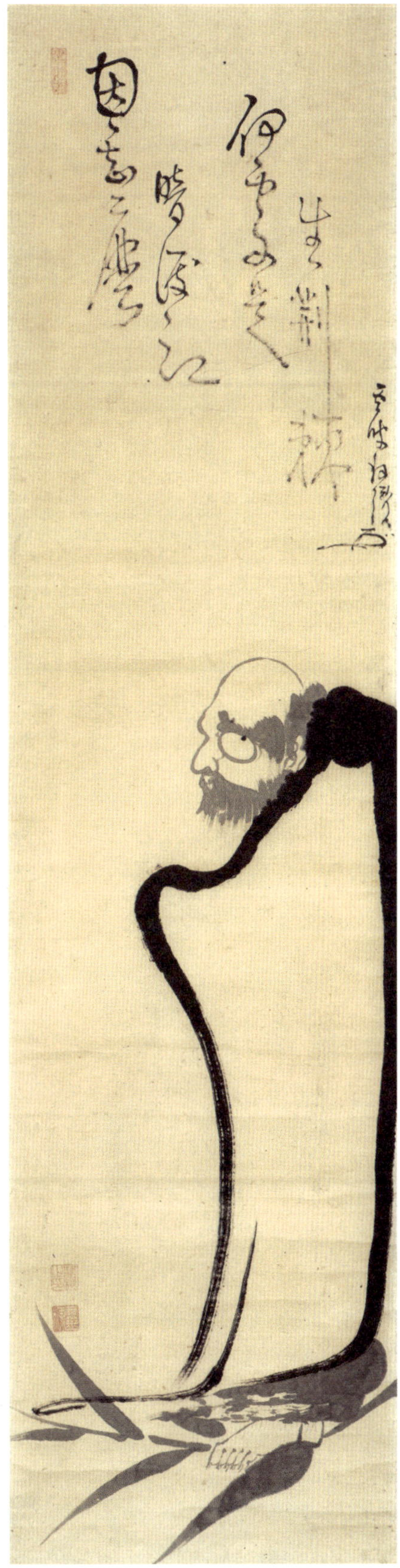

29
REIGEN Eto (1721–1785), painting
ISHIN Eryu (1720–1759), inscription
Rush leaf Daruma
hanging scroll, ink on paper,
114 x 28.7 cm

1. One of Ishin's pen names

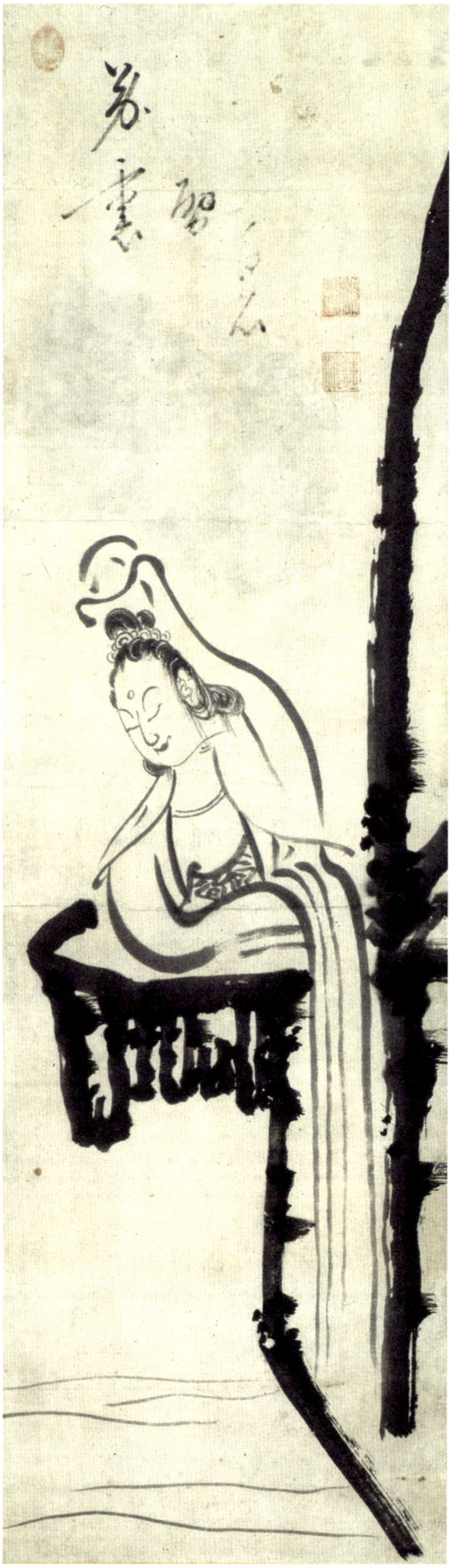

30
REIGEN Eto (1721–1785)
White-robed Kannon
hanging scroll, ink on paper,
94.3 x 27.9 cm
[right] detail

芥裏劈白玉

In the midst of the world's corruption
She is white jade.

This extraordinarily feminine, almost voluptuous portrayal of the bodhisattva Kannon is somewhat unusual. Reigen was skilled at animating his portraits of Daruma and Kannon in a style mid-way between the finely brushed pieces of Hakuin and the cartoon-like strokes of Sengai. As we see here, the effect is quite beautiful and pleasing; her subtle smile gives the appearance of a Zen Mona Lisa.

Reigen is a difficult Zen master to pin down. Silent for much of his life and apparently extremely introspective, this surprising Zen story reveals another side of his character:

> Kaimon, a newly minted Zen Master, met Reigen and announced proudly, 'I received my certificate of enlightenment from the great teacher Daishu Zenjo'. Reigen suddenly shoved Kaimon down with his hands, saying, 'My hands or Buddha's hands – how do they compare?' Before Kaimon could utter a word, Reigen stomped over him and continued walking.

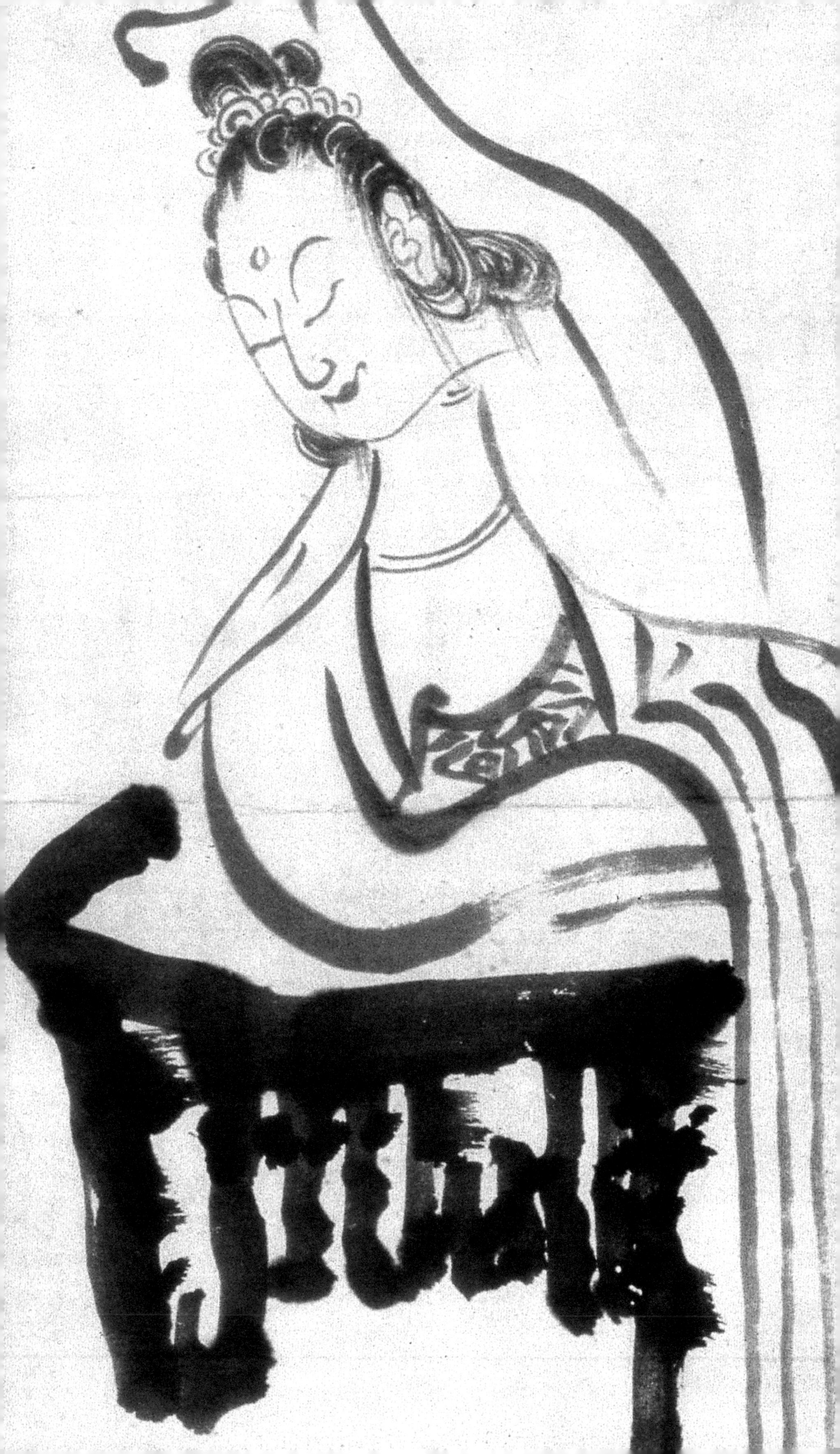

鴉過古村霜

Crows fly past, frost covers the ancient village.

The inscription comes from a line of poetry by Hakuin, evidently written at the end of the meditation session held in the 12th month to mark Buddha's enlightenment. Although Hakuin used this inscription on paintings of Shakyamuni (the historical Buddha), Daruma and (of course) crows, no one is really sure of the meaning. Here, crows fly through a village that looks like it could be experiencing frost, but why would such an inscription be on a painting of Buddha or Daruma? One possible interpretation is that world of nature around us is the same as Buddha-nature, the realm of enlightenment, and if we realise that truth we will be as enlightened as Shakyamuni or Daruma. Indeed, this simple, luminous painting projects a deep sense of serenity and the reassurance that 'all is right with the world'.

31
REIGEN Eto (1721–1785)
Crows in the village
hanging scroll, ink on paper,
120.7 x 28.1 cm

春業試毫
文化十四年丁丑號旦

結果自然成
一華開五葉

One flower opens to five leaves;
Everything is accomplished naturally.

1817, Shunso's first brushwork of the New Year

Shunso, a student of Reigen and Suio, was well-known for his large-scale Zenga of Daruma, Hotei and Fukurokuju, executed in chiselled brushwork. Judging from this powerful Daruma, Shunso must have had an outgoing personality. It has a hard, slightly confrontational edge. The inscription is a common one on Daruma paintings and essentially it means, 'Open up the flower of your mind, expand your consciousness, and enlightenment naturally results'.

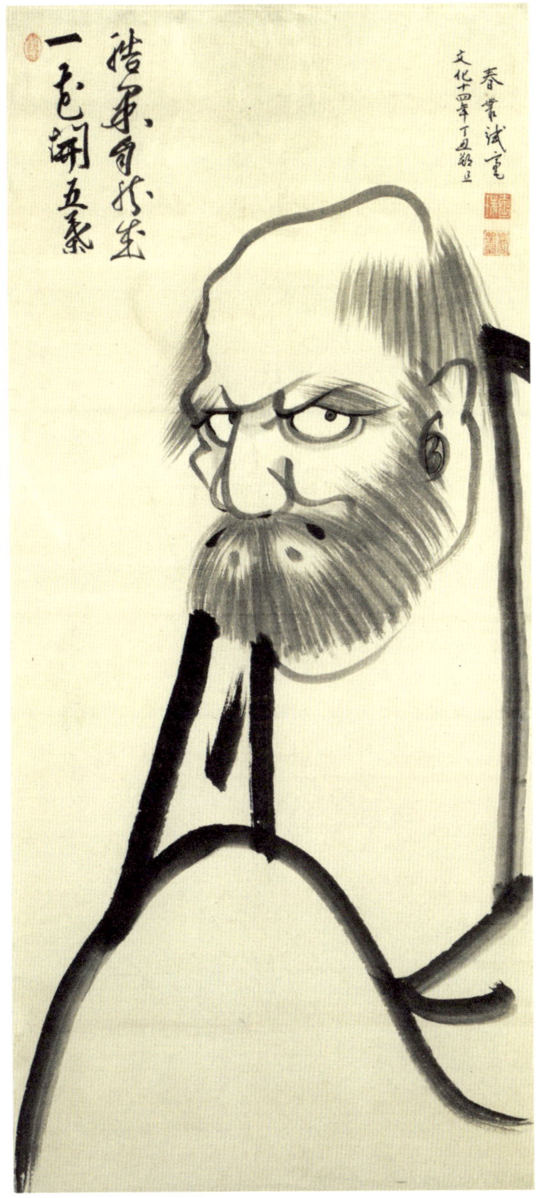

32
SHUNSO Joshu (1750–1839)
Giant Daruma
1828
hanging scroll, ink on paper,
134 x 59 cm

十年
五橋邊二
無人記第
風饗水宿

春叢

Feasting on air and lodging on water,
No one has recorded
The twenty years he lived
Under the Fifth Avenue Bridge.[1]

Shunso

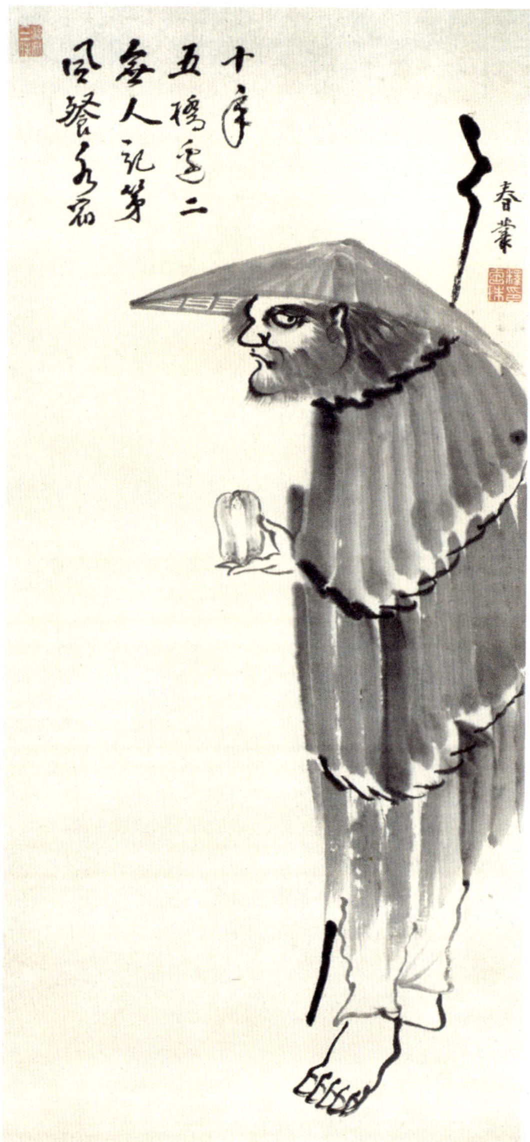

This is another full-scale Zenga by Shunso, depicting the celebrated 14th-century monk Daito (also known as Shuho Myocho). Emulating the Zen heroes of old after his enlightenment experience under the master Daio (also known as Nanpo Jomyo), Daito secluded himself from the world, living as a beggar beneath the Fifth Avenue Bridge in Kyoto. Determined to locate the reclusive monk, the emperor Hanazono sent an aide to lure him out. Knowing that Daito was fond of melons, the aide said, 'This tasty melon is for the first one who can come and get it with a foot'. When Daito responded, 'First, give it without a hand', he was found out. Daito later established Daitokuji, perhaps the most influential Zen temple in Japan. Posthumously, he was proclaimed *kokushi*, 'national teacher'.

Hakuin considered Daito to be head of his lineage, and did several paintings on this theme. Shunso's version is also excellent: Daito's facial expression is especially sharp and the brushwork is big and bold.

33
SHUNSO Joshu (1750–1839)
Daito Kokushi
hanging scroll, ink on paper,
120 x 55 cm

1. These verses are taken from a poem by the 15th-century Zen monk Ikkyu. 'No one has recorded' means 'everyone has forgotten'

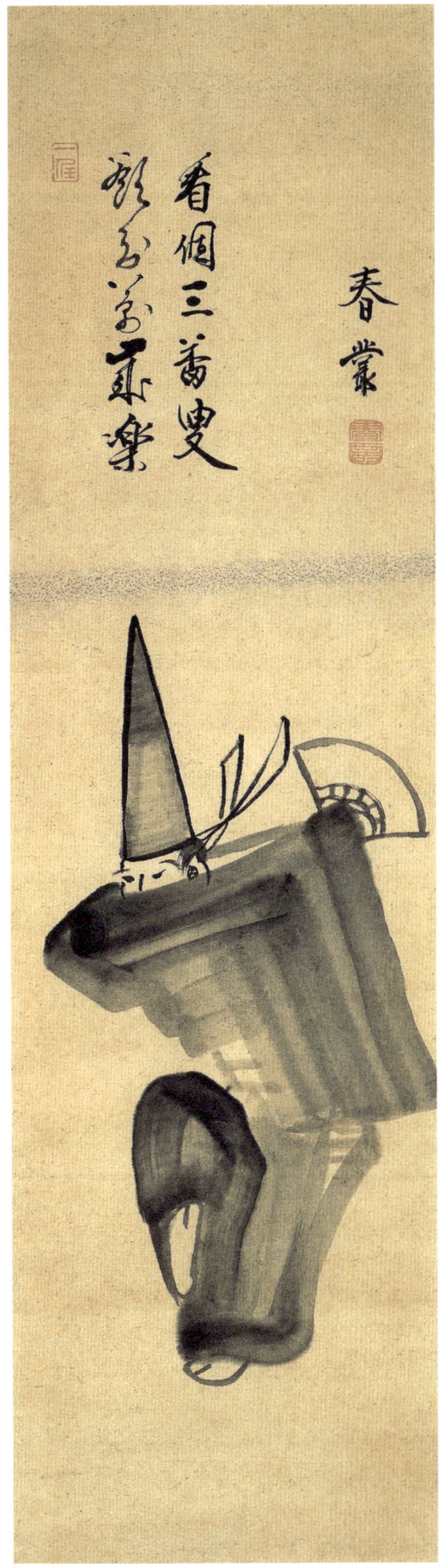

春叢

看個三番叟
観知萬歳楽

If you want a pleasure that will last 10 000 years
Watch a No master perform Sanbaso.

Shunso

Sanbaso is a famous No drama with a dance believed to bring good luck for 10 000 years. No has always been closely associated with Zen – a master performer must harmonise body and mind with the chorus and audience so that they become one. With a minimum of brushstrokes Shunso has recreated all the drama and creative tension of the dance, capturing the 'perfect stillness in the midst of movement', which is the essence of Zen.

34
SHUNSO Joshu (1750–1839)
No dancer
hanging scroll, ink on paper,
100.3 x 27.6 cm

虎

廣壽即非書

KO [TIGER]

[signed]
Brushed by Koju[1] Sokuhi

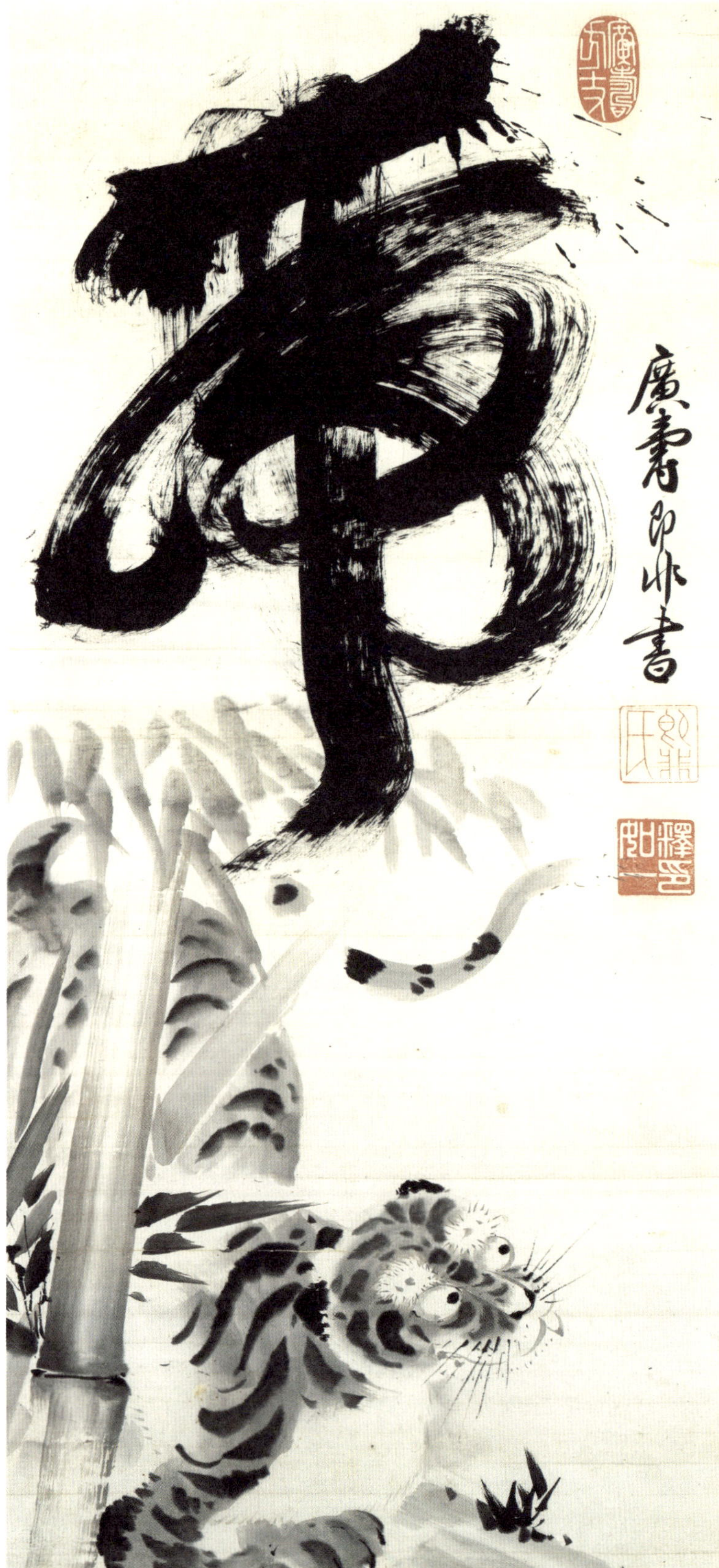

35
Obaku SOKUHI (1616–1671)
Dragon and tiger
pair of hanging scrolls,
ink on paper,
each 113 x 51.1 cm
(overleaf) details

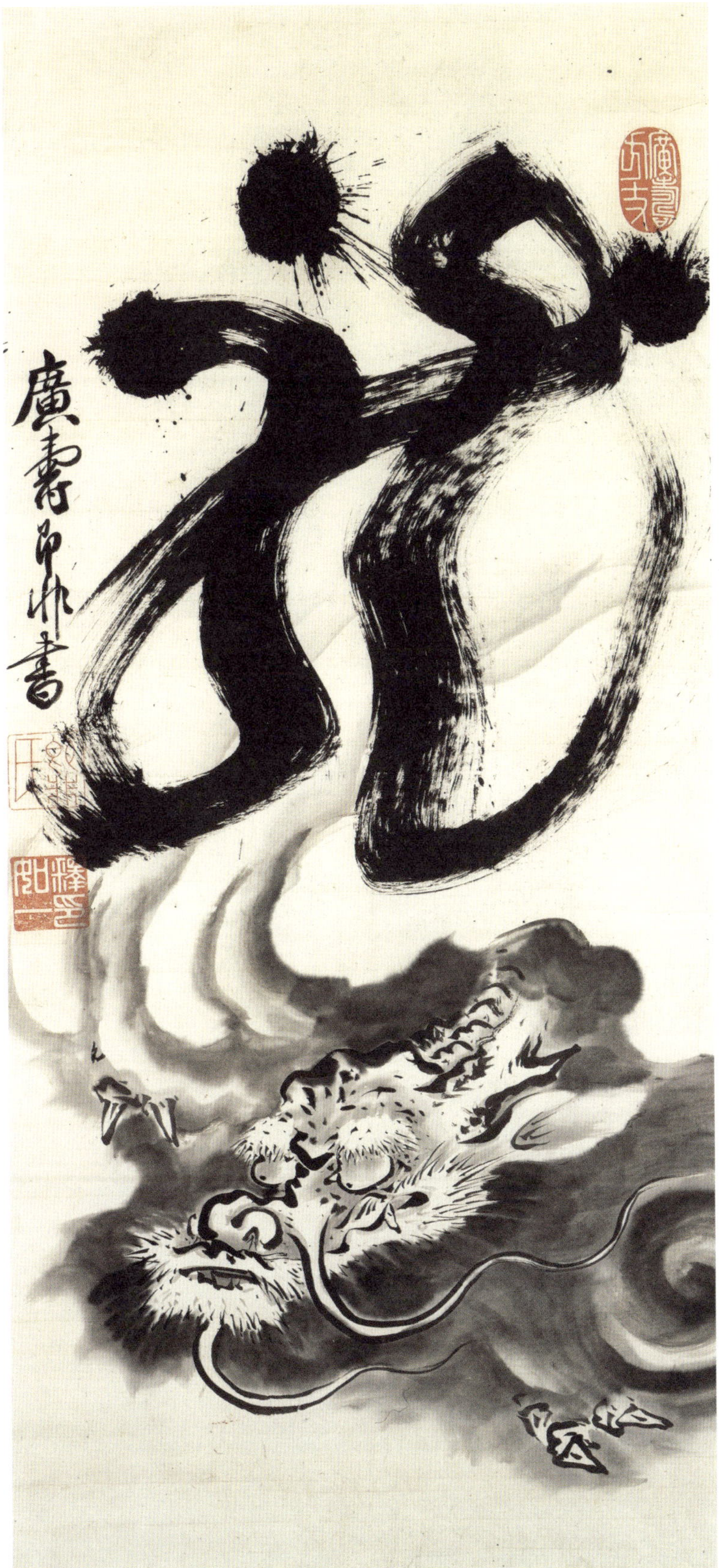

龍
廣壽即非書

RYU [DRAGON]

[signed]
Brushed by Koju Sokuhi

1. Mount Koju, site of the temple of Sofukuji, where Sokuhi lived

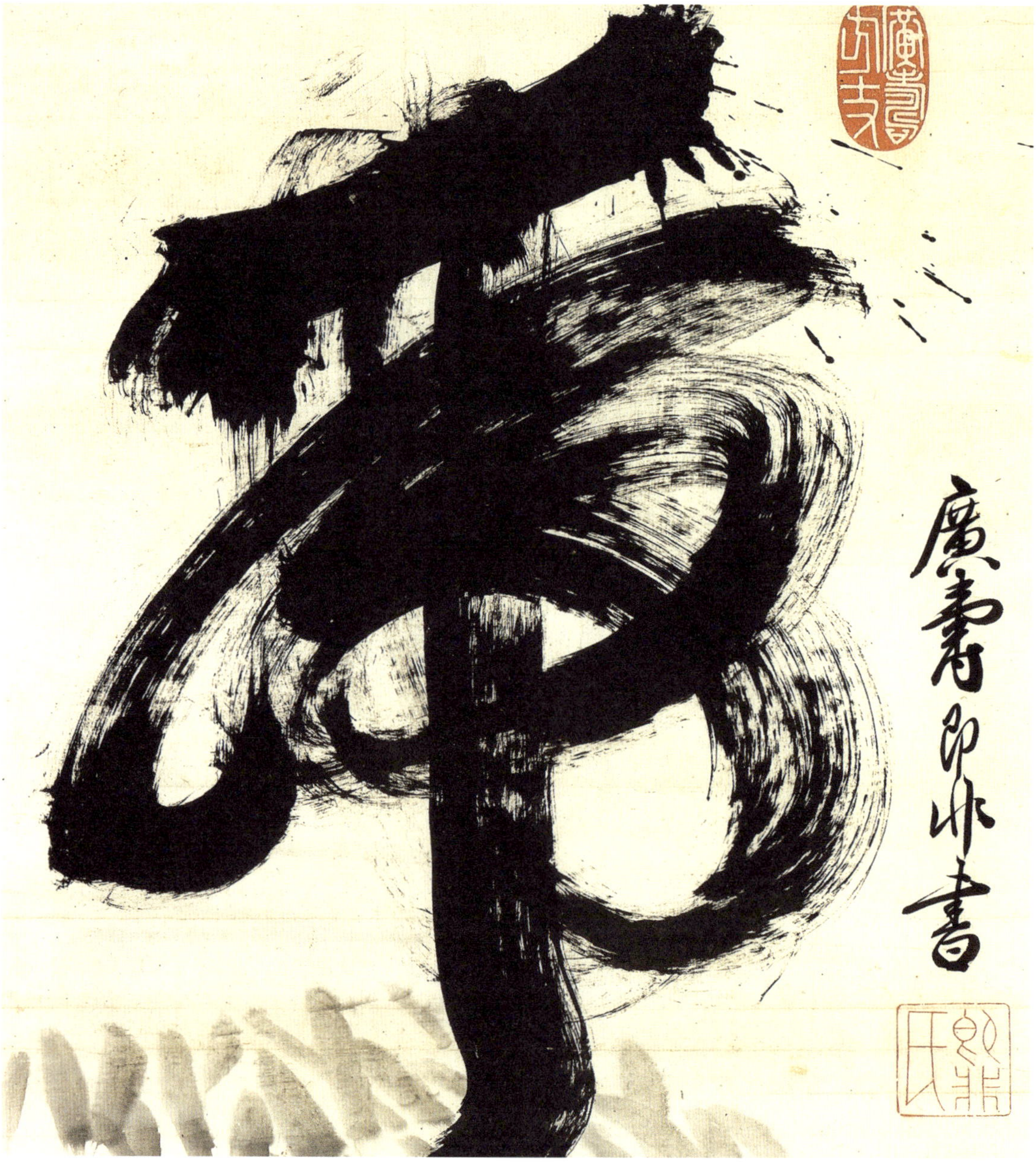
廣壽即非書

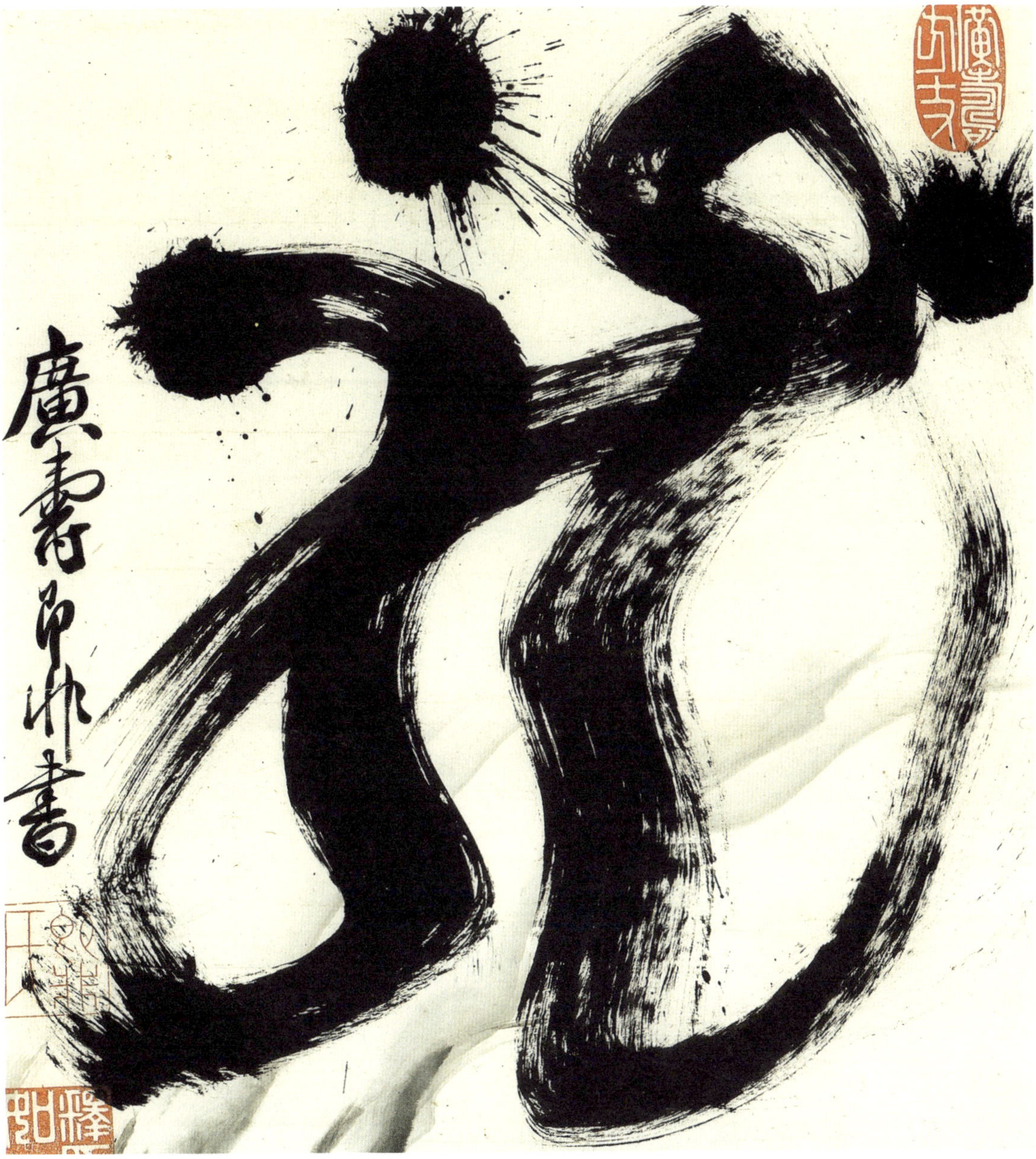

In addition to the Rinzai and Soto streams of Zen in Japan there is the Obaku sect, located at Manpukuji in Uji, south of Kyoto. The Obaku sect was founded by Chinese émigré monks in the 17th century and, even today when the abbot and monks are all Japanese, the sect has a distinctive liturgical and artistic style that is Chinese in influence. Although Sokuhi never became abbot of Manpukuji, he was nonetheless considered a master of the highest rank: Ingen, Mokuan and Sokuhi were the Three Patriarchs of Obaku Zen in Japan.

The dragon flying about in the clouds and the tiger roaming in the bamboo thicket are paired in Asian art as symbols of spiritual power and enlightened wisdom (dragon) and physical strength and courageous living (tiger). In Zen art, the dragon and tiger represent the harmonisation of the spiritual with the physical, heaven with earth. Sokuhi has brushed the two in both their calligraphic (abstract) and pictorial (concrete) forms. The brushwork is bold, dynamic and vivid, with a subtle playfulness that animates the 'on guard' stances of the tiger and dragon.

可憐鬧市無
人識獨自肩
擔布袋歸

［花押］

上天無梯不如坐
遠隔率陀何處歸 應
釣命卒奉塵 玉韻予亦加賛詞云
慎袋子

[Nobutada's inscription]
Such a pity, even in a market place
No one recognises him [as an incarnation of Maitreya Buddha]*;*
So alone he returns
With his sack across his shoulders.

[In the lower right hand corner are Nobutada's cipher and seal]

[Kogetsu's inscription]
[Hotei] *just sits here; there is no ladder to heaven.*
The Tushita heaven where Maitreya resides is too far.
Where can he go?
He still has a mission here in this world.

I was asked to compose a verse
And add it as an inscription.

Shinteishi[1]

The great courtier Nobutada was a contemporary of Fugai (as noted in entry no 1; an art dealer once tried to pass off a Fugai painting as a 'Nobutada'). Though they share a Zen spirit their backgrounds could not have been more different – Fugai lived in caves, Nobutada in the imperial court. In Japan Nobutada is honoured as one of the great calligraphers of all time, but he also produced many paintings in the rough-hewn Zen style. Although Nobutada was a layman with considerable duties as a high-ranking minister, it is said that every morning with a few simple strokes he brushed a portrait of Tenjin, the god of learning. He depicted Daruma, Hotei and other Zen themes (see the next entry) but like Fugai, Nobutada apparently did no portraits of Kannon.

1. One of Kogetsu's pen names

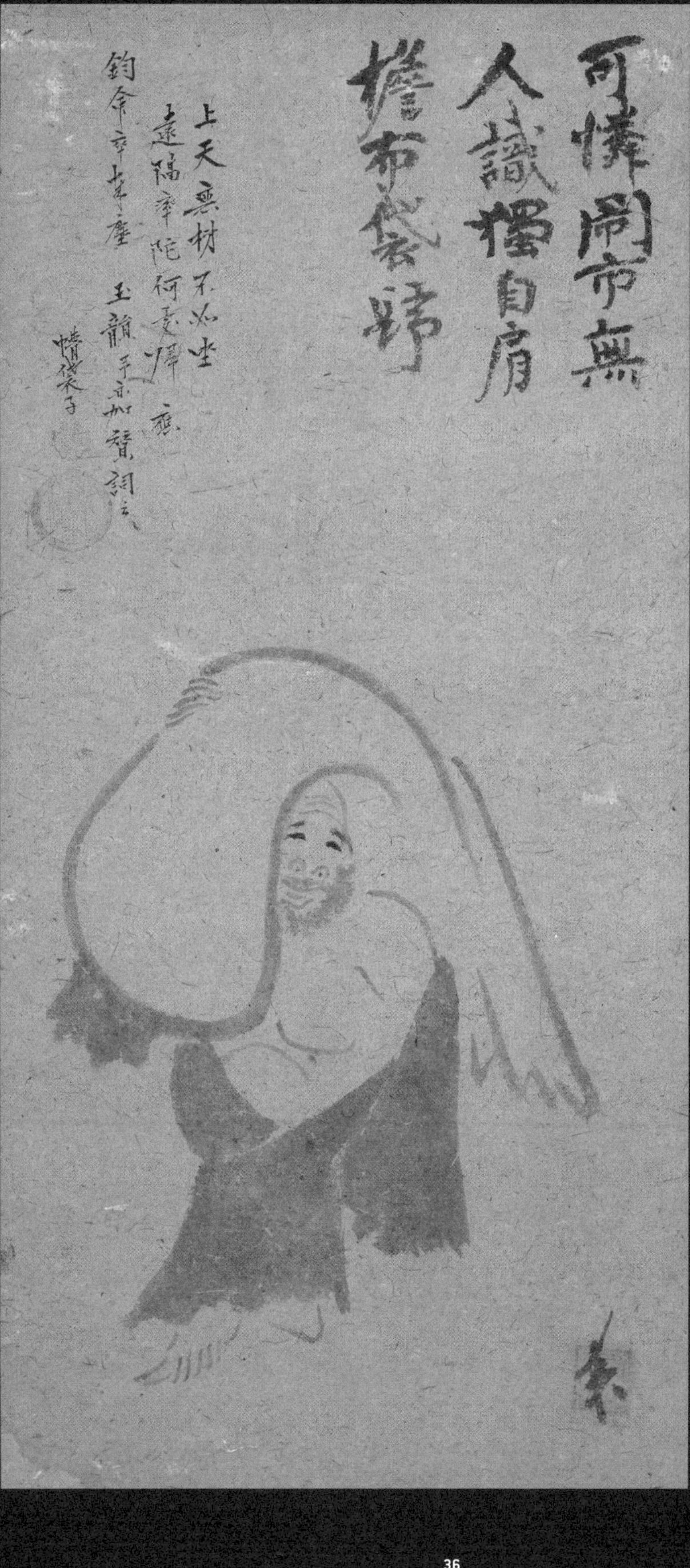

36
Konoe NOBUTADA (1565–1614)
painting and inscription
Daitokuji KOGETSU (1574–1643)
additional inscription

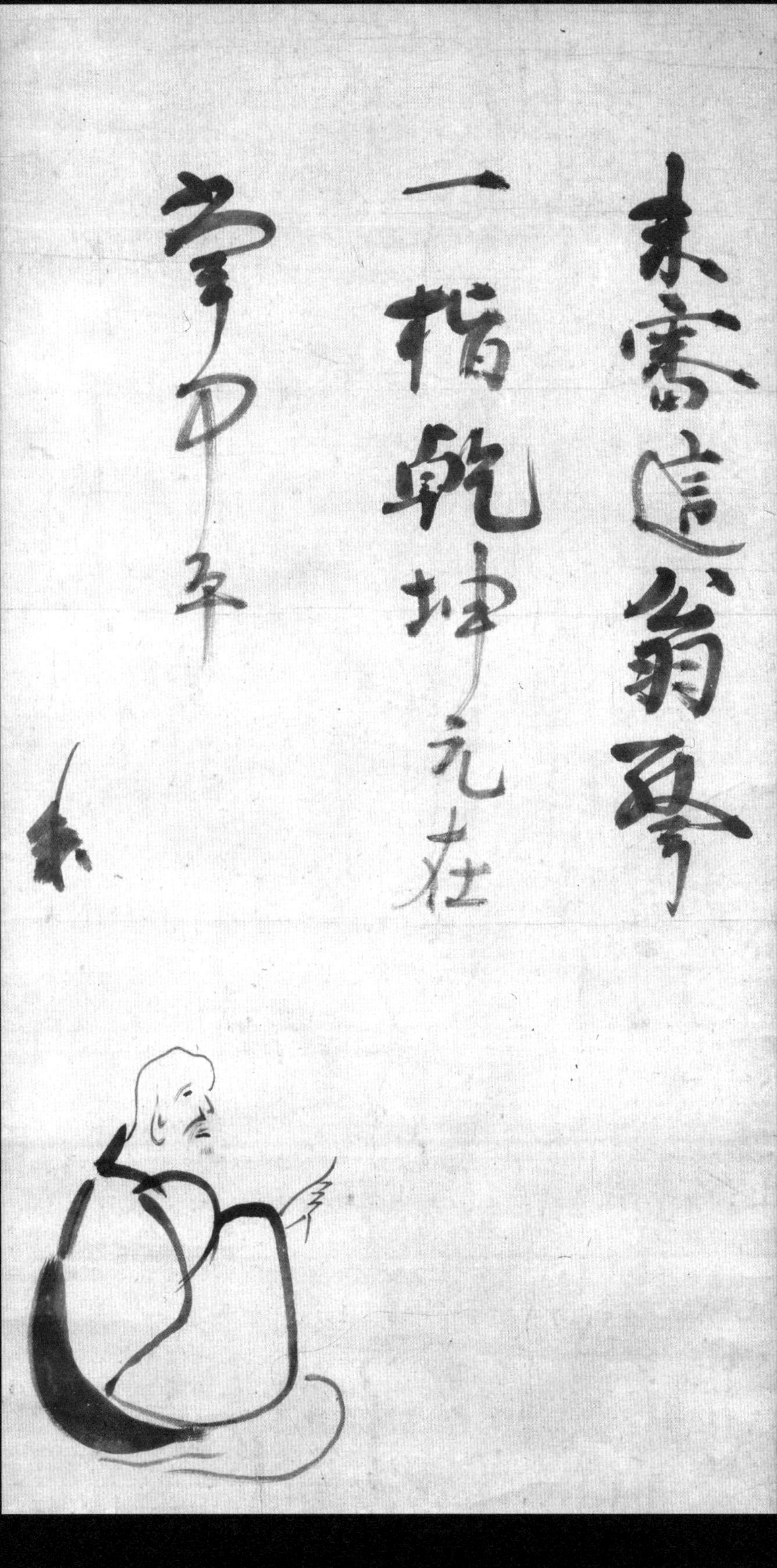

37
Konoe NOBUTADA (1565–1614)
Gutei's one finger
hanging scroll, ink on paper,
55.2 x 28.6 cm

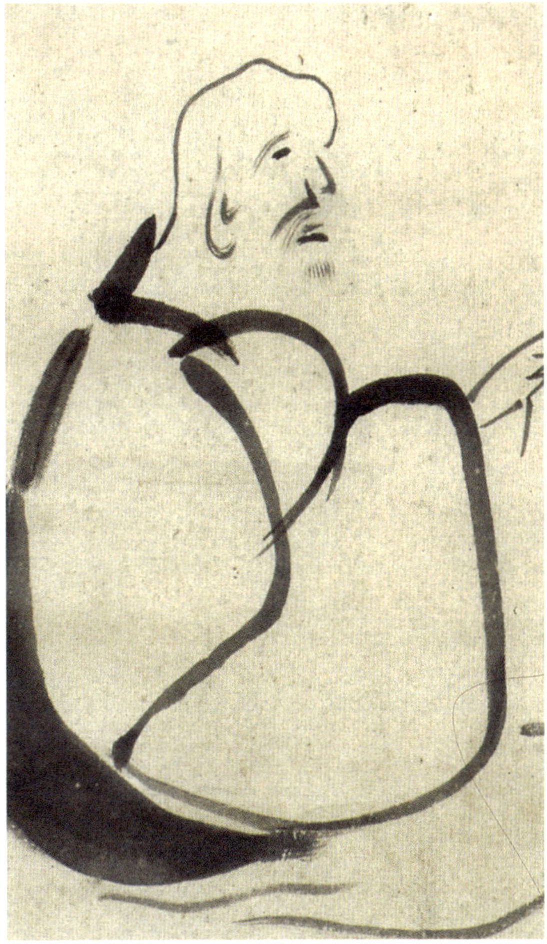

來客這翁聲
一指乾坤元在
掌中卓
[花押]

To all his visitors the venerable master held up one finger and said, 'The cosmos is contained right here!'

[On the left side is Nobutada's cipher]

This story comes from case no 3 of the *Mumonkan*:

> *Whenever Gutei was asked about Zen, the master simply stuck up one finger. One day, a visitor asked an acolyte, 'What is the essential point of your master's teaching?' When Gutei saw the acolyte hold up one finger in reply, Gutei cut off the finger with a knife. As the acolyte ran out of the room screaming in pain, Gutei called to him. When he turned around, Gutei stuck up one finger. The acolyte was enlightened.*

Almost nothing is known about the Chinese master Gutei, not even the dates of his birth and death, but this *koan* is famous in Zen lore and often appears as a theme in Zenga. This is a quite humorous portrayal of Gutei – the master himself appears to be confused about the meaning of 'one finger'.

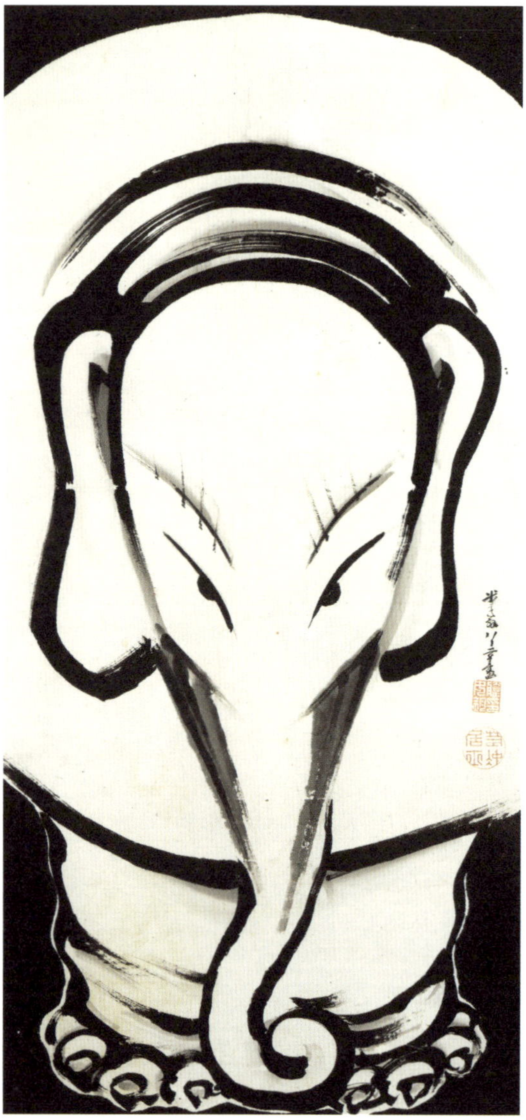

米斗翁八十二書

1795

The 82-year-old fellow Maito[1]

Like Nobutada, Ito Jakuchu was a Zen monk at heart, but because of his many obligations was unable to renounce the world formally to become a Buddhist priest. Jakuchu was head of the family business, a major wholesale store in the greengrocers' district in Kyoto that served more than 3000 retailers. Jakuchu spent more time meditating and painting than shop-keeping, and the business suffered until he finally turned it over to a younger brother in 1775. However, Jakuchu is now considered one of Japan's greatest and most eccentric artists. Jakuchu was particularly known for his depictions of vegetables – his famous *The Vegetable Buddha's entrance into nirvana* in the Kyoto National Museum depicts the dying Shakyamuni as a giant radish and all of his lamenting disciples as vegetables and fruits. Interestingly, there is a Jakuchu painting of a turnip with an inscription by Sengai that says, 'Looks good enough to eat' (Jakuchu's paintings are somewhat akin to the art of the Chinese eccentric Bada Sanren (1626–1705), who also achieved fame as a painter of flowers, vegetables, birds, and small animals in a distinctive and highly unusual style).

Jakuchu left many paintings on Zen themes. While at first glance this painting appears to have little in common with religion, it is in fact a Daruma elephant – the direct head-on, eye-to-eye portrayal is reminiscent of the celebrated *Penetrating gaze Daruma*, by the 17th-century samurai swordsman and painter Miyamoto *Musashi*. Like Daruma, a Zen elephant is irresistible – massive, intent, unstoppable.[2]

38
Ito JAKUCHU (1716–1800)
Elephant Daruma
1795
hanging scroll, ink on paper,
120.9 x 56.8 cm

1. One of Jakuchu's pen names, also sometimes written in reverse, Tomai

2. There are examples of paintings of Daruma riding an elephant by other artists

心如墻壁
日月眼睛
廓然無聖
覿龍現成
丹崖其拝題

A mind like a thick wall,
Eyes as bright as the sun and moon.
Vast emptiness, nothing holy!
Behold a dragon manifest right here!

Respectfully inscribed by Tangai[1]

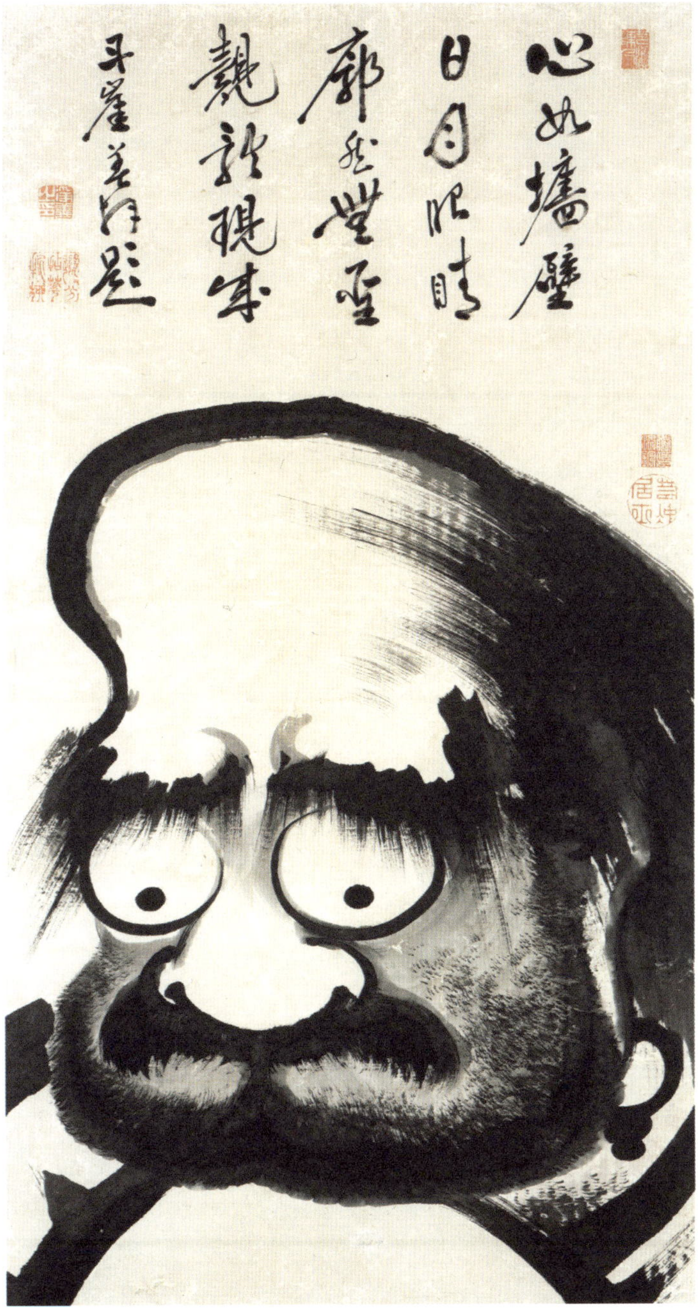

As the inscription states, Daruma is the embodiment of Zen: he has clear vision and a stable, enlightened mind; he is not attached to any doctrine and doesn't make distinctions between the sacred and the profane. In this huge portrait bristling with Zen energy, Jakuchu has brought Daruma to life. There is nothing sanctimonious in this depiction of the grand patriarch; on the contrary, it is laced with Zen humour. Daruma is looking down – a gaze rarely seen in Zen art – and seems surprised, as if he is thinking, 'Even after all these centuries representing Zen, I found something new!' Hidden for centuries, this splendid painting suddenly turned up as this exhibition was in the final planning stages as if to say, 'Include me, too!'

39
Ito JAKUCHU (1716–1800)
painting
TANGAI Musen Jozen (1693–1764)
inscription
Giant Daruma
hanging scroll, ink on paper,
109.9 x 59.4 cm

1. Musen Jozen, an Obaku Zen monk-poet with the pen name of Tangai, inscribed several of Jakuchu's Zen paintings

非是僧非是俗非是聖
非是凡三千界褌一枚
箒掃
海雲盧秀子書

[Jittoku]
Not a monk, not a layman,
Not a saint, not a sinner
In 3000 worlds just a ragamuffin with a straw broom.

Brushed by Roshu of Kaiun

是真是優
這個獨童
面目不相露
髪長似蓮
海雲三代盧秀讃

[Kanzan]
This is true, this is real.
What he recites makes him special.
His original face has not been revealed.
His hair is long, and wild as a lotus flower.

Inscription by Roshu, Third Generation Abbot of Kaiun

These paintings of Kanzan and Jittoku are a classic theme of Zen art, but Jakuchu has the pair facing away from us (whereas his elephant Daruma is coming towards us head-on). Kanzan, with an open scroll, and Jittoku, with his broom, are immediately recognisable, but why do they have their backs to us? Are they showing their disdain for the world? Are they telling us that no one has really seen (understood) them?

The composition is excellent and unusual – although we cannot quite explain why, there is something surreal about Jakuchu's art that catches our attention. Roshu was an Obaku abbot who inscribed several of Jakuchu's paintings.

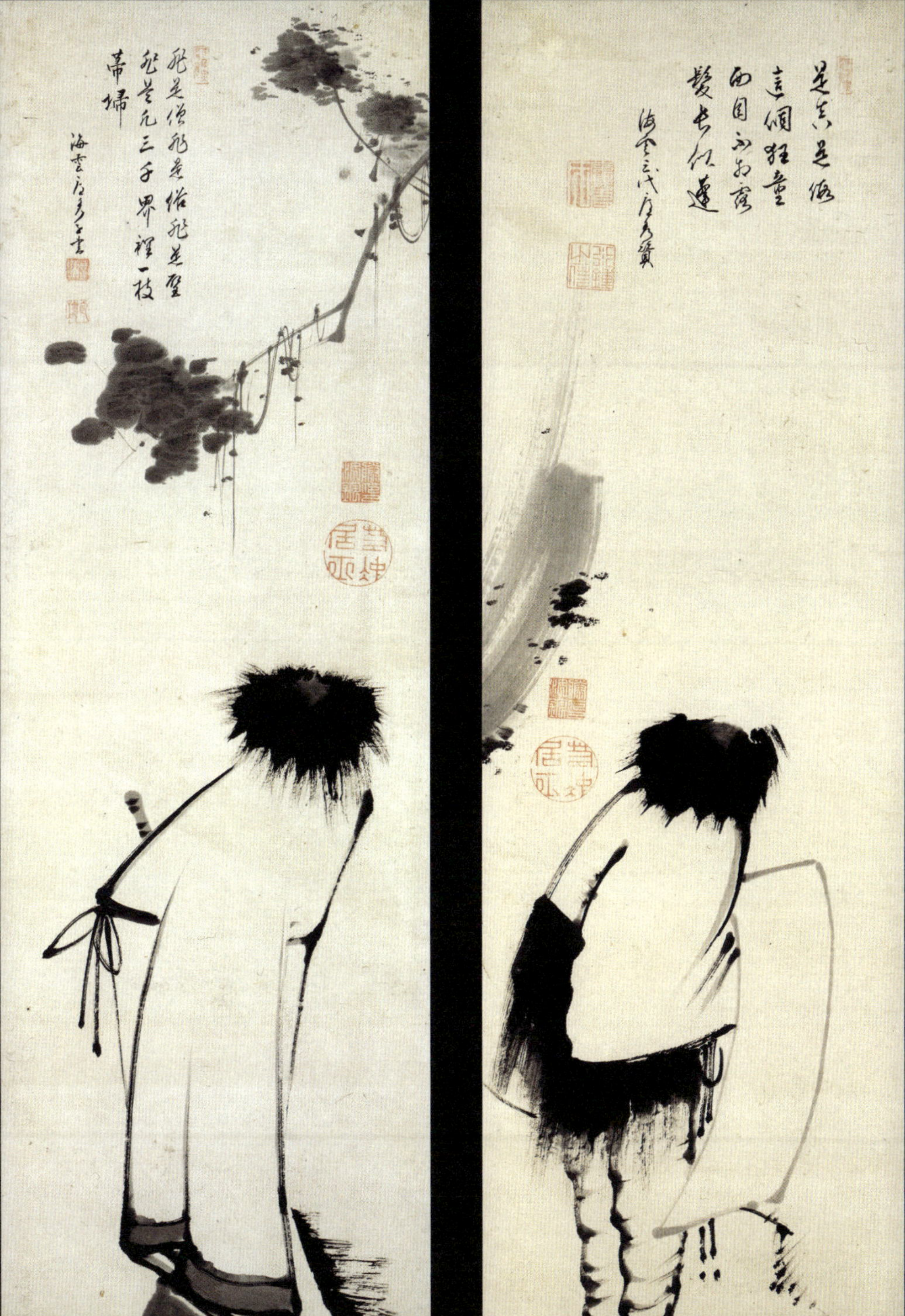

40

Ito JAKUCHU (1716–1800)

painting

ROSHU Ensho (c1769–1789)

無
功
徳

NO VIRTUE! [MUKUDOKU]

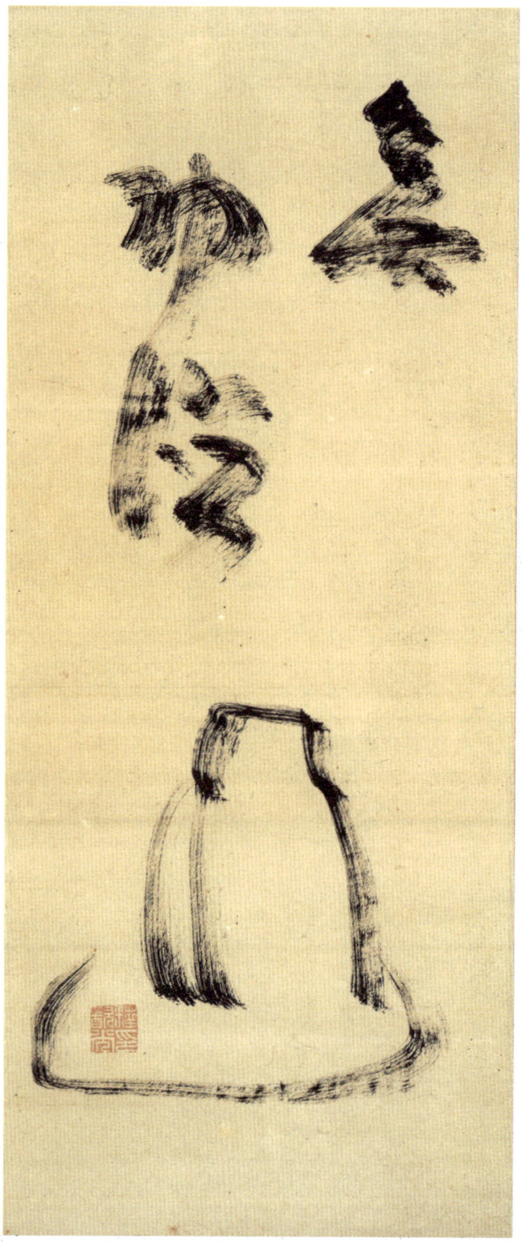

41
JIUN Sonja Onko (1718–1804)
Wall-gazing Daruma
hanging scroll, ink on paper,
64.5 x 26.8 cm

In terms of quality and output Jiun may be considered among the top five Zenga artists of all time (Fugai, Hakuin, Sengai, Jiun and Tesshu). Although he was not a Zen monk, Jiun was ordained into the Shingon Ritsu sect, a small school that emphasised esoteric Buddhism and strict observance of the monastic precepts (Japanese monks in general were lax about their vows. Ikkyu, for instance, openly drank sake, ate fish and had a torrid love affair with a blind minstrel named Lady Mori, and most monks behaved the same way in secret). Jiun, however, took his vows seriously and advocated a return to the original teachings and practices of Buddha.

Jiun trained in Soto Zen under a priest named Daibai (1681–1757) and was familiar with the teachings of Obaku Zen and the calligraphic style of Obaku monks. A prodigious scholar, Jiun was a pioneer of Sanskrit studies in Japan as well as an expert on Shinto doctrine. As with Hakuin, Jiun's literary output is so vast that scholars can unfortunately focus on just his writings and ignore his artwork. In 1797 Jiun established his own sect, the Shobo Ritsu movement. He was a popular teacher, said to have had several hundred monastic disciples and 10 000 lay students. Until then, however, Jiun had lived in seclusion for almost 30 years on Mount Katsuragi. It was at his hermitage in Kokiji that he produced most of his Zenga.

Jiun was not a painter; he brushed only Darumas such as this, *enso* and other simple drawings, but they are expressive and distinctive. This *Wall-gazing Daruma* is a classic Jiun Zenga. He has used a reed rather than an animal-hair brush, hence the rough, 'flying white' effect of the brushstrokes. There are only a few brushstrokes in the entire piece. Although it is not a large scroll, the effect is very powerful. The inscription refers to Daruma's interview with Emperor Wu, and means 'You cannot bribe your way into nirvana with good works; you must first awaken your mind!' The placement of Jiun's seal on the patriarch's robe is a nice touch.

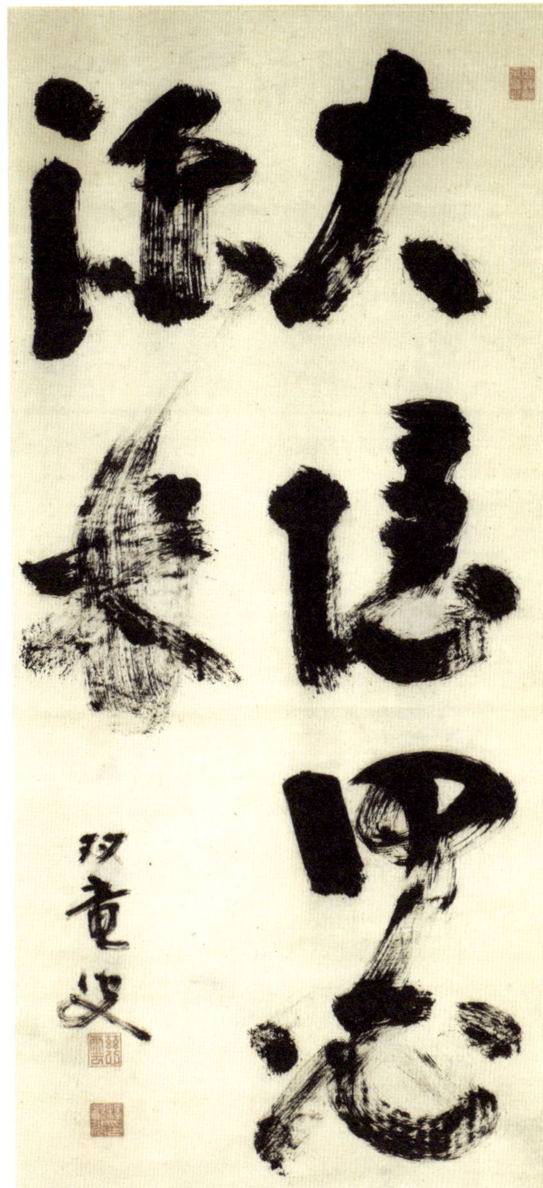

大隠何必
深林
双竜叟

Why is it necessary for a great hermit
To hide in a deep forest?

The old Double Dragon[1]

This kind of bold, rough brushwork is another Jiun trademark. Like Tesshu (see no 58), Jiun did hundreds of pieces of calligraphy at a time. When his disciples pointed out that his calligraphy would not be as valuable, Jiun replied, 'I know. That way no one will be tempted to fake them in the future and fall into the sin of avarice'. Alas, that was not to be. Jiun scrolls are second in value only to Hakuin pieces in the Zenga art market, and imitations abound.

As to the meaning of this calligraphy: a real hermit can maintain inner tranquillity anywhere – in a deep forest or on a street corner. True meditation does not depend on ideal conditions.

1. One of Jiun's many pen names

42
JIUN Sonja Onko (1718–1804)
Two-line calligraphy
hanging scroll, ink on paper,
110.3 x 50 cm

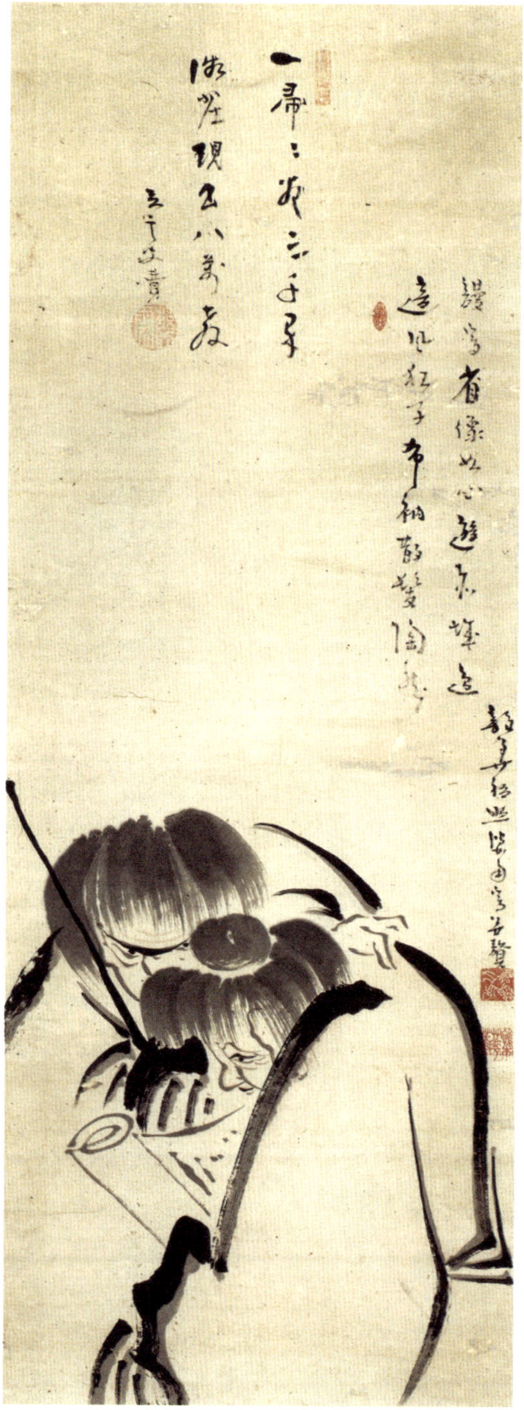

雑華祐照　画写共賛

謾寫省像如心遊赤城邊

這風狂子布衲散髪陶然

一箒二巻三千年

微塵現出八萬教

慈雲叟書

[Yusho's inscription]
Carefree lunatics in rags with dishevelled hair,
gloriously drunk;
This abbreviated sketch only hints at their real purpose.

Painted and inscribed by Yusho of Zakkean Hermitage

[Jiun's inscription]
One broom, two volumes of verse, 3000 years.
Appearing in this world of dust to teach us in 80 000 ways.

Brushed by Jiun

Jiun had a wide circle of acquaintances and was frequently asked to add inscriptions to paintings by others (there is, for example, a Jiun inscription on a Torei painting; it appears that there was interaction between many of the great Zenga artists of that period, or that at least they were aware of each other's work). Nothing is known about Yusho. Here he has painted Kanzan and Jittoku huddled together conspiratorially, apparently indicating their desire to keep their real purpose – teaching the essence of Zen – hidden from coarse outsiders. Their '80 000 ways of teaching' are open only to those who truly understand their madcap ways.

43
JIUN Sonja Onko (1718–1804)
additional inscription
YUSHO Zakkean (dates unknown)
inscription and painting
Kanzan and Jittoku
hanging scroll, ink on paper,
118 x 43 cm

閻魔王前御用心々
八萬四千煩悩主人豪潮画題

時年八十有六

Be careful, be careful when you stand before King Enma!

Painted and inscribed by Gocho, the man of 84 000 passions

This year, eighty plus six [years old]

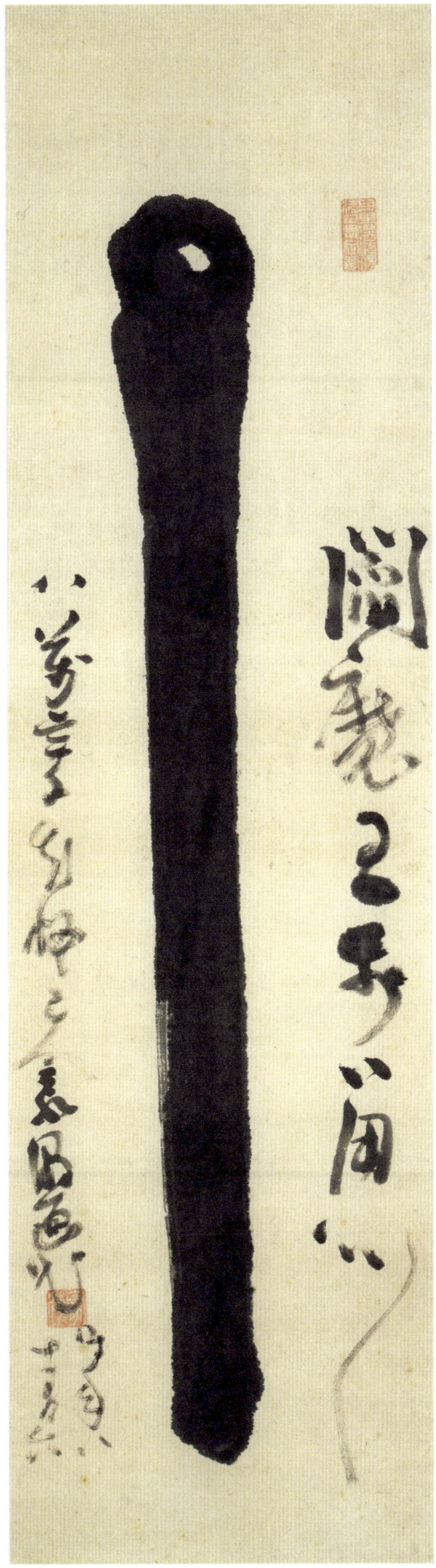

Gocho, an abbot of the Tendai sect, was another non-Zen Zenga artist. Unlike Jiun, however, Gocho was a pre-eminent painter of highly detailed, iconographically correct Buddhist-style paintings. Yet his Zenga were free flowing, almost wild, in the manner of his friend Sengai. Gocho was a famed miracle worker, and his incantations were sought to bring rain and cure disease, even by the Tokugawa shoguns.

The Japanese believed that when a person died, he or she had to face Enma, the king of hell. If the judgment was unfavourable, red demons beat the poor soul with iron rods all the way down to the appropriate Buddhist hell (there were ten levels in all). Thus the message of this Zenga is, if you do not want to get hit with this staff, be good.

44
GOCHO Kankai (1749–1835)
Demon rod
1834
hanging scroll, ink on paper,
106 x 29.4 cm

丙辰冬應
安生醫生需畫共題豪潮
通然天地中
德深流無盡
何辨百薬効
不賞百草毒

He taught us how to avoid 100 poisonous herbs;
He showed us how to apply 100 kinds of effective medicine.
His virtue is a continual stream that cannot be exhausted
Throughout heaven and earth.

Painted and inscribed at the request of Dr Ansei in the winter of 1796

The god of medicine (and agriculture), Shinno is venerated throughout East Asia and is often depicted as half-animal, half-human. Paintings of Shinno serve as a talisman, especially for medical practitioners. This work was commissioned by a Japanese doctor (and now in the 21st century, is owned by another physician, Dr Gitter). Gocho painted this Shinno in the Zenga style, with humour and insight.

45
GOCHO Kankai (1749–1835)
Shinno, god of medicine
1796
hanging scroll, ink on paper,
104.5 x 28.3 cm

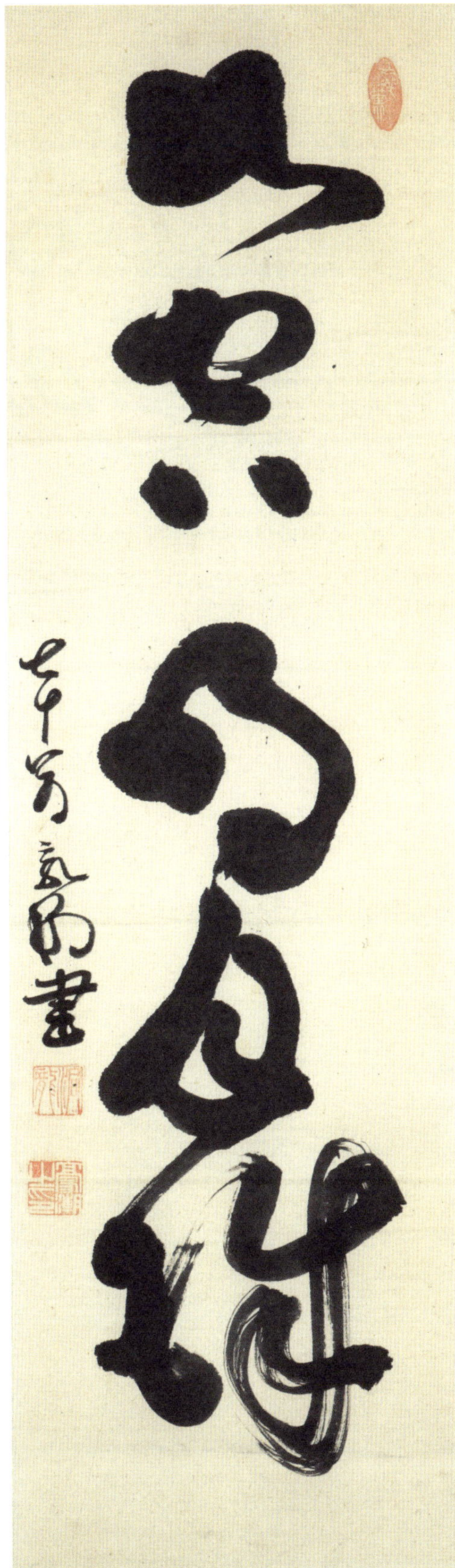

如空明月珠
七十翁豪潮書

Emptiness like the pearl of a bright moon.

Brushed by the 70-year-old fellow Gocho

This is a difficult calligraphy to translate. We are all familiar with the bright moon shining like a pearl in the vast night sky. From the standpoint of Buddhist philosophy, 'the pearl of a bright moon' means the 'enlightened consciousness' that enables us to perceive the universe as 'empty like space', the literal meaning of the first two characters. Normally in one-line Zen calligraphic works the characters are placed together in an unbroken flow, often connected by a long, single brushstroke. Gocho, however, preferred to do his one-line calligraphies in separate groups. Here, for example, 'like space' and then 'bright moon pearl', cause the viewer to go from the universal (space) to the particular (pearl). The brushwork is especially soft and (appropriately) bright.

46
GOCHO Kankai (1749–1835)
One-line calligraphy
1818
hanging scroll, ink on paper,
98 x 28.5 cm

文化戊寅應需画七十六齢牛懶
雙眼欲看無
隻字一聲未
発震百雷
七十翁於尾州萬松
禅窟題豪潮

[Gocho's inscription]
One character cannot be seen even with two eyes.
One roar not yet a hundred peals of thunder.

Inscribed in the Oshu 10 000 Pine Zen Cave[1] by the 70-year-old Gocho

[Chingyu's inscription]

Spring 1818, painted upon request by the 76-year-old Lazy Ox[2]

Gocho had a wide circle of acquaintances and in 1817 the Soto Zen monk Chingyu (see next entry) invited Gocho to come to his temple, Manshoji near Nagoya, to demonstrate his miraculous healing powers. Chingyu was an excellent painter, and the two monks collaborated on several outstanding portraits of Kanzan and Jittoku (note that they are looking at a blank scroll). It is not clear who commissioned this painting but it is an especially fine example.

Gocho used several different versions of this inscription. Here the verse is pregnant with a sense of what is about to happen – suddenly everything will be loud and clear if we just pay attention (to the meaning of Zen) like Kanzan and Jittoku.

1. Manshoji . Chingyu was abbot of this Soto Zen temple in Owari province

2. Chingyu's pen name

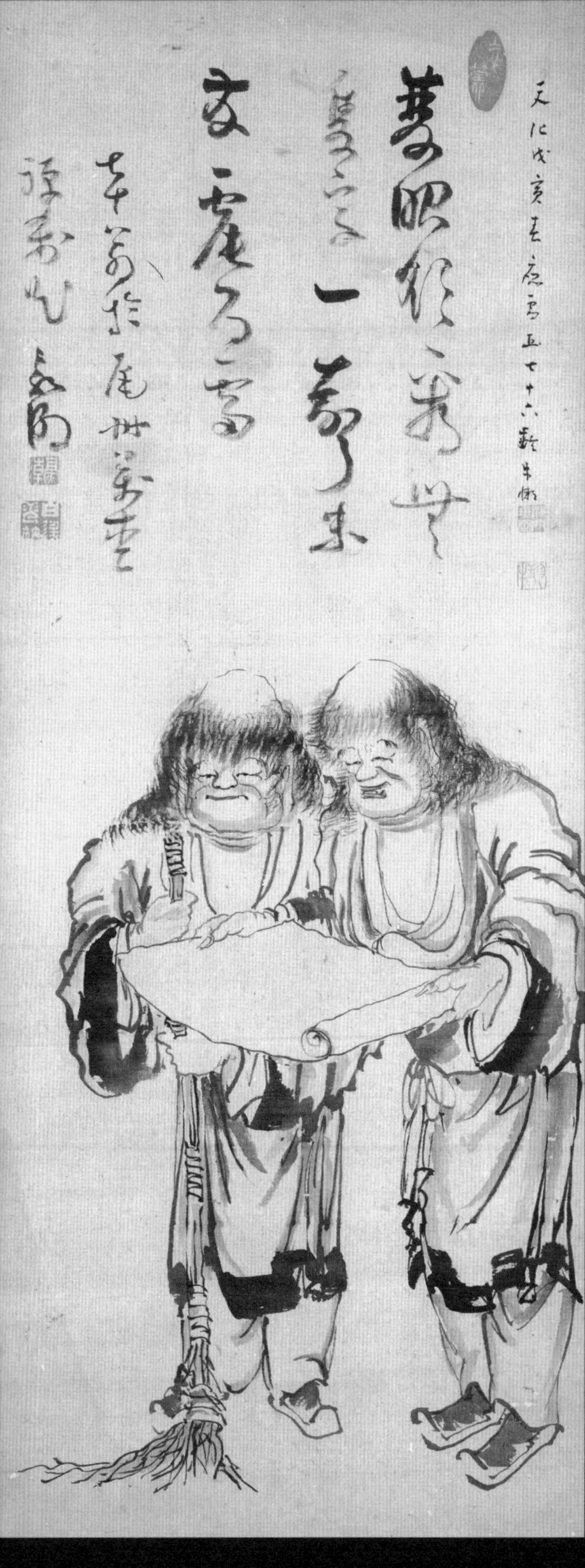

47
GOCHO Kankai (1749–1835) inscription
CHINGYU Zuiko (1743–1822) painting
Kanzan and Jittoku
1818
hanging scroll, ink on silk,
84.5 x 32 cm

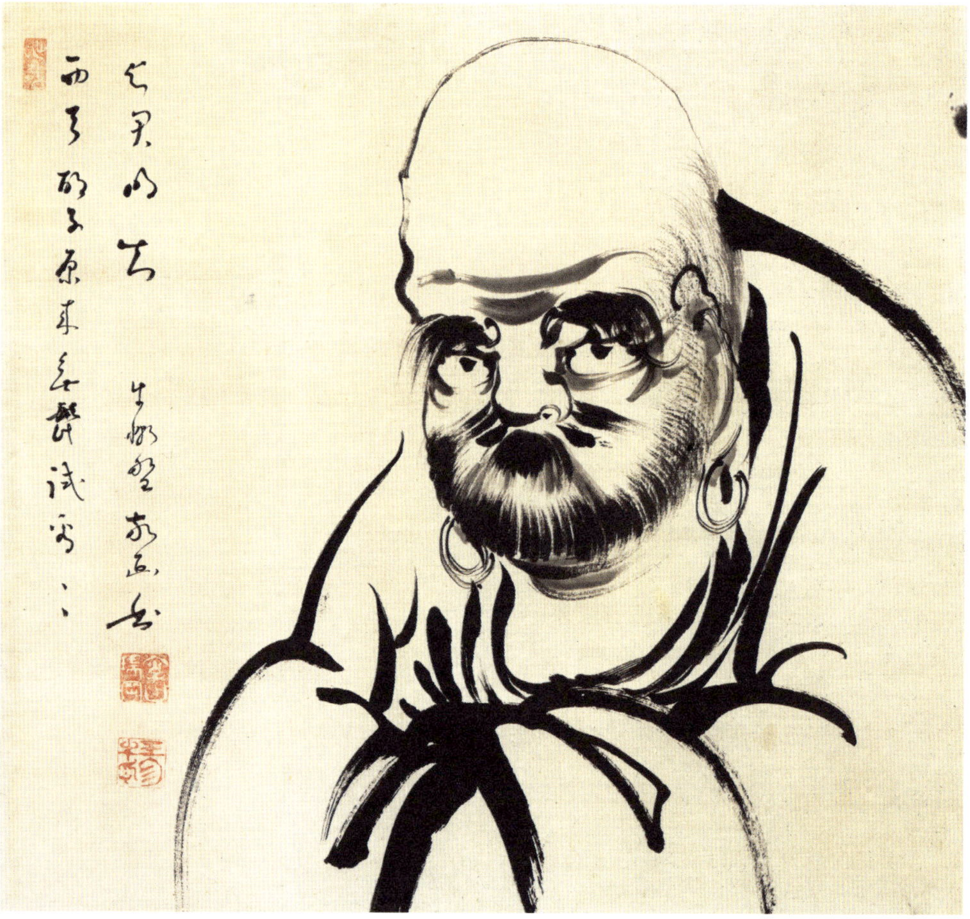

長閑明知　牛懶野敬画書
西天胡子原來無髭試金々

The Western Barbarian [Daruma] *originally has no beard;*
Dig, dig deeper until you elucidate the meaning.

Respectfully brushed by the Lazy Ox[1]

Case 4 in the *Mumonkan* is simply: 'Why has the Western Barbarian no beard?' According to legend, and in every portrait, Daruma has a very thick beard. Chingyu, too, has drawn this Daruma with a heavy, full beard but he still wants to know why there is 'originally no beard'. This is a *koan*, a Zen puzzle for the viewer, and Chingyu is challenging us to explain it in our own words.

This Daruma is immediately attractive – it is powerful and direct; the patriarch is looking right at us and seems to be really present. Chingyu wrote on a similar portrait of Daruma: 'The original face cannot be put anywhere; it cannot be drawn, it cannot be painted', but here too he succeeds in drawing Daruma's 'original face', accomplishing the great paradox of Zenga – manifesting the ineffable Zen mind with the concrete tools of brush, ink and paper. The inscription is well integrated with the painting, and even if we do not know the meaning – most Japanese, too, will not have a clue to what it says – we can still enjoy the brushwork. Knowing what the inscription means is helpful (and challenging) but the visual impact is what makes it a Zenga.

Chingyu became a monk at an early age, and served as abbot of various temples. He seems to have been quite eccentric because he worked as a fishmonger for a time (Buddhist monks are supposed to be vegetarian). Chingyu formally studied painting when he was young and he was a skilled and creative painter – one of the best in the Soto Zen line of Zenga.

48
CHINGYU Zuiko (1743–1822)
Daruma
hanging scroll, ink on paper,
55.5 x 58.1 cm

1. Chingyu's pen name

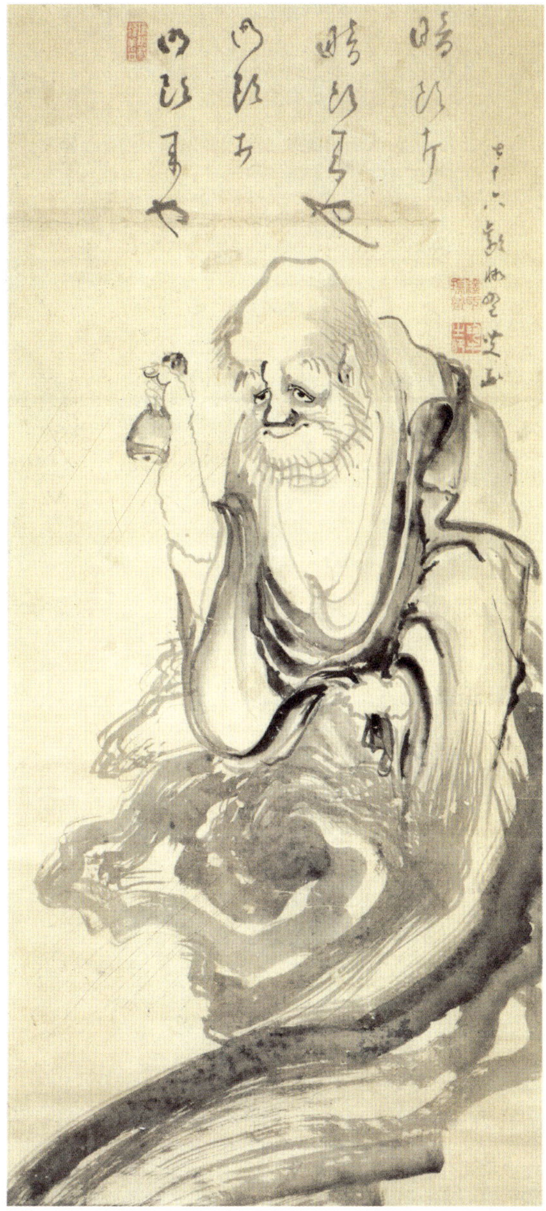

七十六齡懶野叟書
暗頭打
暗頭來也
明頭打
明頭事也

Come in brightness,
I will smash that brightness;
Come in darkness,
I will smash that darkness!

Brushed by the 76-year-old fellow Lazy Ox

Fuke (Puhua) was a Zen vagabond who lived in China during the time of the great 9th-century master Rinzai (Linji). Fuke wandered around town ringing a bell, chanting, 'Come in brightness, and I will smash that brightness; come in darkness, and I will smash that darkness. Come from any direction, come with nothing, and I will smash that to pieces too!' (Fuke's challenge is often used as an inscription on paintings of Zen staffs). At the end of his life, Fuke entered a coffin Rinzai had sent him, and had himself nailed inside. As the coffin was being carried to the cemetery, the bearers noticed it suddenly felt very light. The coffin was opened and found to be empty, but the sound of an invisible bell could be clearly heard.

Here Fuke ascends on a cloud to heaven while ringing his bell, a favourite theme of Zen artists (Daoist immortals are also sometimes portrayed ascending straight to heaven). Chingyu was more technically skilled than many Zen artists, and took more time in creating his pieces. This portrait shows the detail typical of Chingyu's Zenga style.

49
CHINGYU Zuiko (1743–1822)
Monk Fuke
1818
hanging scroll, ink on paper,
112.1 x 49.8 cm

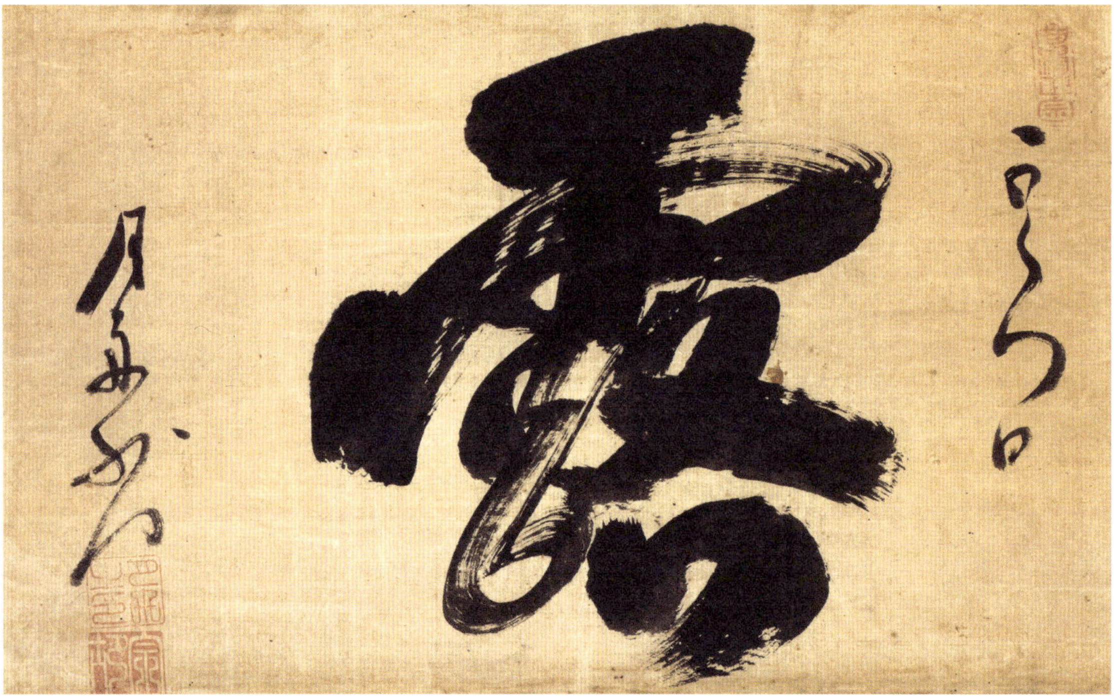

雲門曰
露
月舟翁書

Unmon[1] said

REVEALED! [RO]

Brushed by the old fellow Gesshu

This is a 'one-word barrier', a single large character set off as a visual *koan*. This particular 'barrier' is *ro,* meaning 'dewdrop', but just as a dewdrop reflects like a mirror, the word connotes 'completely revealed', or 'perfectly clear'. The *koan* originated from the Chinese Zen master Unmon, famous for his one-word answers. For instance, Unmon's reply to the question, 'Does this dog have Buddha nature?' was '*mu*' (no!). That *mu* became the central *koan* in Zen tradition. In this case, the question from one of Unmon's disciples was, 'If we kill our parents we can repent before Buddha. But if we kill a Buddha to whom can we repent?' Unmon replied '*ro*', meaning the answer is 'perfectly clear'. One interpretation could be that from the state of enlightenment all things are revealed clearly, so such questions would never even arise in our consciousness. In other words, live in the present and do not waste time on stupid questions.

Gesshu was ordained in the Shingon sect but later became an influential Soto Zen abbot. He did not paint but his calligraphy was highly valued and he loved to do such one-word barriers. Not long ago, a wonderful half-calligraphy by Gesshu sold for a very high price on the art market. The calligraphy had originally been displayed in a temple which caught fire. The head priest rushed in and grabbed the burning Gesshu scroll but only managed to save half of it.

50
GESSHU Soko (1618–1696)
Revealed
hanging scroll, ink on paper,
32 x 50.1 cm

1. Chinese Zen master Unmon (Yunmen, d949)

城中乞食了得々携囊帰々來
知何處家在白雲涯　良寛

After finishing my begging rounds in the town,
I carry a full bag;
Where do I return? Back to my hut among the
white clouds.

Ryokan

Ryokan is one of Japan's greatest poets and calligraphers and ranks with Ikkyu and Hakuin as a popular religious figure. Ryokan's life, poetry and artwork are still avidly studied in Japan, and now also in the Western world. After training as a Soto Zen monk and wandering about the country for years, Ryokan returned to his native Niigata prefecture. Here he spent his days as a mendicant monk, playing with children, drinking sake with the villagers and farm folk, composing poems in Chinese and Japanese and practising calligraphy, especially in the style of Huaisu, an 8th-century Chinese monk. Ryokan spent most of his years in Niigata living in a tiny hut deep in the forest.

This poem describes a typical day in his life, most likely in autumn, when the harvest was in and people were generous with their alms. Even when he was alive it was difficult to acquire a Ryokan calligraphy. It was impossible to buy, and many tales tell of the devious lengths people went to to get him to write something: a barber shaved only half of Ryokan's head (the monk's hair grew long over the winter confinement) and demanded a piece of calligraphy to do the other half; someone pulled the ladder away when Ryokan was up in a tree picking persimmons, refusing to bring it back until he promised to write something; calligraphies were wagered on games of *go*.

This calligraphy wanders all over the paper as if it were Ryokan on his begging rounds. The brushwork flows freely, almost entirely beyond form. Yet it is still legible, a trademark of Ryokan's calligraphy.

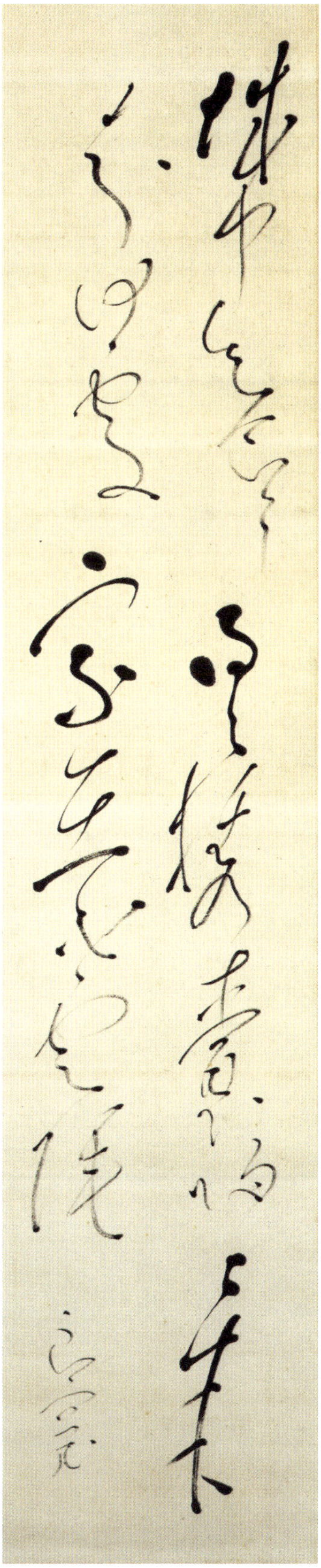

51
RYOKAN Daigu (1758–1831)
Two-line calligraphy
hanging scroll, ink on paper,
130 x 27 cm

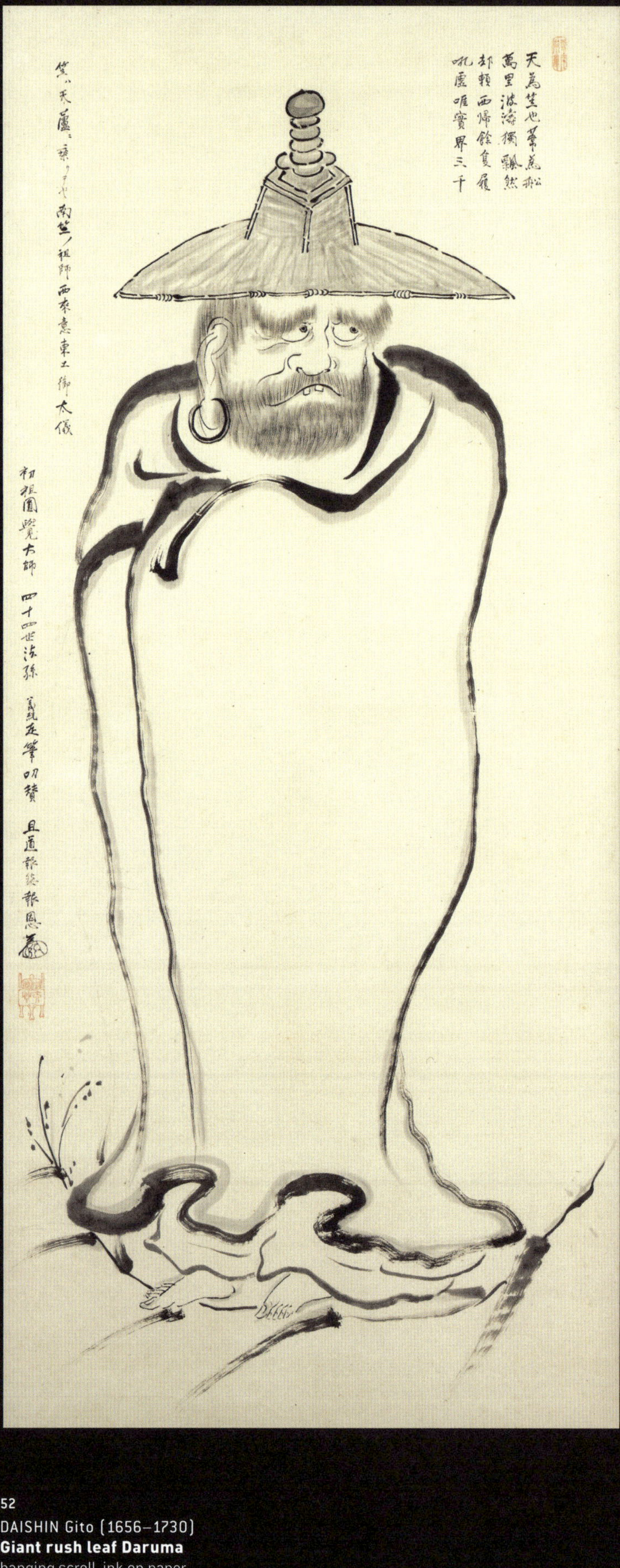

52
DAISHIN Gito (1656–1730)
Giant rush leaf Daruma
hanging scroll, ink on paper,
132.7 x 57.9 cm

天為笠也葦為舩
萬里波濤獨飄然
却頼西帰餘隻履
吼虎唯實界三千

笠ハ天蘆二製リテャ南竺ノ祖師西來意東土御太儀

初祖圓覺大師　四十四世法孫　義統是筆口讃　且道報徳報恩

[upper right corner]
Using heaven as a hat and a reed as a boat,
He floated across 10 000 leagues of waves.
When he went back to the west he left a single sandal;
He roared like a tiger in 3000 worlds.

[left side]
He wears a thick straw hat; know the principle behind the meaning of the First Patriarch's coming from the west in India to here in the east

The First Patriarch Engaku Daishi
Brushed and inscribed by his 47th descendant with deep gratitude and respect

[Daishin's cipher and seal]

Associated with the Rinzai Zen temple of Daitokuji in Kyoto, Daishin was an influential cultural figure who produced many fine Zenga, usually in a creative, uninhibited style.

This is perhaps the most important work Daishin produced and is a unique example of his painting in a more formal style. Daishin usually brushed simple portraits of Daruma and the great 7th-century Japanese poet Hitomaro, and other rough, sketchy drawings, but this is a huge full-scale painting. It was almost certainly commissioned by a major Zen temple. Daruma is wearing a large *kasa* (straw hat) adorned with a *stupa* (symbolising the enlightened mind); this image of Daruma originated with Chinese Obaku painters. The face is wonderfully expressive but the feet are too small, probably because it was Daishin's first – and last – full-length portrait of Daruma. The inscription on the right refers both to Daruma's coming to the east on a reed, and his return to the west (after he died, there were reports of him being seen heading back to India carrying one sandal; his tomb was opened and all that was found was a single sandal). The formality of the inscription along the left side suggests the painting's importance to Daishin.

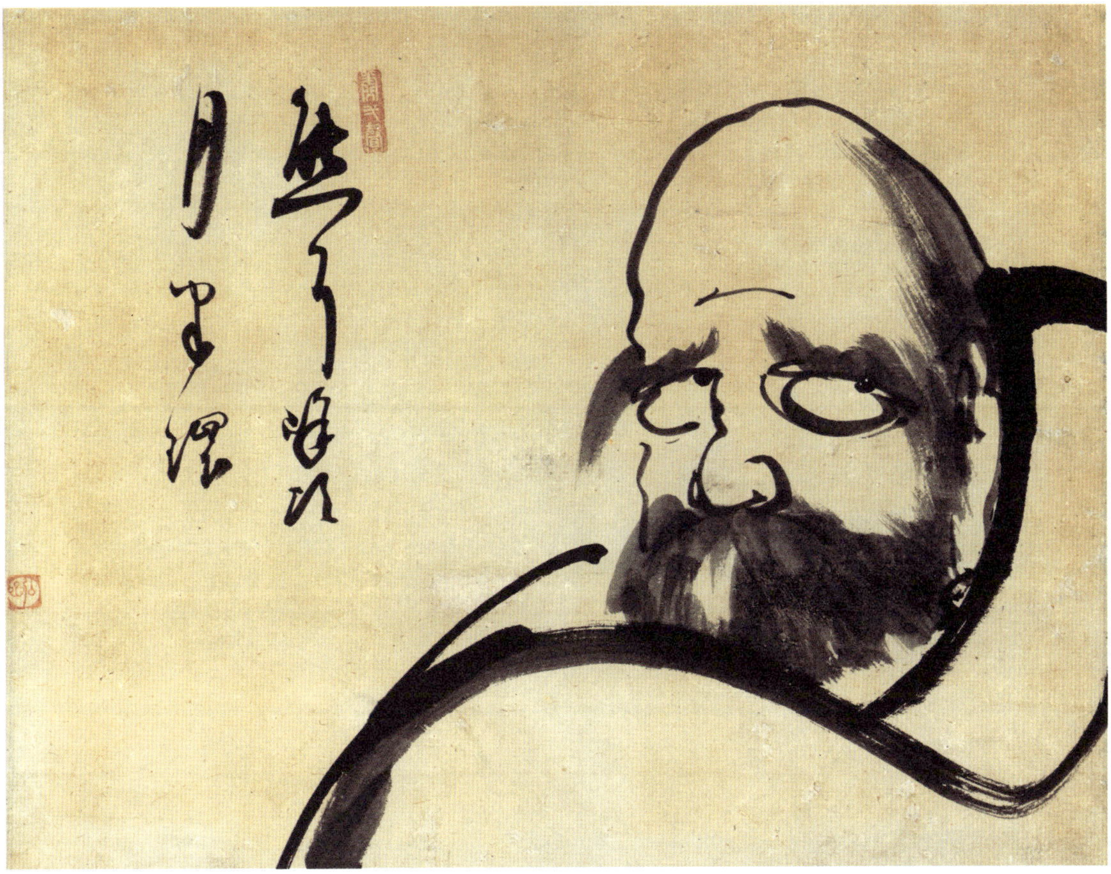

熊耳峰頭
月半輪

A half moon above the peak of Bear Ear Mountain.

Kogan studied with Hakuin, but as the master was near the end of his life Kogan finished his training with Suio and Sokai, two of Hakuin's direct disciples. In 1784, Kogan became abbot of Kogenji in Tanba province.

Like Hakuin and Suio, Kogan used Zenga as a teaching vehicle. He was a prolific artist who painted all kinds of subjects and may have been the first Zen artist to paint mendicant monks out on their rounds, a theme that later became standard. This painting depicts Zenga's most common subject, Daruma, but the inscription is puzzling. Bear Ear Mountain is the location of Daruma's tomb in China. The inscription states that above the mountain there is a half-moon (that is not visible in the painting). Is the painting of Daruma the other half of the moon that is visible? Together with other invisible half, does that indicate complete enlightenment – an enlightenment that never dies?

53
KOGAN Gengei (1748–1821)
Daruma
hanging scroll, ink on paper,
33 x 41.5 cm
(left) detail

六十八翁物外
此畫尊像
三日酒書
此話議得
之人者莫
請達磨
大師

1861

I did this venerable image
After three days of drinking.
To those who do not
Understand this meaning,
Just ask the Great Teacher Daruma.

The 68-year-old fellow Motsugai

Here we have a Daruma by someone intoxicated after three days of drinking (despite the monastic prohibition of alcohol, Japanese Zen monks are great imbibers of rice wine; they call it euphemistically *hannya-to*, 'hot water of transcendental wisdom'). Motsugai was one of Japan's prominent martial artists, founder of his own style, the Fusen school, and famous for his strength. Nicknamed 'Monk Fist', he could crack thick *go* boards with his bare hands.[1] Like Tesshu (see no 58), another extremely powerful man, Motsugai had a light and soft touch with the brush. As well as being a martial artist, Motsugai was a monk of the Soto Zen sect and an excellent scholar. He produced many Zenga, both paintings and calligraphy.

1. Motsugai had only one draw among his martial art contests; he called it quits after a one-day battle with Lady Shuei, who was armed with a 68kg iron halberd

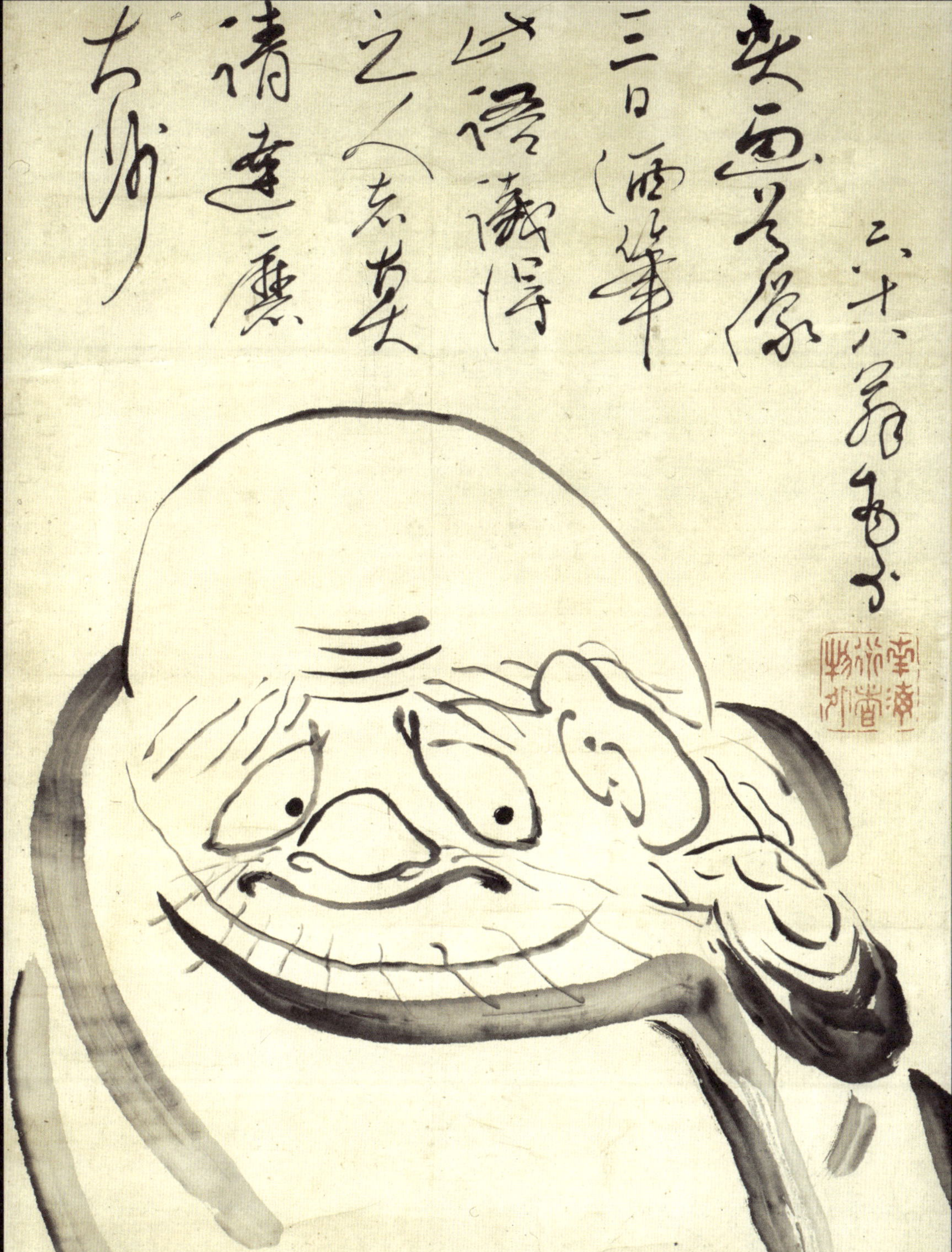

54
MOTSUGAI Fusen (1794–1867)
Drunk Daruma
1861
hanging scroll, ink on paper,
75.7 x 52.6 cm

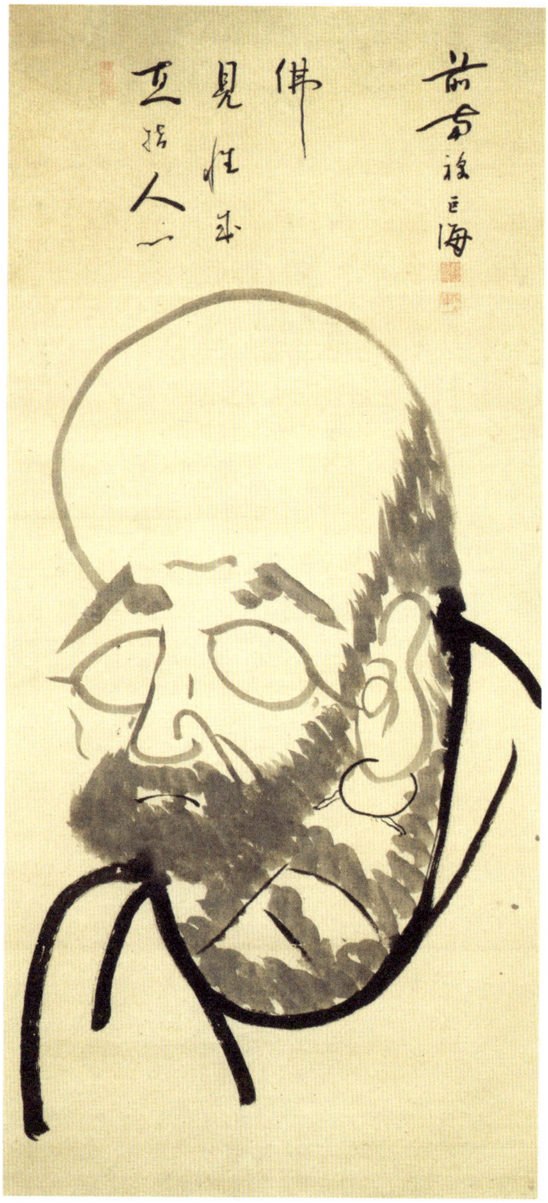

前南禅臣海
佛
見性成
直指人心

Direct pointing to the human heart,
See your nature, become Buddha.

The former abbot of Nanzen [monastery] Kokai

Although the inscription is standard, the Daruma is brushed in Kokai's distinctive style – big brushstrokes throughout the composition but the tiniest of dots for Daruma's pupils. Kokai belongs to the Kogetsu stream of Zen and consequently his brushwork is soft and light hearted, graced with good humour.

During the tumultuous years of the fall of the Tokugawa shogunate in the third quarter of the 19th century, Kokai was in Kyoto at the centre of the action. Nevertheless, he attended to his traditional duties as abbot of Nanzenji for nearly 20 years during the uncertainties of that period. Kokai's Daruma paintings were in high demand: it is said that even the most restless child or disturbed adult would be assured of a sound sleep with one in their room.

55
KOKAI Jiko (1800–1874)
Daruma
hanging scroll, ink on paper,
133.4 x 61 cm

正法山主蘇山書
一刀兩段任偏頗
頼得南泉能學令
撥動烟塵不奈何
兩堂倶是社禅和

The elders from two halls were discussing Zen
When a dispute arose between them.
Nansen demanded an answer that showed
their understanding.
One cut, two halves, an end to their discrimination!

Brushed by the Master of Mount Shobo[1]

Nansen (Nanchuan, 748–834) was a great Chinese master and this *koan* (case 14 in the *Mumonkan*, case 63 in the *Hekiganroku*) immortalised him. In Chinese monasteries there was a western hall for monks who meditated and an eastern hall for administrative monks. Cats were kept in a temple to keep the grounds free of rats, which nibbled on scrolls and sutras. As can be imagined, the monks were always arguing about something. During one dispute, Nansen came by, picked up a nearby cat, and demanded, 'Give me a word of Zen, you babbling monks, or I will kill this cat!' When no one replied, Nansen sliced the cat in two (the case in the *Mumonkan* goes on to say that when Joshu, Nansen's student, heard of his teacher's action, he put his sandal on his head and walked away. Nansen responded, 'If you had been there, the cat would have been saved').

Probably because of its shock value, Zenga artists loved the tale, and brushed it often. Sozan served as abbot of Myoshinji and received the honour of a purple robe from the emperor. Although not technically gifted, Sozan was an enthusiastic and important Zen artist who specialised in paintings of Kannon.

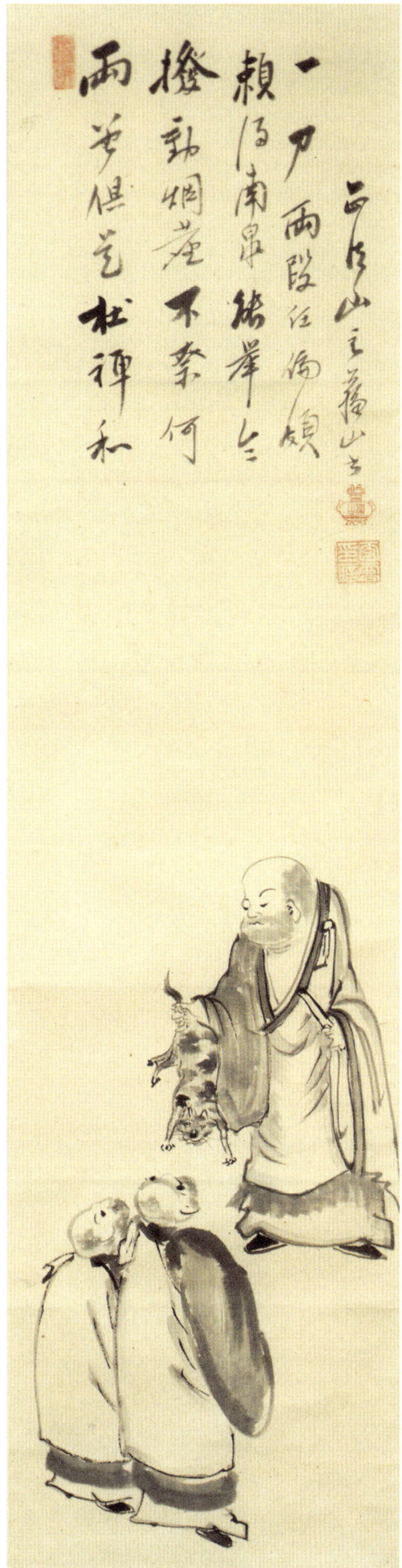

56
SOZAN Genkyo (1799–1888)
Nansen cuts the cat
hanging scroll, ink on paper,
106 x 27.1 cm

1. The 'mountain name' for Myoshinji. Every Zen temple has both a mountain and temple name

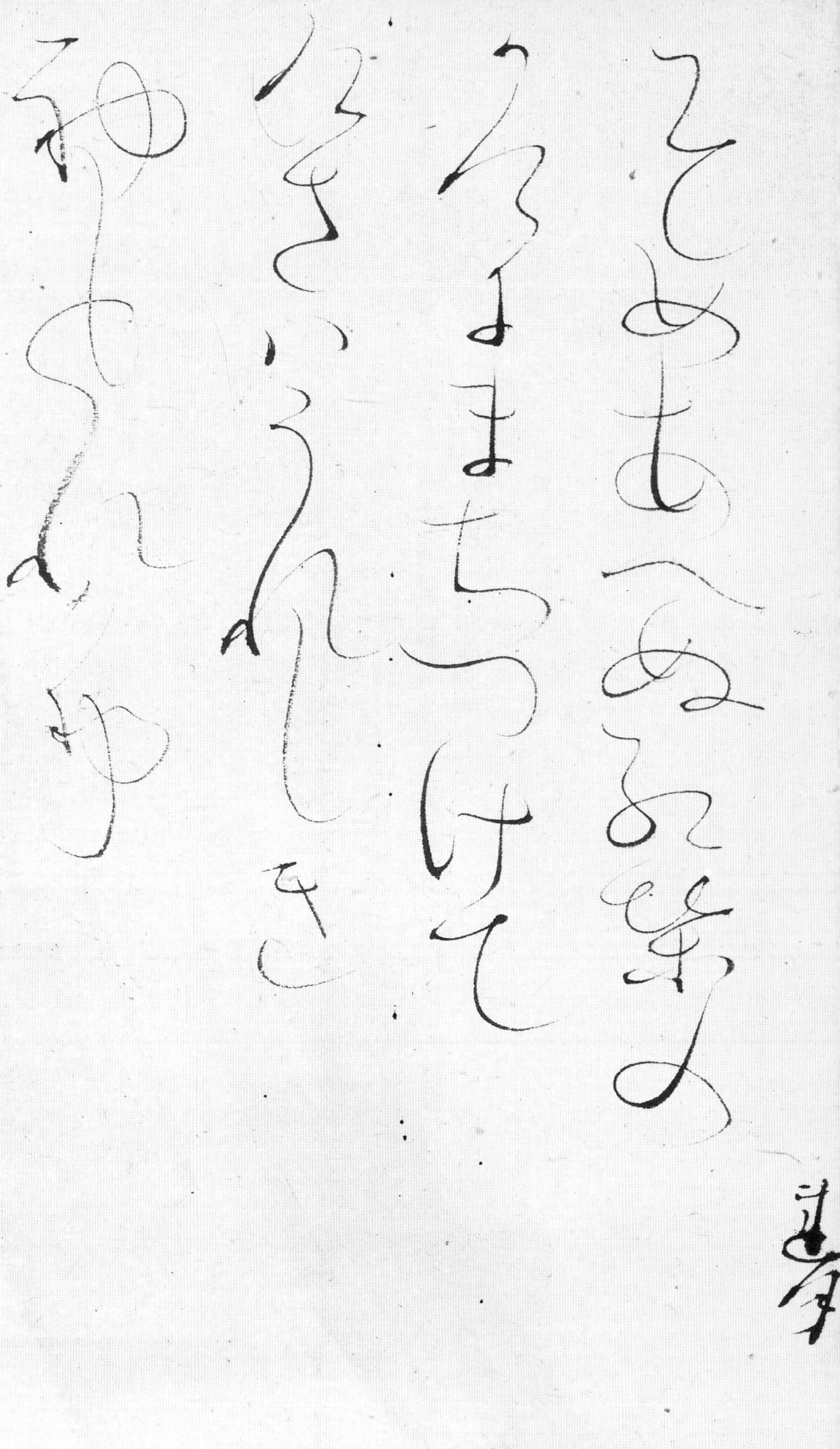

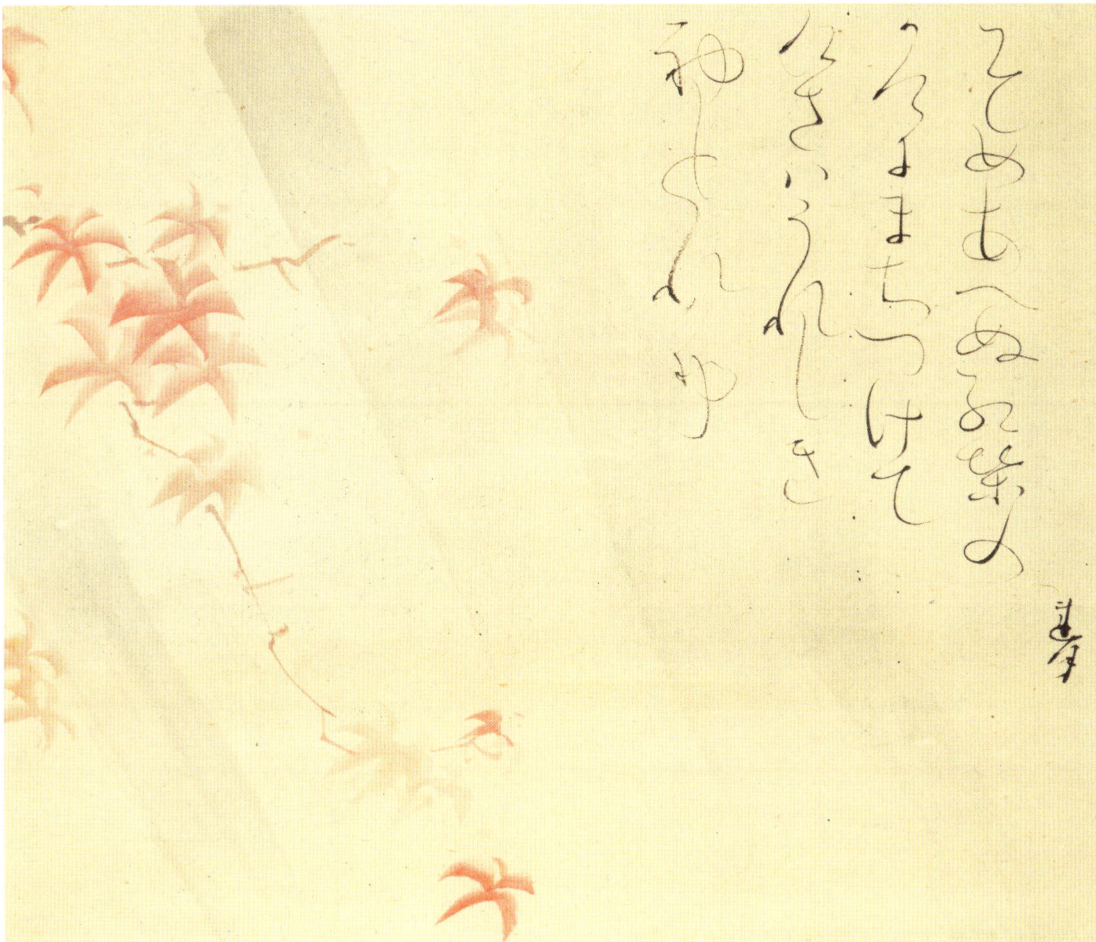

そめあへぬ紅葉の
可介尓まちつけて
介さハうれしき
初しぐれ(可)那

蓮月

Still crimson,
In the shadow of the maple leaves,
I take cover;
Today, such a happy event –
The first rain of late autumn.[1]

Rengetsu

Although not a Zen painter, and this is not a Zenga per se, the Buddhist nun Rengetsu was associated with Zen people such as Tesshu (see no 58) and was one of the most remarkable women in Japanese (and indeed in world) history. Her two husbands and several children all died before she turned 33. She supported herself by making pottery inscribed with her poetry and was a prolific composer of Japanese *waka* poetry, like the poem inscribed on this painting. The poem dances across the paper in supple yet firmly centred brushwork. It is believed that Rengetsu produced more than 50 000 pieces of art in her long life – pottery, paintings, poem cards and joint works with other artists. She died in a temple in a tea ceremony room on the night of a full moon.

During a visit to the Kimura family's residence in Niigata prefecture to do research on Ryokan, I once commented on a fine Tesshu calligraphy signboard in the entrance hall. 'Oh yes', they responded, 'Our family loves Tesshu. But his brushwork is not as strong as that of Rengetsu – hers is more powerful'.

1. 'Shigure' is a Japanese term for the light, cold showers of late autumn/early winter

57
Otagaki RENGETSU (1791–1875)
Maple leaves
hanging scroll, ink on paper,
29 x 33.6 cm
(left) detail

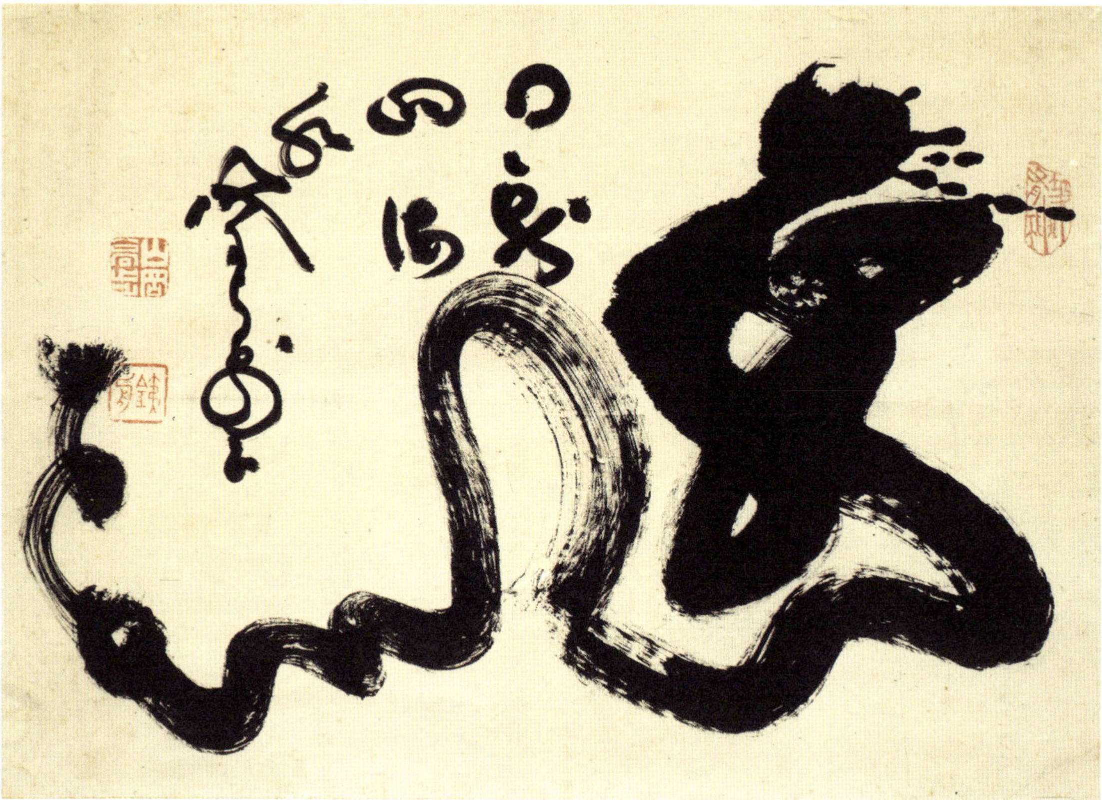

龍
日献
四海
水
鉄舟高歩書

DRAGON
Feasts on the sun
And the water of the four seas.

Brushed by Tesshu Koho[1]

Although an excellent calligrapher and painter, a sympathetic Zen master and one of Japan's greatest swordsmen, Tesshu is not as well known overseas as other Zen artists. Tesshu had a comparatively short life but he produced more Zen art than anyone in history – at least a million pieces. These he created to provide endowments for temples, to finance good works and to meet the great demand for his brushwork. A lay Zen master, Tesshu received his certificate from Tekisui of Tenryuji. Tesshu served a number of years as Emperor Meiji's most trusted aid – an aid, it is said in a famous tale, who did not hesitate to throw and pin to the floor the drunken emperor when Meiji misbehaved. Also a master swordsman, he founded the Muto (No-sword) School and was a tireless promoter of the 'Zen and the sword are one' philosophy.[2]

This wonderful calligraphic dragon is typical Tesshu – powerful, strong brushstrokes projecting a tremendous energy: the dragon actually seems to be moving. It would have been brushed as a talisman to protect a family against flood, fires and other disasters. Another interpretation of this inscription is 'Dragon offers to the sun the water of the four seas', but I prefer the more dynamic image of the dragon drawing sustenance from the sun and the oceans.

58
Yamaoka TESSHU (1836–1888)
Talismanic dragon
hanging scroll, ink on paper,
44.5 x 60.3 cm

1. One of Tesshu's pen names

2. It was with Takuan and Tesshu that the Zen/swordmanship connection became strongly emphasised. Once, it is said, Tesshu was brushing calligraphy when a deranged student suddenly attacked him from behind. Tesshu slid to the side to avoid the attack and the sword stuck in the mat. Tesshu calmly finished the brushstroke, telling the other startled disciples with a smile, 'See what I mean – this is the secret of swordsmanship'

お前百迄和しや九十
九迄とも尓白髪の者へるま伝
鉄舟高歩書

You will live to be one hundred, I will last to ninety-nine as our hair turns white together.

Brushed by Tesshu Koho

This is a wonderful interpretation of *Takasago*, a No play about an old couple, Jo and his wife Uba. The pair lived for decades in connubial bliss, and died at a great old age. With just a few masterful brushstrokes, Tesshu has created two elderly lovers who sit in quiet contentment together. The husband offers to go first, but the couple, as close in death as in life, will likely pass away within a few days of each other. This kind of Zenga served as a good luck charm for married couples. Often Tesshu pieces can be overwhelming but here there is a pleasant sense of warmth and light. This particular style of depicting *Takasago* appears to have originated with Tesshu and thereafter become a standard theme in Zenga.

Tesshu had a large family and a huge circle of friends, disciples and just plain hangers-on. It is said he turned no one away who was in need, and his family often fed 50 or 60 people during meal times. Tesshu also wrote dog tags for stray dogs – 'This dog belongs to Tesshu' – to prevent them from being bludgeoned to death by city officials. Tesshu regularly distributed food to the local beggars, and he kept giving the money Emperor Meiji provided him for new clothes to the poverty-stricken.

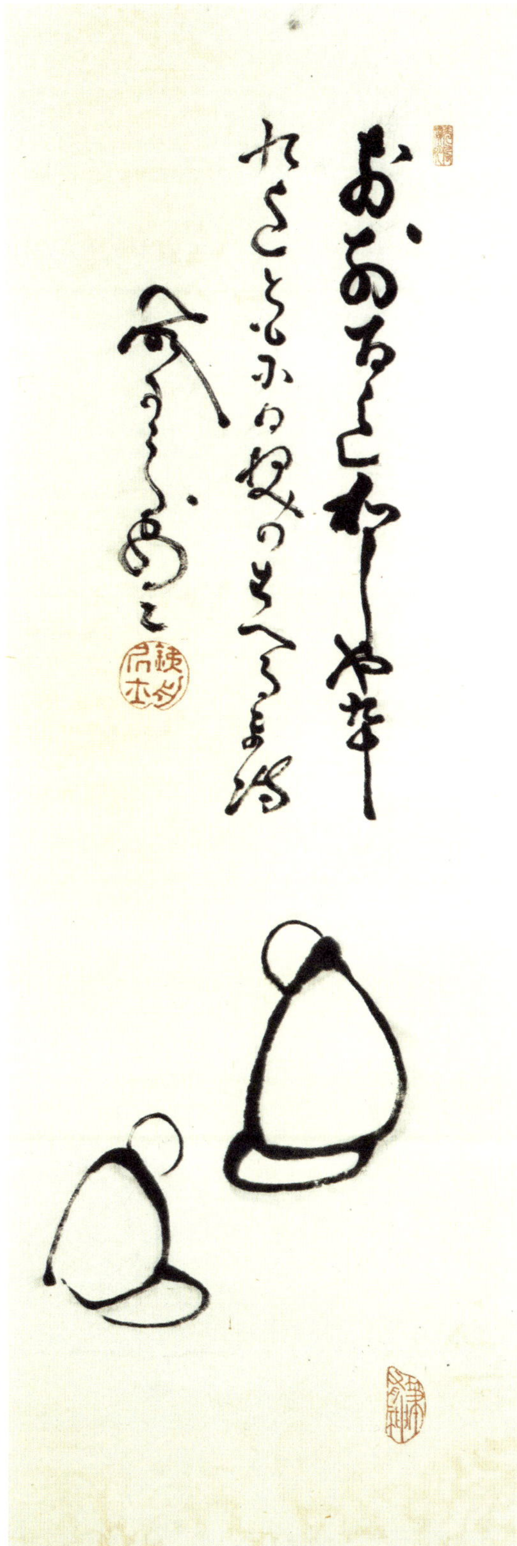

59
Yamaoka TESSHU (1836–1888)
Zen couple
hanging scroll, ink on paper,
104.2 x 34.9 cm

廓然無聖
古希加三
南天棒鄧州

Vast emptiness, nothing holy!

The 70+3-year-old Nantenbo Toju[1]

The colourful monk Nantenbo looked and acted the part of a curmudgeon Zen master throughout his long life of 86 years. Nantenbo claimed his Zenga output at 100 000 pieces, 'a lot more than Tesshu' (Tesshu, in fact, did a 100 000 pieces a year). At its best, however, Nantenbo's brushwork is quintessential Zen art – rough, direct and powerful – and a delight to behold.

This framed portrait of Daruma with a long Mount Fuji-like robe is one of Nantenbo's best. It was done in his vigorous 70s and the brushwork is fresh and bright. The inscription is Daruma's answer to the Chinese emperor's question, 'What is the first principle of Buddhism?'

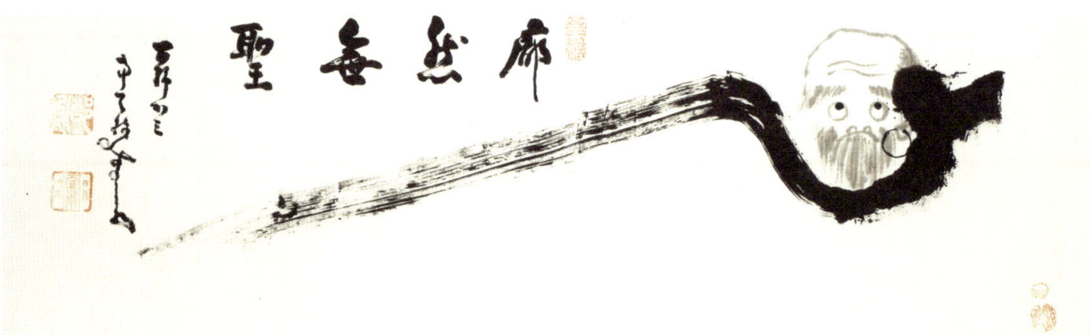

60
Nakahara NANTENBO (1839–1925)
Daruma
1911
framed leaf, ink on paper,
33.2 x 108.8 cm

1. Toju was Nantenbo's monastic name

道得南天棒道不得南天

棒

為鈴木隠潭氏清嘱南天棒鄧州

Speak [and you will get] *Nanten's staff; do not speak* [and you will still get] *Nanten's STAFF!!!*[1]

Brushed at the request of Mr Suzuki Intan by Nantenbo Toju

This is Nantenbo's trademark: 'Speak glibly of Zen and you will get a good whack of my stick; feigning understanding by staying mute won't fool me either – you will still get a good whack'. Many students, Nantenbo believed, needed sense beaten into them, and he never spared the rod (his stick had a cover with calligraphy by Tesshu). Note that the two inscriptions on either side of the big staff in the centre form miniature staffs. Nantenbo brushed hundreds of 'staff' paintings, but this example, probably brushed in his late 60s and for a particular person, is scintillating with Zen energy.

61

Nakahara NANTENBO (1839–1925)

Nanten's staff

hanging scroll, ink on paper,
131.3 x 33 cm

1. The staff itself is both a painting and a substitute for the character that forms part of the inscription

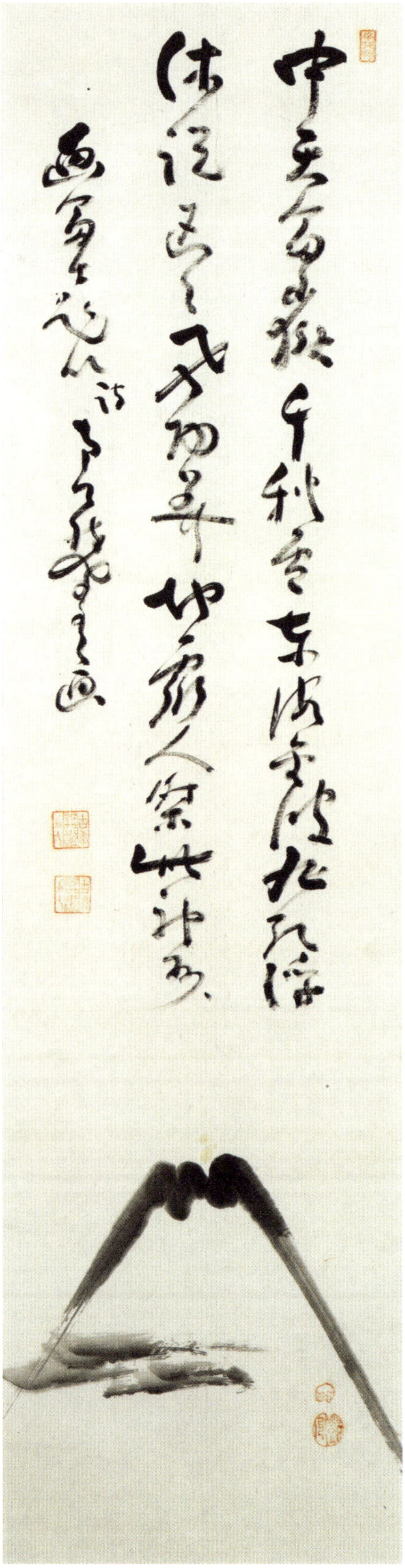

中天富嶽千秋雪東海金波旭影浮
休説区々風景美地霊人傑此神州
画富士 詩 南天棒鄧州画

Fuji's peak pierces the heavens,
draped with the snow of a thousand years,
and tinted with the golden rays of the rising sun of Tokai
[eastern Japan]
as it floats serenely [above the clouds].
Stop trying to extol its incomparable beauty –
this heroic symbol of our sacred land.

Fuji poem originally composed by General Nogi.
Inscription and painting by Nantenbo Toju.[1]

The famous general Nogi Maresuke[2], one of Nantenbo's Zen students, composed this poem for a Mount Fuji painting brushed by Nantenbo in January of 1911 (or 1910 according to some sources). Nantenbo often used it thereafter as the primary inscription on his many Fuji paintings. Usually Mount Fuji is most prominent but here the calligraphy takes precedence in the composition. The calligraphy flows up and down gracefully in the space above Fuji. The mountain is formed with rich, luminous brushstrokes. This is a splendid example of Nantenbo's Zenga.

62
Nakahara NANTENBO (1839–1925)
Mount Fuji
1915
hanging scroll, ink on paper,
127.5 x 33.8 cm

1. From one of the seals we know this was brushed in Nantenbo's 77th year

2. In a dramatic act famous in modern Japanese history, General Nogi Maresuke (1849–1912) and his wife Shizuko committed ritual suicide upon the death of Emperor Meiji

八十三翁南天棒鄧州
塞翁
馬
人間萬事

In all human affairs
Remember Old Man Sai's
HORSE[1]

The 83-year-old fellow Nantenbo Toju

This is the story of Old Man Sai, who lived near the border of ancient China. One day, his favourite horse ran away. His neighbours said, 'Bad luck'. Sai just smiled. A few days later, his horse returned home with another magnificent wild stallion. 'Good luck', his neighbours congratulated him. Sai just smiled. Sai's son tried to break in the new horse but was thrown and broke his leg. 'Bad luck', his neighbours commiserated. Sai just smiled. War broke out in the district and all the young men in the village were pressed into military service except for Sai's son, who was laid up. Many perished in the fighting but Sai's son was safe. 'Good luck', everyone told Sai. He just smiled.[2]

In short, good fortune and bad luck are sisters, and all of us experience various ups and downs in the course of our lives. From the Zen perspective, we should retain our equanimity, accepting the good along with the bad regardless of what befalls us.

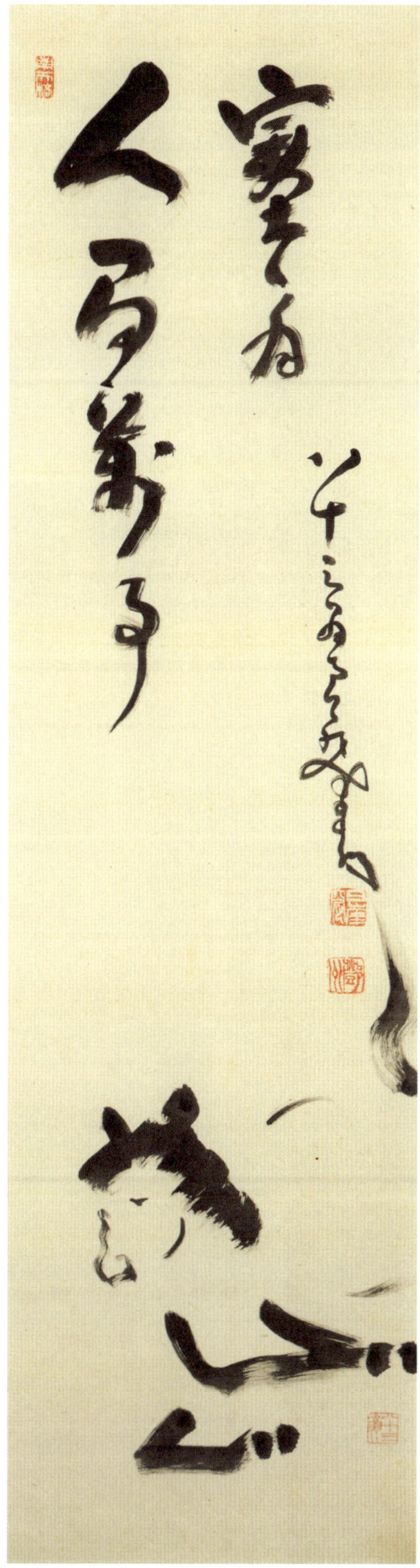

63
Nakahara NANTENBO (1839–1925)
Zen horse
1921
hanging scroll, ink on silk,
124.8 x 33.6 cm

1. The painting of the horse also serves as the last character of the inscription

2. From *Huainanzi* (Huainan philosophers), compiled by Liu An (179–122 BCE), adviser to Emperor Wu of the Han dynasty

四海雲水
鉢盂如雷
鳥藤
圓笠
化機村帰
八十五翁
南天棒鄧州

Trainee monks of the four seas
Their bowls resounding like thunder
And wearing round straw hats
[Come and] *go to transform the village.*

The 85-year-old fellow Nantenbo

This is a classic Zenga theme: young mendicant monks marching in unison and chanting together to beg alms in the local village. For the monks, begging is part of their Zen training; for the people in the village it is an opportunity to show their generosity and earn merit. Both the monks and the villagers can be 'transformed' by their actions. Normally the monks are shown 'coming' and 'going' on two separate scrolls (see no 67) but here Nantenbo has cleverly painted them both front and back on one sheet of paper to convey the idea of continual marching and stress the endless, timeless aspect of religious mendicancy, a practice that dates from the time of Buddha himself.

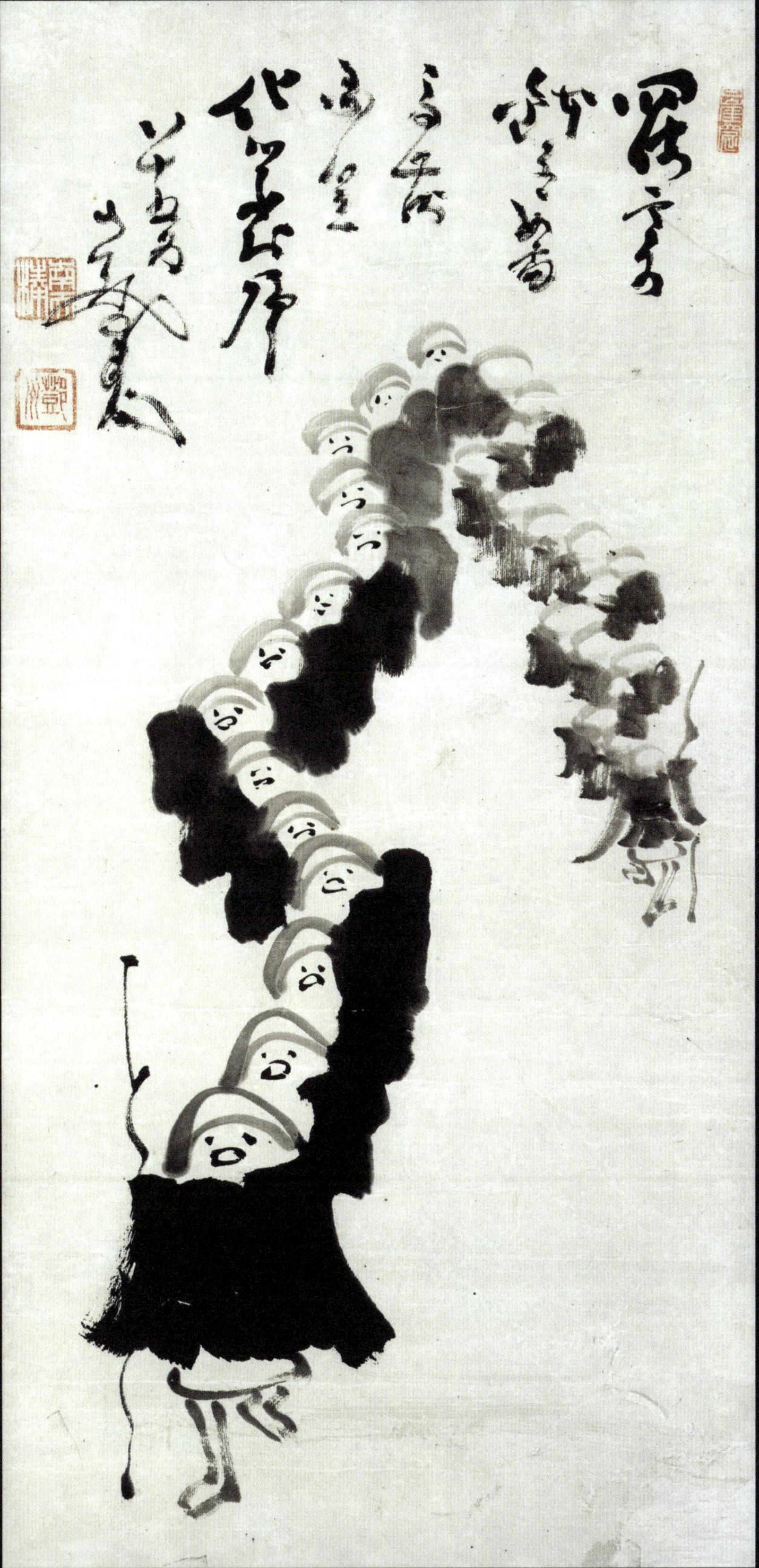

64
Nakahara NANTENBO (1839–1925)
Procession of monks
1923
hanging scroll, ink on paper,
65.5 x 31.5 cm

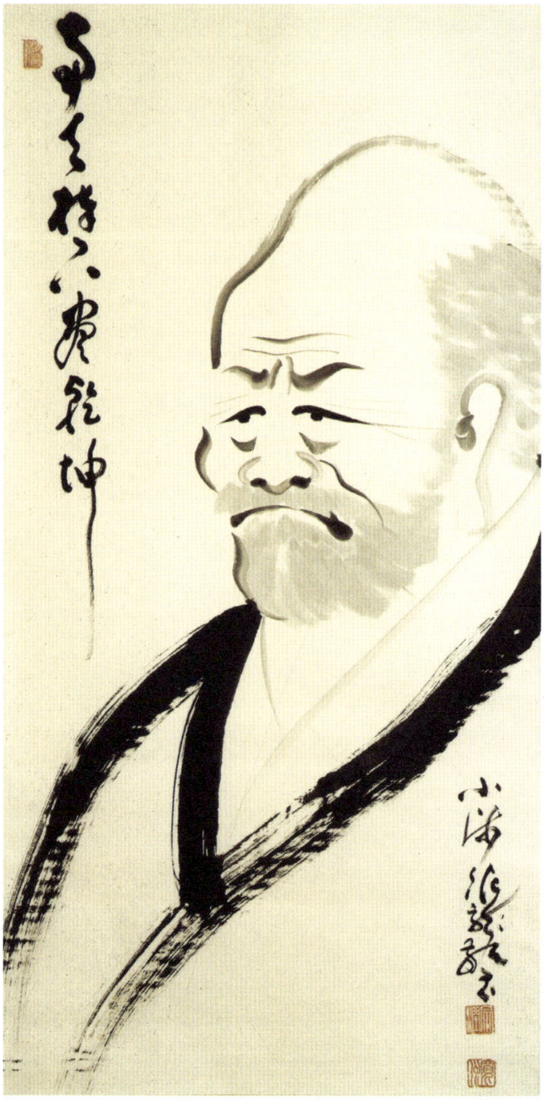

南天棒下盡乾坤

小師泥龍敬書

Nantenbo has used up heaven and earth!

Respectfully brushed by Monk Deiryu[1]

Deiryu, whose real name was Izawa Kanju, was Nantenbo's chief disciple. In addition to his duties as a Zen priest, Deiryu was a martial artist (accomplished in both *kendo* fencing and *kyudo* archery), who practised the tea ceremony and was skilful with a brush. There is an amusing story told about Deiryu. When Nantenbo accused him of making 'Nantenbo' fakes, he responded, 'Why should I copy you? My own calligraphy is much better'. Nevertheless, Deiryu greatly respected his master, and did many portraits of Nantenbo that purposely emulate portraits of Daruma. This may be the largest and most majestic. The inscription refers to the grand scale of Nantenbo's Zen teaching.

65
DEIRYU Kutsu (1895–1954)
Portrait of Nantenbo
hanging scroll, ink on paper,
125 x 61.8 cm

1. Deiryu ('Mud Dragon') was his Zen master name

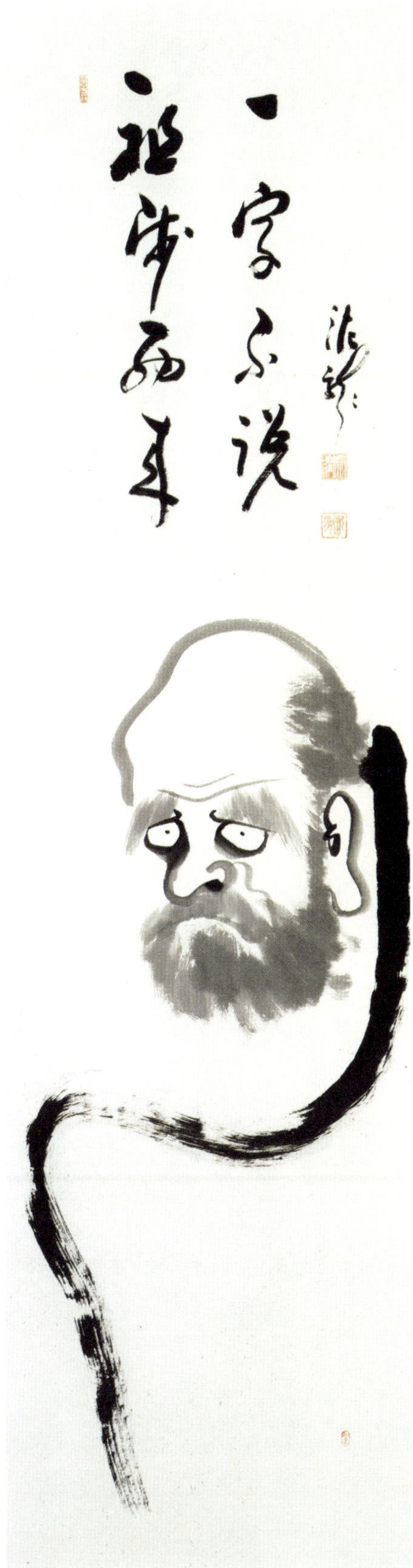

祖師西來
一字不説
泥龍

The First Patriarch came to the west
But did not explain a single world.

Deiryu

This is Deiryu's version of Daruma: Daruma did not come from India to China (and beyond) to give us more theory; he came to teach the experience of meditation – the physical and spiritual realisation of Buddha-nature in the here and now – an experience that cannot be explained no matter how many words are used. Deiryu's brushwork is softer and suppler than Nantenbo's, reflecting Deiryu's more gentle character.

66
DEIRYU Kutsu (1895–1954)
Daruma
hanging scroll, ink on paper,
128.5 x 34 cm

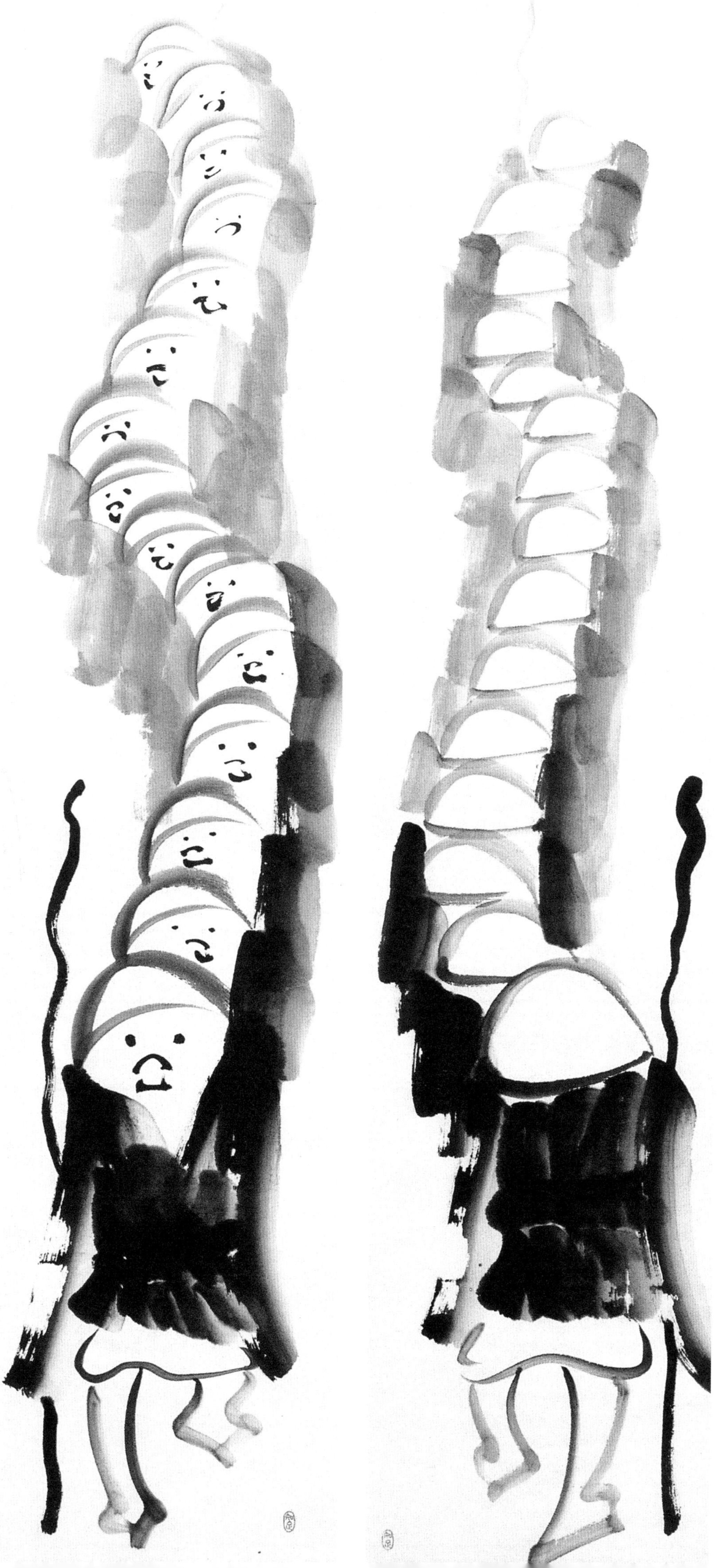

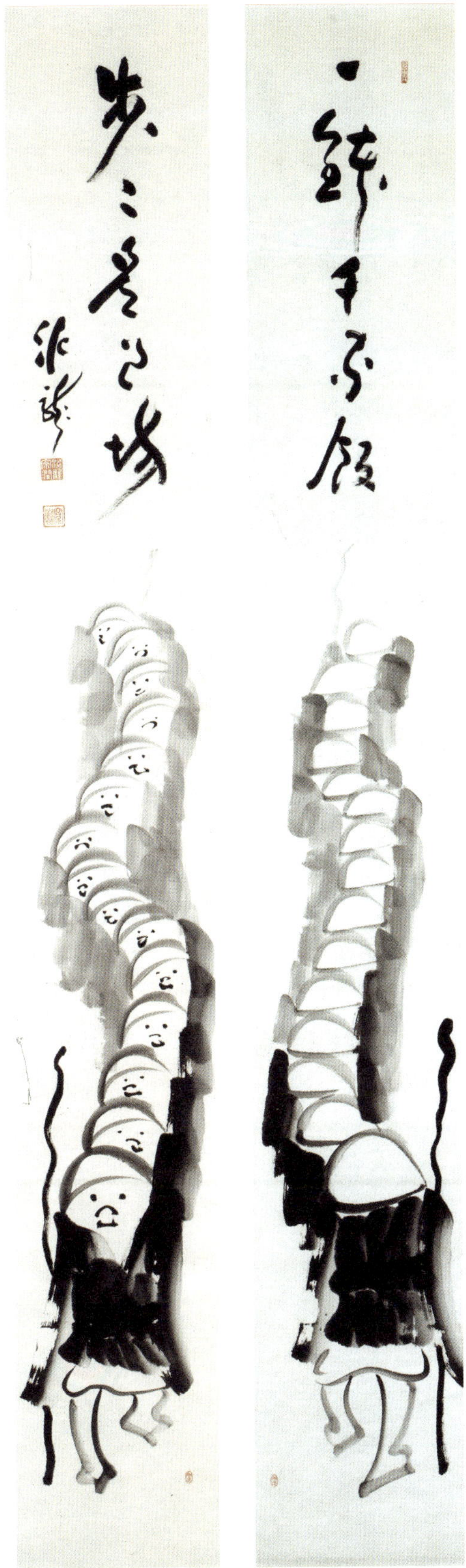

一鉢千家飯
歩々是道場
泥龍

[Monks coming]
Step by step we are practicing the Way

Deiryu

[Monks going]
Each begging bowl full of rice from a 1000 homes.

This portrayal of the theme of begging monks is typical in Zenga: on two scrolls, with the monks coming on the left and going on the right (see also Nantenbo's version, no 64). Although the mendicant rounds to the village are intended for trainee monks, it is said that even when Deiryu was abbot of Enpukuji in Kyoto he would join the monks, leading the procession himself. The theme of mendicant monks was popular in both Nantenbo's and Deiryu's Zenga.

67
DEIRYU Kutsu (1895–1954)
Procession of monks
pair of hanging scrolls,
ink on paper, each 162 x 22.4 cm
(left) detail

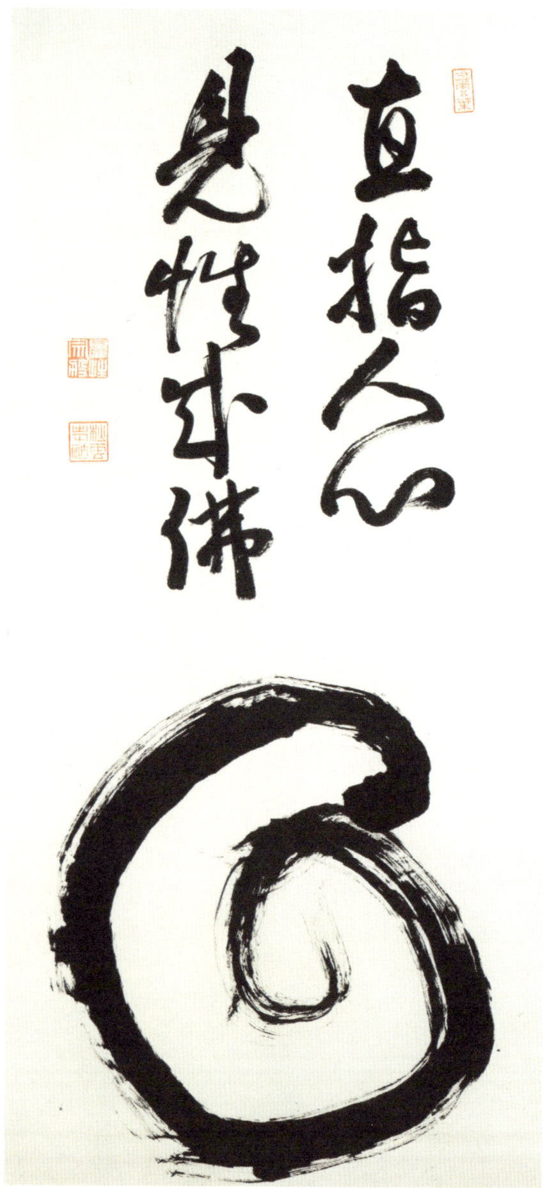

直指人心
見性成佛

Direct pointing
To the human heart
See your nature
Become Buddha.

Sohan Genpo is better known by his Zen master name Shoun ('Pine Cloud') and signed most of his works in this way. Because he was rather heavy-set and liked to dress informally – even though he was abbot of Daitokuji, perhaps the most important Zen temple in Japan – he was also nicknamed 'Hotei', after the legendary hobo Zen monk. In fact his dress was so shabby that he was once arrested as a beggar.

Also a leading disciple of Nantenbo (and associate of Tesshu), Shoun was a prolific calligrapher and painter who created many Zenga. This type of wall-gazing Daruma was his specialty, where Daruma resembles a traditional Japanese tumbler doll – a round-bottomed doll that immediately pops up when knocked over. This Daruma is also a kind of *enso*, or Zen circle.

68
SHOUN Sohan Genpo (1848–1918)
Wall-gazing Daruma
hanging scroll, ink on paper,
141.5 x 64.2 cm

妙心管長碧松敬書
結果自然成
一華開五葉

One flower opens to five leaves,
All things are accomplished naturally.

Brushed by Myoshin Abbot Hekisho[1]

Said to have been a gentle and considerate Zen master, Rozan was abbot of Tokugenji in Nagoya and for five years served as primate of the entire Myoshinji branch of Rinzai Zen. His Daruma portraits are often roughly drawn like the one here, but Rozan was quite skilled with a brush and also capable of producing detailed paintings in colour. In both styles Rozan was very creative, using a wide range of subjects in his Zenga. Rozan is now recognised as one of the most important 20th-century Zen artists.

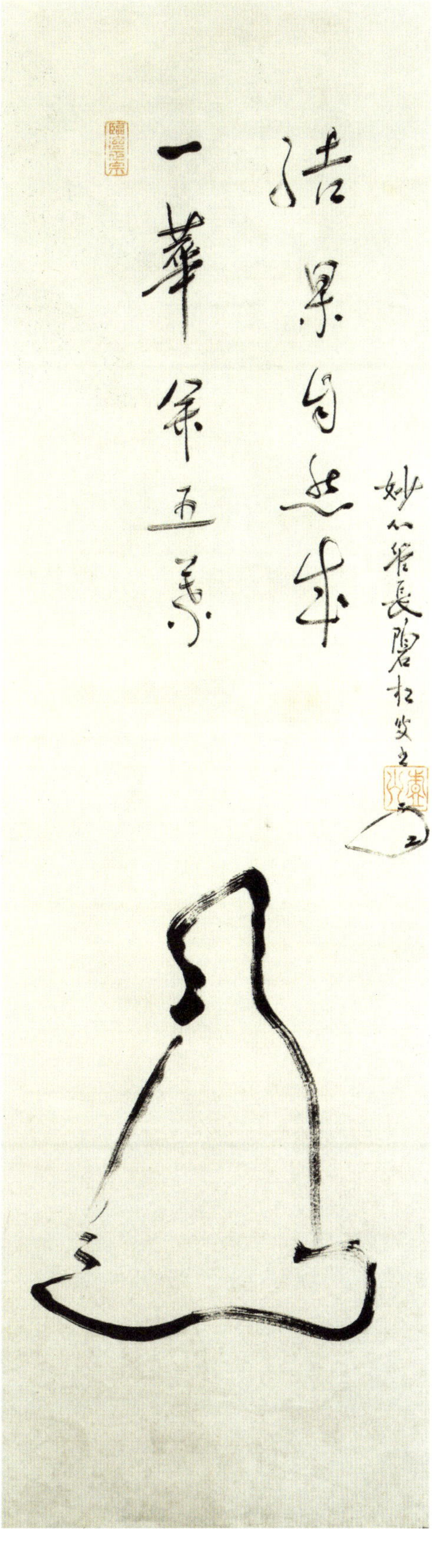

69
ROZAN Eko (1865–1944)
Wall-gazing Daruma
hanging scroll, ink on paper,
104.7 x 29.3 cm

1. Rozan's Zen master name

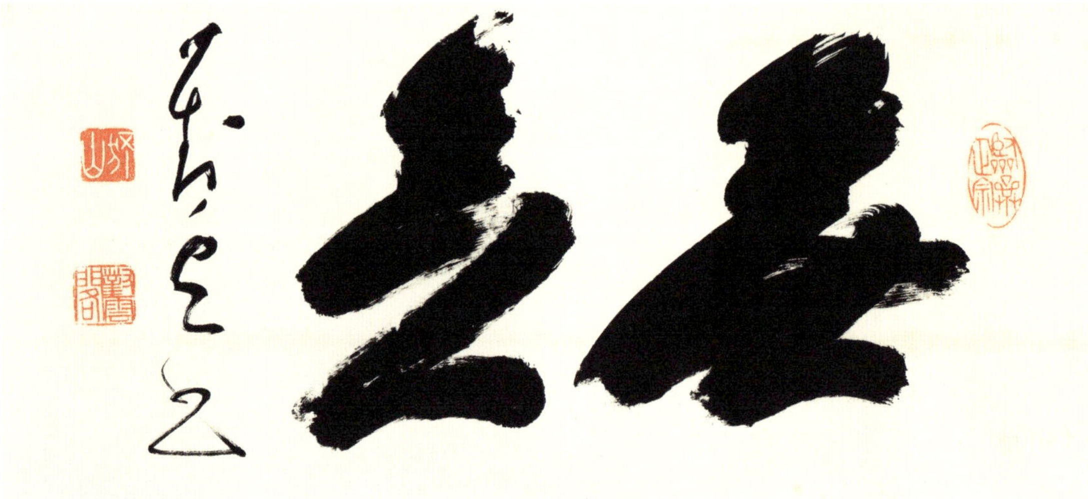

無念
対雲書

MU NEN (NO THOUGHT)

Brushed by Taiun[1]

Unlike most of the Zenga artists in this exhibition, Dokusan was more of a painter-priest than a priest-painter – he studied art professionally with the renowned scholar and artist Tomioka Tessai (1836–1924) before running away to become a Zen monk. Dokusan eventually served as abbot for a period at Shokokuji, a major Zen temple in Kyoto. While Dokusan is known mostly for his finely composed paintings, his calligraphy is wild, almost manic. Perhaps his calligraphy expressed a different aspect of his character. His brushwork here of *mu nen*, 'no thought' – a key concept in both Zen and the martial arts – is comparatively subdued, but other examples by Dokusan are nearly illegible. However, both his paintings and calligraphy are prized.

70
Hashimoto DOKUSAN (1869–1938)
No thought
hanging scroll, ink on paper,
30.5 x 67.3 cm

1. One of Dokusan's many pen names

不識
精拙

DON'T KNOW!

Seisetsu

'Don't know!' was of course Daruma's reply to Emperor Wu's question, 'Who are you?' (see p 21). It is a common inscription on Daruma paintings. In Buddhism, there is nothing that can be construed as a permanent self. Daruma was free of such 'self-conceit' and refused to be confined within a rigid framework of 'this' or 'that' person. Here, Daruma sits in deep Zen meditation while remaining perfectly aware.

Seki Seisetsu was abbot of Tenryuji in Kyoto, and a prolific Zen artist. While not as skilled technically as Dokusan, Seisetsu was just as enthusiastic, producing many portraits of Daruma in different styles (some in colour). It is said whenever Seisetsu felt tired or out of sorts, all he had to do was brush a Daruma painting to reinvigorate himself.

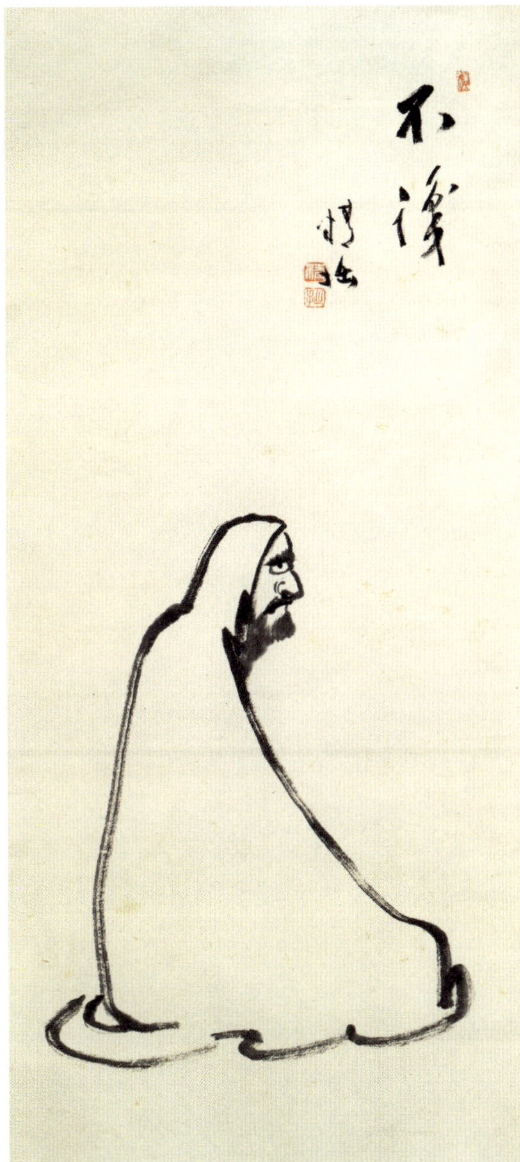

71
Seki SEISETSU (1877–1945)
Wall-gazing Daruma
hanging scroll, ink on paper,
64.5 x 29.2 cm

無盡蔵
記志功

MU JIN ZO (AN INEXHAUSTIBLE TREASURE)

Recorded by Shiko MU JIN ZO

Woodblock print artist Munakata Shiko, one of the founders of the modern *mingei* folk craft movement in Japan (together with Yanagi Soetsu, Serizawa Keisuke, Hamada Shoji and Kawai Kanjiro), also did big brush calligraphy, almost always on Buddhist themes. Because of his poor eyesight, Munakata had to put his face right against his woodblocks to carve, but with calligraphy this was unnecessary. His brushstrokes project a sense of being etched rather than drawn. In Zenga, 'an inexhaustible treasure' is used as an inscription on *enso*, typically in the phrase: 'Within not one thing an inexhaustible treasure'. It also can stand alone as Zen calligraphy, as we see here. All three characters seem to be a single solid construction, a kind of massive barrier the viewer must penetrate in order to discover, from the Zen perspective, the emptiness that gives birth to all things.

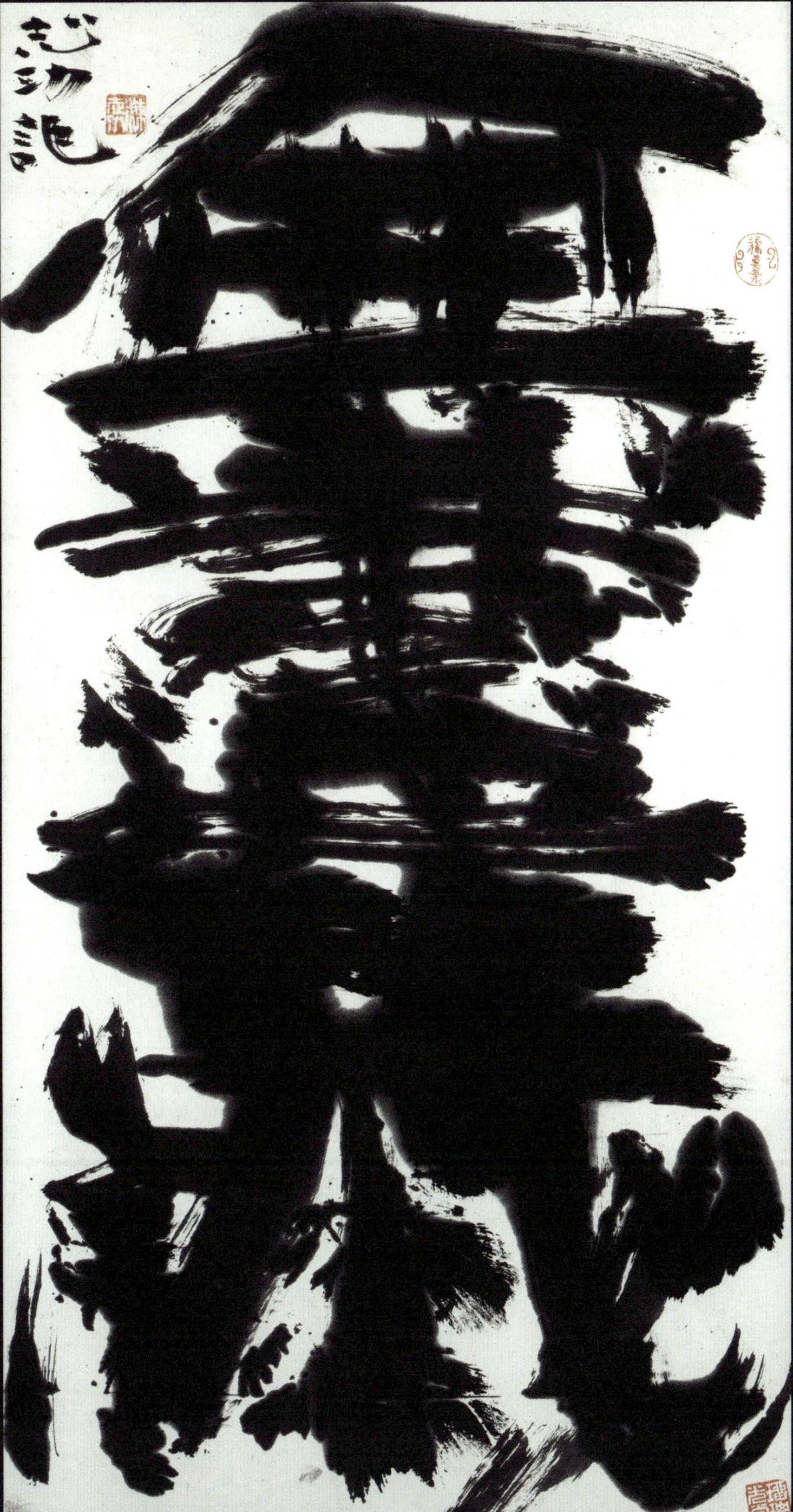

72
MUNAKATA Shiko (1903–1975)
An inexhaustible treasure
hanging scroll, ink on paper,
93.2 x 47.7 cm

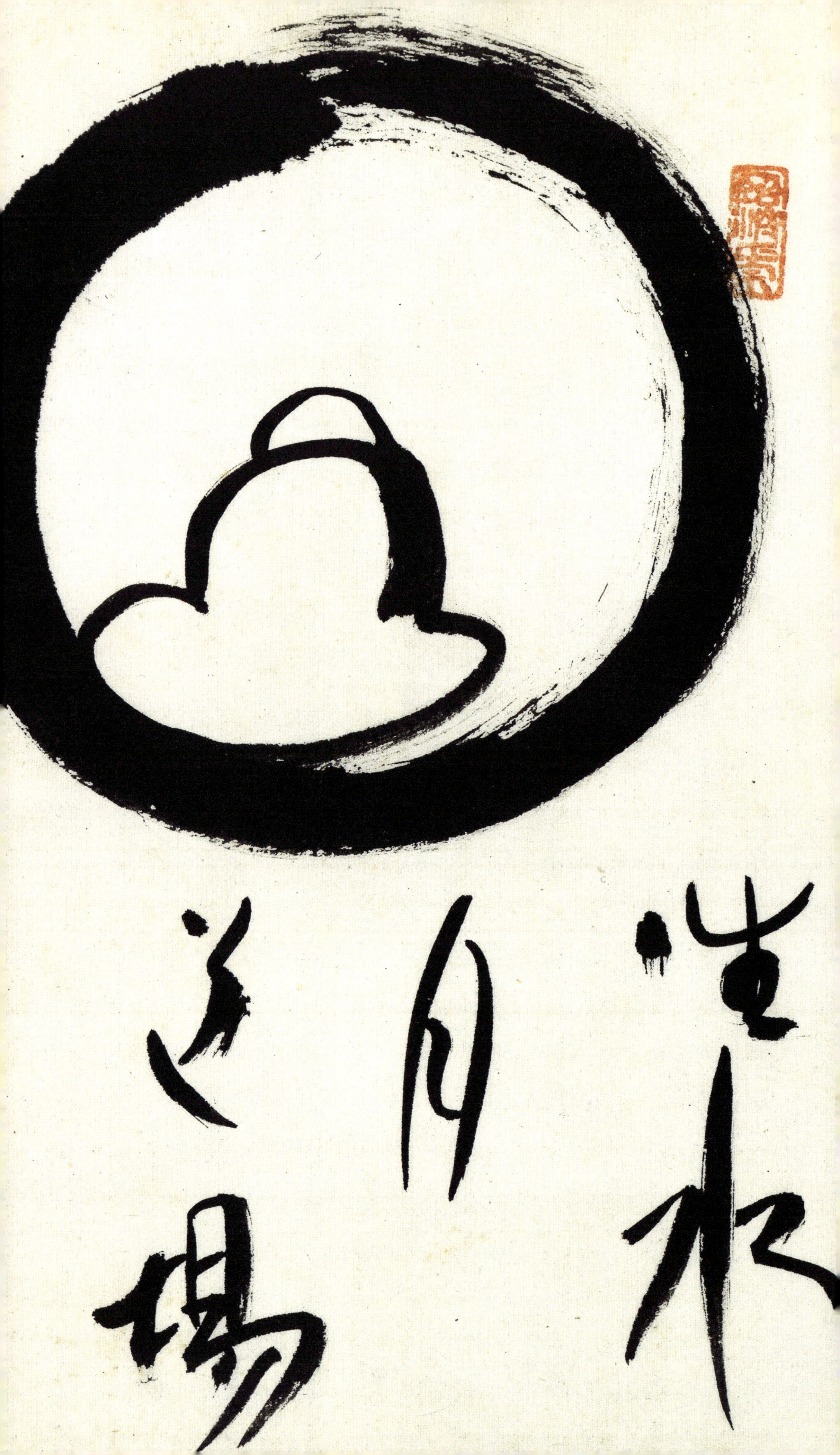

円相

ENSO

the circle of Zen

ENSO

the circle of Zen

JOHN STEVENS

The symbol supreme of Zen art is the *enso*, a circle. From the beginning of Buddhism, enlightenment has been compared to the 'bright full moon' and a 'great round mirror'. It is said that the 1st-century patriarch Nagarjuna, often considered a 'second Buddha', was transformed into a luminous circle whenever he taught in public to reveal, according to his biography, 'the true form of Buddha-nature, that is neither large or small, neither wide nor narrow, neither good nor bad, neither transient nor eternal'. Bodhidharma was called the Great Teacher of Circle Enlightenment. In a 6th-century text from China, the *Shinjinmei* (verses on the believing mind), the Way of Buddhism is described as 'a circle-like space, lacking nothing, nothing in excess', and this phrase is still used as an inscription for *enso*.[1] In the early days of Zen in China, *enso* were formed in the air or drawn in the dirt.

In the *koan* collection the *Shoyoroku* (book of serenity) case 77 contains many stories of Zen circles including this verse:[2]

> Before the birth of your father and mother,
> One solid circle;
> Even Buddha did not understand it –
> How could his greatest disciples transmit it?

In the *Hekiganroku* we have two such cases. The first is case 33:

> Minister Chinso went to see Zen master Shifuku. Shifuku drew a circle in the air. Chinso said, 'I came here with no ulterior motive. Why bother drawing a circle?' Shifuku slammed the door.

The second is case 69:

> Nansen, Kisu, and Mayoku were on their way to visit the national teacher Chu. When they were halfway there, Nansen drew a circle on the ground and said, 'If you can say a word, I will go on with you'. Kisu sat down in the middle of the circle. Mayoku curtsied like a woman. Nansen said, 'Then I will not go!' Kisu said, 'What are you thinking?'

The earliest reference to an *enso* brushed on paper occurs in the 11th-century *Keitoku dentoroku* (record of the transmission of the lamp)[3] and concerns the Master Kyozan (814–890):

> A monk asked Kyozan for something concrete to help him with his Zen studies. Kyozan brushed a circle and said, 'Thinking about this and then

understanding it is second best; not thinking and understanding it is third best'.

First best, presumably, is seeing Zen right in front of your face, and not needing any aids. However, *enso* paintings eventually did become aids, valuable visual tools for awakening the mind. An early *enso* appears in the *Ten ox-herding pictures* that originated in China around the 11th century and became popular in Japan. Picture number eight in this series, *Both man and ox forgotten*, was simply a painting of an *enso*. Other than this, few *enso* paintings from before Hakuin exist in Japan (or China).[4] Hakuin himself did a small number of *enso* but after him the Zen circle, together with portraits of Daruma, became the most important themes in Zenga.

Enso were brushed in all kinds of ways – from the top, from the bottom, clockwise, anti-clockwise, in two half circles. There was a Zen tradition that 'Even when an *enso* is painted, it is not really painted', and it is certainly true that many *enso* appear to have emerged spontaneously rather than have been consciously created with a brush and ink. Occasionally an *enso* stands alone as a kind of mirror, but most have an accompanying inscription that gives us a Zen hint (most Daruma portraits also have an accompanying inscription). The *enso* can be a symbol of the mind, the moon, the universe, zero, eternity, a jewel, the whirl of existence, enlightenment, Buddha, Daruma, a rice cake, a monk's shaven head, or just the top of an empty bucket. The most common inscription on an *enso*, however, is the three-character phrase, 'What is this?'

1. The *Shinjinmei*, known in the original Chinese as the *Xinxinming*, is one of the earliest and most influential Zen writings, consisting of 146 Chinese verses directly expressing the Zen spirit in a simple, compact form

2. The *Shoyoroku*, known in the original Chinese as the *Congrong lu*, is a collection of *koans* associated with the Caodong (Soto) school. It was compiled in the 12th century and included introductions, commentaries and verses for each *koan*

3. Compiled in 1004 by Chinese Zen master Daoxuan, the *Jingde Chuandeng lu* (as it was known in the original Chinese) details the lineage of Zen Buddhism handed down from the Seven Buddhas of the Past through Indian and Chinese Zen patriarchs up to the 10th century

4. The author has in his possession an *enso* brushed by Jakuan Josho (d1302), possibly the earliest extant *enso* in Japan

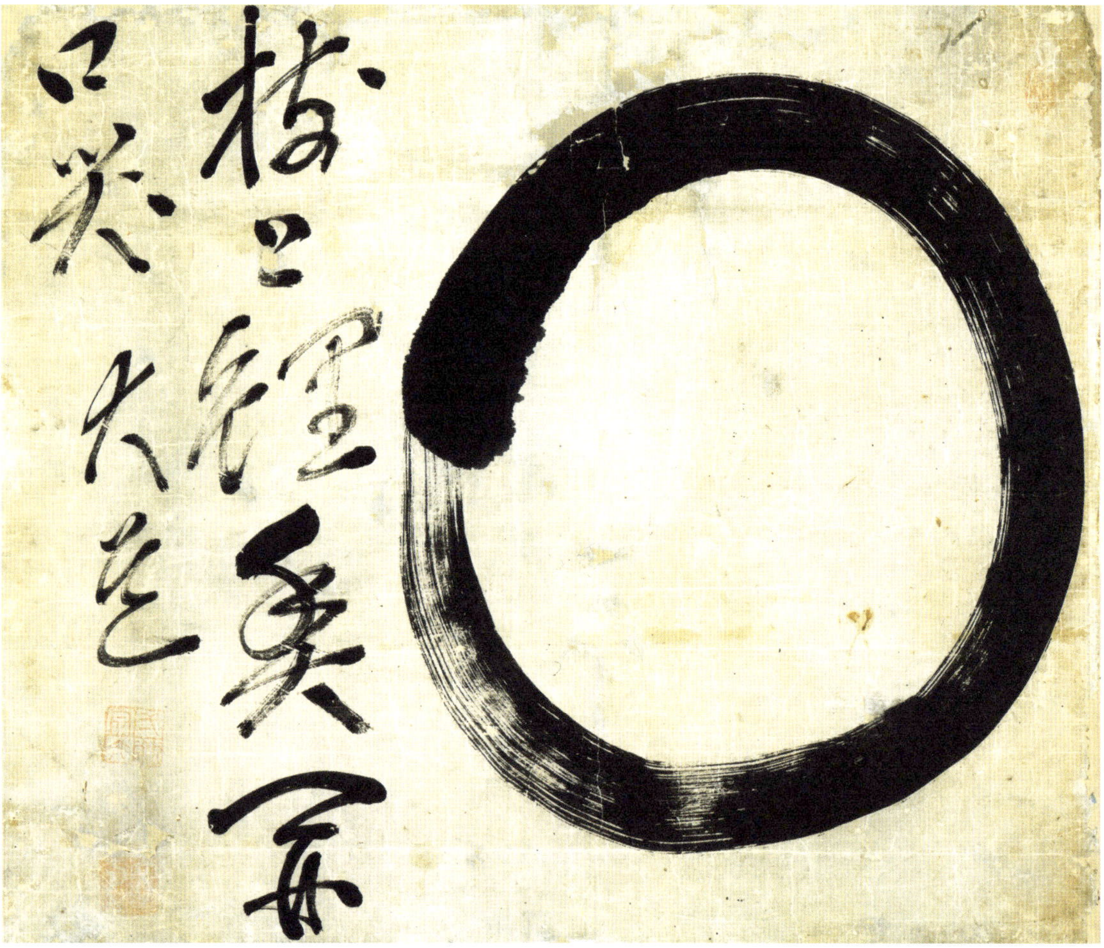

Daido was the first great *enso* painter in Japanese Zen, and he painted the subject often. Despite the toll taken on the paper by the ravages of time, in this example his brushwork is extraordinarily bold and powerful, and the calligraphy remains fresh, direct and vital. The inscription is a *koan*: humorous, surprising, indeed surreal – challenging us to transcend the logical and mundane and see everything from a universal perspective. The accompanying verse to this phrase is, 'A stone tortoise sits next door blinking his eyes '.

Daido had an eclectic approach to Zen. He trained under masters from different schools (Obaku, Kogetsu and the branch of Zen founded by the unorthodox 17th-century master Bankei) and as a young monk lived as a hermit, practising meditation from morning till night. Later, as a Zen master himself, he was very strict ('Demon Daido' was his nickname). In a verse written on his deathbed, he observed: 'When death comes, die; when life comes, live. Past and present, coming and going, the moon is bright, the wind pure'.

樹上鯉魚開
口笑　大道

A trout with a huge smile sits atop a bamboo pole!

Daido

73
DAIDO Bunka (1680–1752)
Enso
hanging scroll, ink on paper,
45 x 51.9 cm

天上天下唯我
独尊 東嶺

In heaven and earth
I alone am the Honoured One!

Torei

Suddenly all inner doubts are resolved and everything is seen as it really is. That is one definition of enlightenment, and a Zen circle reflects this transforming experience – feeling perfectly empty yet at the same time completely full, infinite, aware. The inscription repeats Buddha's dramatic declaration at birth – that each and every one of us is a miniature universe, containing all things within our bodies. Enlightenment, symbolised by this *enso*, consists of realising that fact.

Enso were Torei's favourite theme, and he created some of the best in Zen art. His biography records an occasion when Torei brushed *enso* for each of more than 200 people present at a large gathering.

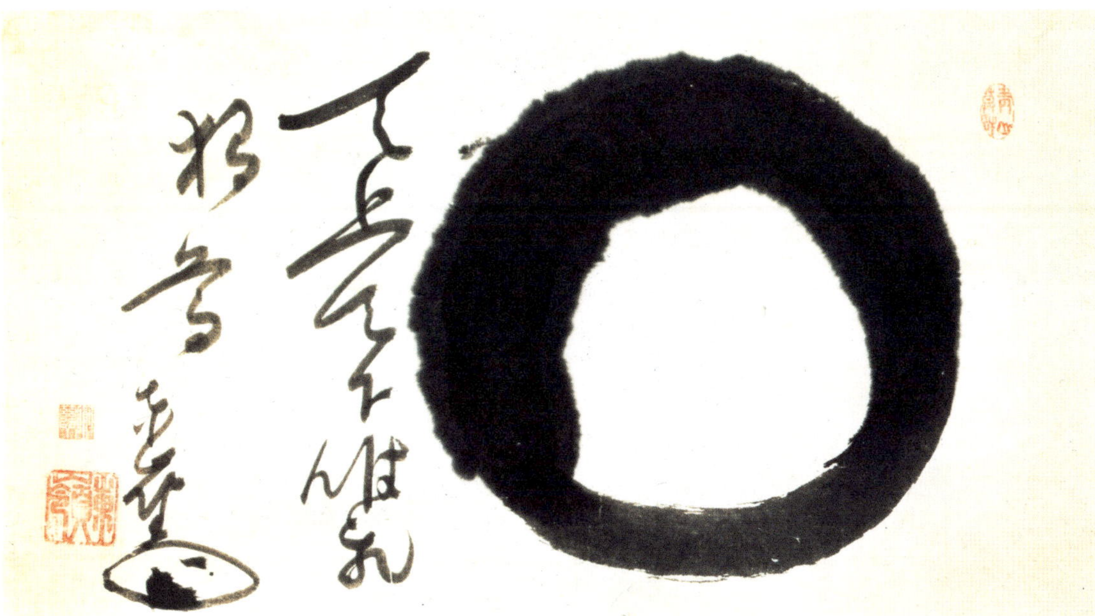

74
TOREI Enji (1721–1792)
Enso
hanging scroll, ink on paper,
31.5 x 55.5 cm

One evening a well-known tea master is said to have visited Seisetsu to take part in a tea ceremony. Seisetsu came out of his hut to greet the master and drew a big circle in the air with his finger. The tea master nodded in agreement, and immediately returned home. This is the same type of Zen circle, only written on paper with brush and ink. The *enso* is soft and luminous, and projects a deep sense of calm. There is also a very pleasing balance between the circle and the calligraphic inscription. The placement of Seisetsu's signature suggests that he is off to the side quietly enjoying the moon's brilliance.

Seisetsu, originally from Shikoku, became a Zen acolyte at age seven. As was the custom, Seisetsu spent his teens as a wandering monk and was eventually accepted as a disciple of Gessen Zen'e, who was also Sengai's master. Seisetsu was invited to the temple of Engakuji in Kamakura, where he served as head monk of the training hall for 28 years. Late in life, he was abbot of several temples in Kyoto. Seisetsu had hundreds of disciples and great influence as a Zen master. A cultured person with many talented friends, he was skilled in calligraphy, painting and poetry.

誰やら可心に似り
秋の月
誠拙

Who says my heart is like
the autumn moon?

Seisetsu

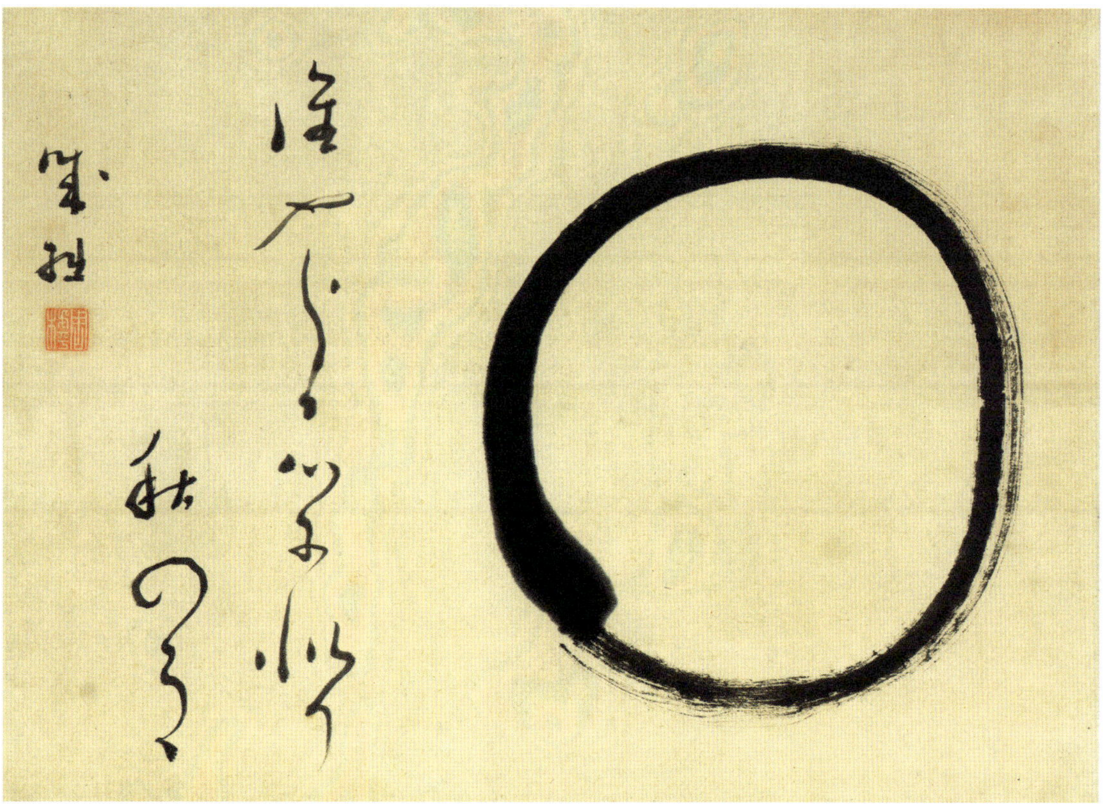

75
SEISETSU Shucho (1745–1820)
Enso
hanging scroll, ink on paper,
42.9 x 55.9 cm

此月可落たら屋らふとつて見よ
八十六翁
南天棒鄧州

When this moon falls who will try and catch it?

[signed] *The 86-year-old fellow Nantenbo Toju*

In his long career as a Zen artist, Nantenbo brushed many *enso*. This particular inscription seems to have originated with Sengai: 'Enlightenment is coming towards us. Who is bold enough to step forward to attain it?'

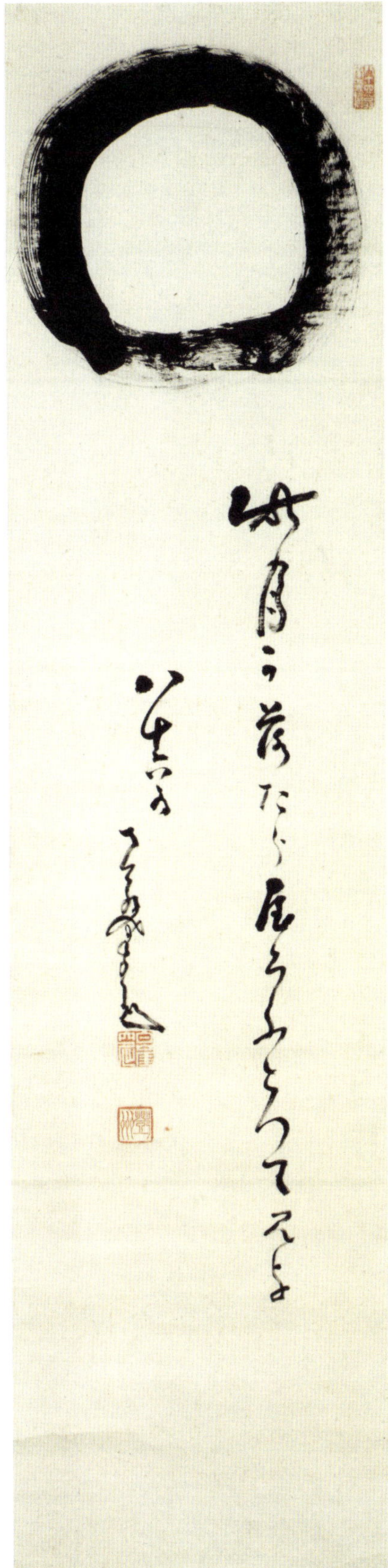

76
Nakahara NANTENBO (1839–1925)
Enso
hanging scroll, ink on paper,
194.5 x 43.8 cm

This beautiful *enso* is by one of the most colourful Buddhist monks of the modern era. Ashizu Sekiren was originally a Tendai scholar-priest who represented that school of Buddhism at the famous World Parliament of Religions at the Chicago World's Fair in 1893. Sekiren later switched to Rinzai Zen and became abbot of Eigenji, continuing to advocate the essential unity of all Buddhist sects. Sekiren was also a good friend of Yamaoka Tesshu and worked with that master to promote Buddhism at all levels of society. Although Sekiren was a talented and creative artist, his work has been largely forgotten in Japan.

'My heart is like the autumn moon', a popular inscription on *enso*, is a line from a well-known poem by the Zen eccentric Kanzan. However, here Sekiren is saying, 'Yes, Kanzan's heart is like the autumn moon, but what about your own heart? Isn't it also like the autumn moon? Instead of using another's thoughts, create your own!' It is interesting to compare Seisetsu's and Sekiren's *enso*: Seisetsu, a traditionally trained Zen monk, had only the slightest hint that there was a world outside Asia; Sekiren was an activist priest who travelled to the West and was familiar with the challenges and opportunities of the modern age. Yet they both put the same inscription on their *enso*; such circles of enlightenment were the original Zenga, first brushed 1500 years ago.

誰やら我心に似たり
秋の月
永源石蓮叟

Who says my heart is like
the autumn moon?

The old fellow Sekiren of Eigen
[Eigen temple]

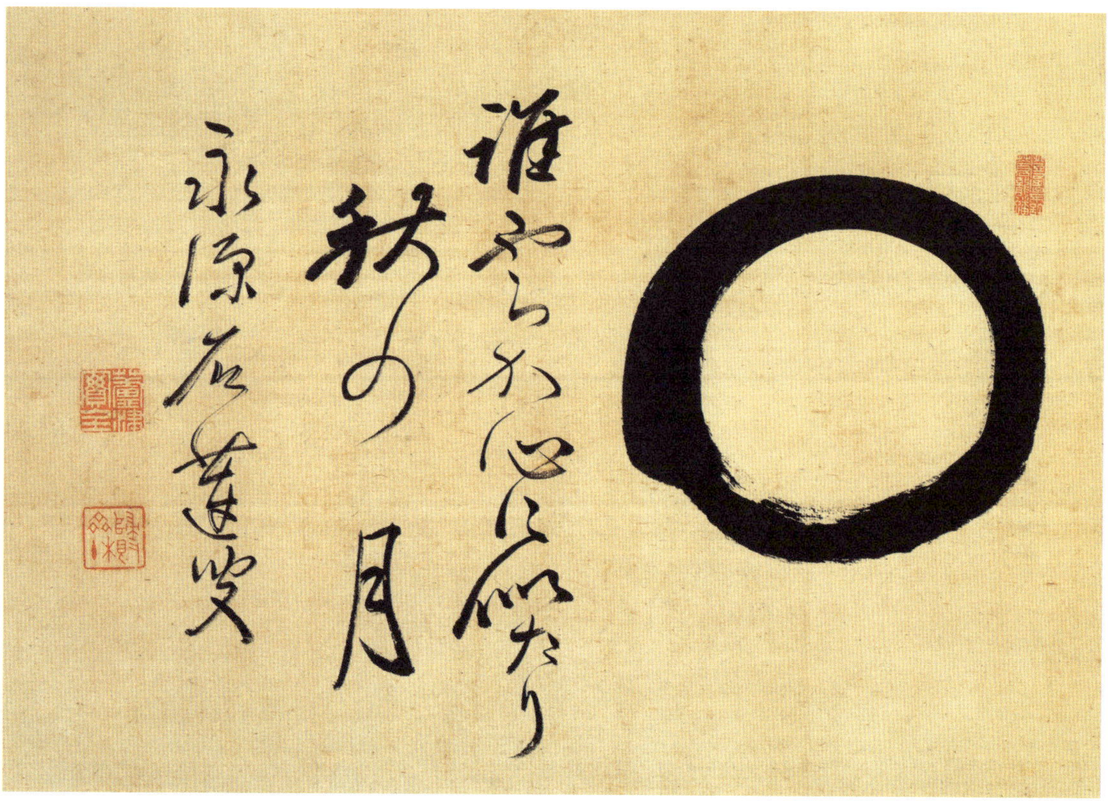

77
Ashizu SEKIREN (1850–1924)
Enso
hanging scroll, ink on paper,
41.3 x 56.5 cm

坐水
月
道場
般若

Sitting in the water moon dojo.

Hannya[1]

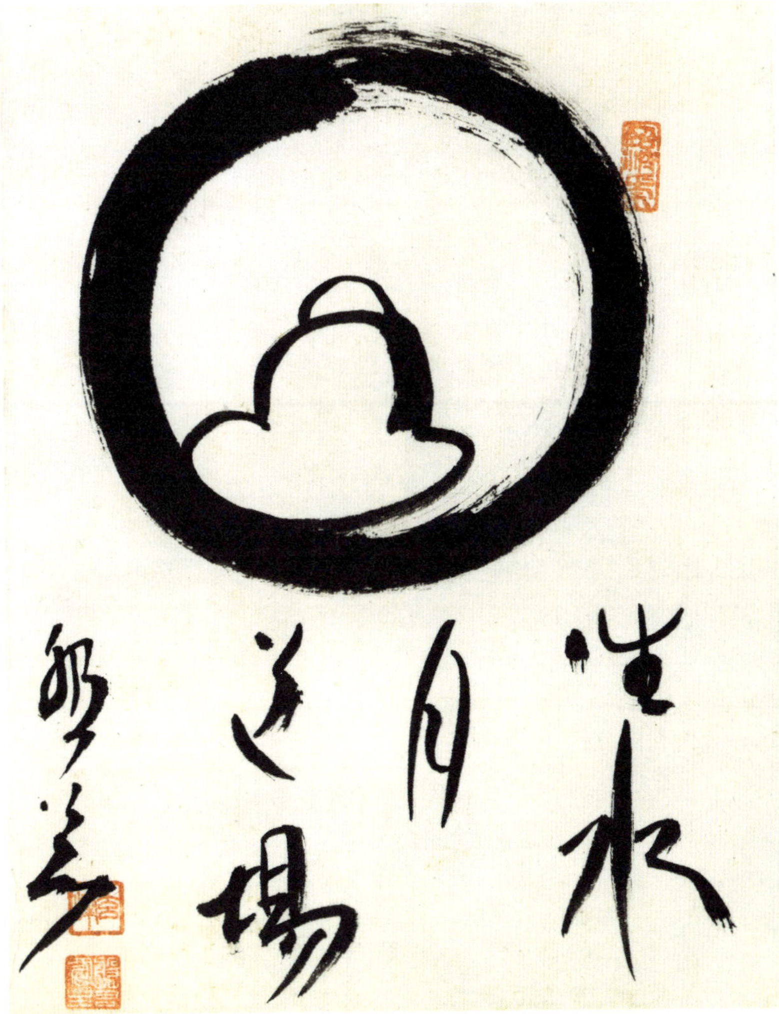

The best known 20th-century Zen master, Genpo was abbot of Ryutakuji in Mishima, a small but important temple. As an infant, he was left to die near a hot spring but was rescued by a good samaritan. Genpo had poor eyesight and never attended school, so he learnt to read and write late. In his 30s, he educated himself by reading the *Hekiganroku* and *Record of Rinzai* over and over, and using a dictionary to look up each character. Later a prolific Zen artist, he brushed simple paintings and easy-to-read characters that were an important aspect of his teaching. His brushwork is childlike but very bright and refreshing, and pieces by Genpo are cherished.

This is a Daruma/self-portrait sitting inside an *enso*. *Dojo*, 'place of enlightenment', is the name for a training hall used for meditation or martial arts practice. 'Water moon' (*suigetsu*) has many important meanings in Zen and the martial arts, but here it means the 'appearance rather than the reality of things'. The entire phrase means, 'Remain centred within the constant whirl of illusion'.

78
Yamamoto GENPO (1886–1961)
Enso
hanging scroll, ink on paper,
23.7 x 18.1 cm

1. This is Genpo's Zen master name

LIST OF WORKS

ABBREVIATIONS OF PUBLICATION TITLES

MAL *A myriad of autumn leaves: Japanese art from the Kurt and Millie Gitter collection*, Stephen Addiss, Michael R Cunningham, Pat Fister, William J Rathbun, Melinda Takeuchi, New Orleans Museum of Art, New Orleans 1983

Z&N *Zenga and Nanga paintings by Japanese monks and scholars*, Stephen Addiss, New Orleans Museum of Art, New Orleans 1976

ZBOE *Zen: brushstrokes of enlightenment*, John Stevens, Alice Rae Yelen, New Orleans Museum of Art, New Orleans 1990

ZRFA *Zen, return from America: Zenga from the Gitter-Yelen collection*, Yamashita Yuji, Asano Laboratories, Tokyo 2000

AEV *An enduring vision: 17th to 20th century Japanese painting from the Gitter-Yelen collection*, Kobayashi Tadashi, Lisa Rotondo-McCord, New Orleans Museum of Art & University of Washington Press, New Orleans / Seattle 2002

1 FUGAI Ekun (1568–1654)
Half-body Daruma
hanging scroll, ink on paper,
63.5 x 30.5 cm
1989.1
Published ZRFA

2 FUGAI Ekun (1568–1654)
Smiling Hotei
hanging scroll, ink on paper,
47.3 x 23.9 cm
1999.3
Published ZRFA

3 FUGAI Ekun (1568–1654)
Frowning Hotei
hanging scroll, ink on paper,
52.2 x 21.6 cm
2003.3

4 FUGAI Ekun (1568–1654)
Lazy San, the potato monk
hanging scroll, ink on paper,
32.7 x 44 cm
2005.14

5 HAKUIN Ekaku (1685–1768)
Giant Daruma
hanging scroll, ink on paper,
130.8 x 55.2 cm
1973.2
Published Z&N, ZBOE, ZRFA, AEV

6 HAKUIN Ekaku (1685–1768)
White-robed Kannon
hanging scroll, ink on paper,
93.5 x 26.3 cm
2003.11

7 HAKUIN Ekaku (1685–1768)
Lotus pond Kannon
hanging scroll, ink on paper,
44.2 x 13.9 cm
2004.27

8 HAKUIN Ekaku (1685–1768)
Zazen Hotei
hanging scroll, ink on paper,
88.9 x 26.7 cm
2004.7

9 HAKUIN Ekaku (1685–1768)
Running Hotei
hanging scroll, ink on paper,
40.9 x 52.4 cm
2003.19

10 HAKUIN Ekaku (1685–1768)
Fukurokuju
hanging scroll, ink on paper,
173.5 x 38 cm
1998.11
Published ZRFA

11 HAKUIN Ekaku (1685–1768)
Seven Gods of Good Fortune
hanging scroll, ink on paper,
57.8 x 89.4 cm
2000.1
Published ZRFA, AEV

12 HAKUIN Ekaku (1685–1768)
Blind men crossing a log bridge
hanging scroll, ink on paper,
28 x 83.8 cm
1975.1
Published MAL, ZBOE, ZRFA, AEV

13 HAKUIN Ekaku (1685–1768)
Fan
hanging scroll, ink on paper,
32.7 x 44.7 cm
2001.25

14 HAKUIN Ekaku (1685–1768)
Renshobo on his horse
hanging scroll, ink on paper,
118 x 56 cm
2003.1

15 HAKUIN Ekaku (1685–1768)
Dragon staff with fly whisk
(enlightenment certificate)
1762
hanging scroll, ink on paper,
127.1 x 28.8 cm
1996.1
Published ZRFA

16 HAKUIN Ekaku (1685–1768)
Always remember Kanzeon
hanging scroll, ink on paper,
132.7 x 27.9 cm
1989.11
Published ZBOE, ZRFA

17 HAKUIN Ekaku (1685–1768)
Virtue
hanging scroll, ink on paper,
117.3 x 55.2 cm
1974.1
Published MAL, Z&N, ZBOE, ZRFA, AEV

18 HAKUIN Ekaku (1685–1768)
One hundred times 'longevity'
1767
hanging scroll, ink on paper,
124.1 x 54.3 cm
2004.55

19 SENGAI Gibon (1750–1837)
Hotei wakes from a nap
hanging scroll, ink on paper,
29.5 x 48.4 cm
1981.24
Published MAL, ZBOE, ZRFA, AEV

20 SENGAI Gibon (1750–1837)
Laozi riding an ox
hanging scroll, ink on paper,
78.4 x 27.9 cm
1989.6
Published ZBOE, ZRFA

21 SENGAI Gibon (1750–1837)
Kanzan and Jittoku
pair of hanging scrolls, ink on paper,
each 94 x 29 cm
1973.10a/b
Published Z&N, ZRFA

22 SENGAI Gibon (1750–1837)
Shoki, the demon-queller
hanging scroll, ink on paper,
123 x 53.4 cm
2004.26

23 SENGAI Gibon (1750–1837)
Bamboo
hanging scroll, ink on paper,
59.2 x 63.7 cm
1999.18
Published ZRFA

24 SUIO Genro (1716–1789)
Side-view Daruma
hanging scroll, ink on paper,
96.5 x 29.2 cm
1989.12
Published ZBOE, ZRFA

25 SUIO Genro (1716–1789)
The sixth patriarch's rice-pounder
hanging scroll, ink on paper,
32 x 50.6 cm
2000.12

26 SUIO Genro (1716–1789)
Kanzan and Jittoku
hanging scroll, ink on paper,
113.5 x 24 cm
1973.9
Published Z&N, ZRFA

27 SUIO Genro (1716–1789)
painting
GESSEN Zenne (1701–1781)
inscription
Bukan and the tiger
hanging scroll, ink on paper,
129.3 x 41.9 cm
2001.14
Published AEV

28 TOREI Enji (1721–1792)
Calligraphic talisman
hanging scroll, ink on paper,
128.9 x 27.6 cm
1979.9
Published ZBOE, ZRFA

29 REIGEN Eto (1721–1785)
painting
ISHIN Eryu (1720–1759)
inscription
Rush leaf Daruma
hanging scroll, ink on paper,
114 x 28.7
1998.61
Published ZRFA

30 REIGEN Eto (1721–1785)
White-robed Kannon
hanging scroll, ink on paper,
94.3 x 27.9 cm
1986.3
Published ZRFA

31 REIGEN Eto (1721–1785)
Crows in the village
hanging scroll, ink on paper,
120.7 x 28.1 cm
1997. 18

32 SHUNSO Joshu (1750–1839)
Giant Daruma
1828
hanging scroll, ink on paper,
134 x 59 cm
1972.3
Published Z&N

33 SHUNSO Joshu (1750–1839)
Daito Kokushi
hanging scroll, ink on paper,
120 x 55 cm
1974.10
Published Z&N, AEV

34 SHUNSO Joshu (1750–1839)
No dancer
hanging scroll, ink on paper,
100.3 x 27.6 cm
1989.10
Published ZBOE

35 Obaku SOKUHI (1616–1671)
Dragon and tiger
pair of hanging scrolls, ink on paper,
each 113 x 51.1 cm
1984.12 a/b
Published ZBOE

36 Konoe NOBUTADA (1565–1614)
painting and inscription
Daitokuji KOGETSU (1574–1643)
additional inscription
Hotei
hanging scroll, ink on paper,
69.8 x 32.2 cm
2005.18

37 Konoe NOBUTADA (1565–1614)
Gutei's one finger
hanging scroll, ink on paper,
55.2 x 28.6 cm
1993.3

38 Ito JAKUCHU (1716–1800)
Elephant Daruma
1795
hanging scroll, ink on paper,
120.9 x 56.8 cm
2003.100

39 Ito JAKUCHU (1716–1800)
painting
TANGAI Musen Jozen (1693–1764)
inscription
Giant Daruma
hanging scroll, ink on paper,
109.9 x 59.4 cm
2005.47

40 Ito JAKUCHU (1716–1800)
painting
ROSHU Ensho (c1769–1789)
inscription
Kanzan and Jittoku
pair of hanging scrolls, ink on paper,
each 104.1 29.2 cm
2004.9

41 JIUN Sonja Onko (1718–1804)
Wall-gazing Daruma
hanging scroll, ink on paper,
64.5 x 26.8 cm
2004.37

42 JIUN Sonja Onko (1718–1804)
Two-line calligraphy
hanging scroll, ink on paper,
110.3 x 50 cm
1980.9
Published MAL, ZBOE, ZRFA

43 JIUN Sonja Onko (1718–1804)
additional inscription
Zakkean YUSHO (dates unknown)
inscription and painting
Kanzan and Jittoku
hanging scroll, ink on paper,
118 x 43 cm
1999.9

44 GOCHO Kankai (1749–1835)
Demon rod
1834
hanging scroll, ink on paper,
106 x 29.4
2003.7

45 GOCHO Kankai (1749–1835)
Shinno, god of medicine
1796
hanging scroll, ink on paper,
104.5 x 28.3 cm
1997.30
Published ZRFA

46 GOCHO Kankai (1749–1835)
One-line calligraphy
1818
hanging scroll, ink on paper,
98 x 28.5 cm
1997.17

47 GOCHO Kankai (1749–1835)
inscription
CHINGYU Zuiko (1743–1822)
painting
1818
Kanzan and Jittoku
hanging scroll, ink on silk,
84.5 x 32 cm
2003.5

48 CHINGYU Zuiko (1743–1822)
Daruma
hanging scroll, ink on paper,
55.5 x 58.1 cm
2004.30

49 CHINGYU Zuiko (1743–1822)
Monk Fuke
1818
hanging scroll; ink on paper,
112.1 x 49.8 cm
1997.1
Published ZRFA

50 GESSHU Soko (1618–1696)
Revealed
hanging scroll, ink on paper,
32 x 50.1 cm
1996.11

51 RYOKAN Daigu (1758–1831)
Two-line calligraphy
hanging scroll, ink on paper,
130 x 27 cm
2002.11

52 DAISHIN Gito (1656–1730)
Giant rush leaf Daruma
hanging scroll, ink on paper,
132.7 x 57.9 cm
2004.42

53 KOGAN Gengei (1748–1821)
Daruma
hanging scroll, ink on paper,
33 x 41.5 cm
2003.8

54 MOTSUGAI Fusen (1794–1867)
Drunk Daruma
1861
hanging scroll, ink on paper,
75.7 x 52.6 cm
1998.37
Published ZRFA

55 KOKAI Jiko (1800–1874)
Daruma
hanging scroll, ink on paper,
133.4 x 61 cm
1989.2
ZBOE, ZRFA

56 SOZAN Genkyo (1799–1888)
Nansen cuts the cat
hanging scroll, ink on paper,
106 x 27.1 cm
1991.8

57 Otagaki RENGETSU (1791–1875)
Maple leaves
hanging scroll, ink on paper,
29 x 33.6 cm
1982.41

58 Yamaoka TESSHU (1836–1888)
Talismanic dragon
hanging scroll, ink on paper,
44.5 x 60.3 cm
1986.5
Published ZBOE, AEV

59 Yamaoka TESSHU (1836–1888)
Zen couple
hanging scroll, ink on paper,
104.2 x 34.9 cm
2003.18

60 Nakahara NANTENBO (1839–1925)
Daruma
1911
framed leaf, ink on paper,
33.2 x 108.8 cm
1997.31
Published ZRFA

61 Nakahara NANTENBO (1839–1925)
Nanten's staff
hanging scroll, ink on paper,
131.3 x 33 cm
2003.20

62 Nakahara NANTENBO (1839–1925)
Mount Fuji
1915
hanging scroll, ink on paper,
127.5 x 33.8 cm
2004.21

63 Nakahara NANTENBO (1839–1925)
Zen horse
1921
hanging scroll, ink on silk,
124.8 x 33.6 cm
1998.54

64 Nakahara NANTENBO (1839–1925)
Procession of monks
1923
hanging scroll, ink on paper,
65.5 x 31.5 cm
2004.14

65 DEIRYU Kutsu (1895–1954)
Portrait of Nantenbo
hanging scroll, ink on paper,
125 x 61.8 cm
1999.2

66 DEIRYU Kutsu (1895–1954)
Daruma
hanging scroll, ink on paper,
128.5 x 34 cm
2001.24

67 DEIRYU Kutsu (1895–1954)
Procession of monks
pair of hanging scrolls,
ink on paper,
each 162 x 22.4cm
1993.1a/b
Published ZRFA

68 SHOUN Sohan Genpo (1848–1918)
Wall-gazing Daruma
hanging scroll, ink on paper,
141.5 x 64.2 cm
2003.4

69 ROZAN Eko (1865–1944)
Wall-gazing Daruma
hanging scroll, ink on paper,
104.7 x 29.3 cm
1998.51

70 Hashimoto DOKUSAN (1869–1938)
No thought
hanging scroll, ink on paper,
30.5 x 67.3 cm
2004.3

71 Seki SEISETSU (1877–1945)
Wall-gazing Daruma
hanging scroll, ink on paper,
64.5 x 29.2 cm
2004.20

72 MUNAKATA Shiko (1903–1975)
An inexhaustible treasure
hanging scroll, ink on paper,
93.2 x 47.7 cm
2004.45

ENSO

73 DAIDO Bunka (1680–1752)
Enso
hanging scroll, ink on paper,
45 x 51.9 cm
2001.5

74 TOREI Enji (1721–1792)
Enso
hanging scroll, ink on paper,
31.5 x 55.5cm
1972.1
Published Z&N, ZBOE, ZRFA, AEV

75 SEISETSU Shucho (1745–1820)
Enso
hanging scroll, ink on paper,
42.9 x 55.9 cm
2005.48

76 Nakahara NANTENBO (1839–1925)
Enso
hanging scroll, ink on paper,
194.5 x 43.8 cm
1998.40

77 Ashizu SEKIREN (1850–1924)
Enso
hanging scroll, ink on paper,
41.3 x 56.5 cm
2004.22

78 Yamamoto GENPO (1886–1961)
Enso
hanging scroll, ink on paper,
23.7 x 18.1 cm
2004.49

GLOSSARY

Amida Buddha (Sanskrit: Amitabha) The Buddha who presides over the Western Paradise and the focus of Pure Land Buddhism, which holds that salvation is assured for anyone who recites Amida's name with sincere faith.

bodhisattva A 'being of awakening'; in Mahayana Buddhism a person who has achieved enlightenment but who has chosen to remain in this world to help others to achieve it.

Bodhidharma (Japanese: Daruma) The Indian credited with establishing Zen Buddhism in China during the early 6th century CE.

Bokuseki 'ink traces', traditional term used primarily to describe calligraphy of the early Zen masters of China and Japan and the abbots of Daitokuji.

Daodejing (the book of the Way and its virtue) This compilation of axioms, traditionally ascribed to Laozi, the legendary founder of Daoism, is one of the most important literary works of Chinese philosophy and the basis of Daoism.

Daoism A set of Chinese philosophical teachings and religious practices which arose in the 6th century BCE, based on the Dao, or 'the Way' – the unchanging principle of reality behind the universe. It aims to achieve harmony with all things and advocates the idea that creative inactivity is better than frenetic activity.

Daruma See Bodhidharma

Emperor Wu[di] (502–49) The first emperor of China's short-lived Liang dynasty and an ardent Buddhist. According to Buddhist tradition he is famed for his enigmatic encounter with Bodhidharma upon the patriarch's arrival in China around 520. It is believed that one of the reasons Emperor Wu was overthrown was his excessive spending on Buddhist causes.

Enso In Zen a brushed-ink painting of a circle, usually depicted in a single brushstroke. Among its many meanings, the *enso* represents the infinite void, the true nature of existence and enlightenment.

Fukurokuju God of good fortune, wealth and longevity. Sometimes called Jurojin.

Hebi ichigo (English: wild strawberries) One of Hakuin's best-known works, written in 1754 in the form of a letter to the lord of Okayama domain, outlining the virtues of wise government and condemning the extravagant and self-indulgent lifestyles of the *daimyo*.

Hekiganroku (Chinese: Biyan lu; English: blue cliff record). A collection of 100 *koans* associated with the Linji (Rinzai) school. It was originally compiled in the 11th century by the Zen monk Xuedou, who added his own verses and remarks. In the 12th century Yuanwu added introductions and commentaries.

Hotei Good-natured, fat-bellied hobo Zen monk in 10th-century China, who came to represent freedom from worldly cares and enlightenment within the midst of everyday life. Thought to have been a manifestation of Maitreya, the Future Buddha, and often called the 'Laughing Buddha', he eventually became popular in China and Japan as a folk god of good luck.

-ji Suffix meaning 'temple', as in Daitokuji (Daitoku Temple).

Kannon (Kanzeon) Bodhisattva of compassion.

Kanzan and Jittoku (Chinese: Hanshan and Shide) A pair of enlightened Zen eccentrics of Tang dynasty China, immediately recognisable from their attributes, a broom and a blank scroll.

Kanzeon See Kannon.

Koan A riddle-like puzzle used for teaching in Zen Buddhism. It cannot be solved by reason, but instead forces the student to solve it through a flash of insight. Its solution requires that students directly and intuitively perceive the true nature of reality.

Kogetsu Zen One of the two main streams of Rinzai Zen along with the Hakuin line. Founded by Kyushu monk Kogetsu Zenzai (1667– 1751).

Mahayana Buddhism Literally the 'great vehicle', the dominant Buddhist tradition of East Asia. It recognises a large number of divinities, available for all to worship: simple faith in these divinities is enough to lead to salvation. Mahayana Buddhism itself has many different schools.

Mumonkan (Chinese: Wumenguan, English: the gateless gate) One of the two most famous collections of *koan*, along with the *Hekiganroku*. Composed in 1229 by Chinese Zen master, Wumen Huikai, it contains 48 *koans*, commentaries and 'praises'.

No drama A major form of classical Japanese drama that has been performed since the 14th century. Involving music, song, dance and wooden masks, it uses symbolism and stylised gestures to suggest the essence of human experience.

Obaku Zen The smallest of the three surviving lineages of Japanese Zen (the other two are Soto and Rinzai), founded in the 17th century by Chinese émigré monks of Huangbo school.

Pure Land Buddhism Form of Mahayana Buddhism focused on Amida Buddha. It emphasises faith in Amida, meditation on and recitation of his name, and the religious goal of being reborn in the Pure Land or Western Paradise over which he presides.

Rinzai Zen One of the two major Japanese Zen sects (the other being Soto). Rinzai is the Japanese branch of the Chinese Linji school, which was founded during the Tang dynasty and brought to Japan by the monk Eisai in 1191. The Rinzai school is known for its emphasis on sudden enlightenment and the use of methods such as the *koan*, studied during *zazen*, to achieve this end.

Satori Zen enlightenment, or 'awakening', characterised by a sudden, all-encompassing vision or complete understanding of the nature of reality. According to some Zen masters, this state of illumination may be lost and regained.

Sakyamuni The Historical Buddha, Siddhartha Gautama. 'Sakyamuni' means 'wise one of the Sakya', the clan into which the Buddha was born.

Shingon Buddhism A major school of Japanese esoteric Buddhism, brought from China by the Japanese monk Kukai in the early 9th century. Its mystical teachings emphasise the use of rituals, mantras and other symbolism.

Soto Zen One of the two main lineages of Japanese Zen Buddhism (the other being Rinzai). Soto is the Japanese branch of Caodong sect of Zen, brought to Japan by the Chinese monk Dogen in the early 13th century. The tradition stresses '*mokusho* Zen' (the Zen of silent awakening), so called because it is based on *zazen* practice that does not rely heavily on verbal instructions or *koan* training.

Sutras Buddhist scriptures, the sermons attributed to Sakyamuni Buddha (and less often to one of his immediate disciples).

Tendai Buddhism The Japanese lineage of the Chinese Tientai school, brought to Japan by the monk Saicho (762–822). It emphasises the Lotus sutra and incorporates elements of esoteric and Zen Buddhism.

Yoga Literally 'yoke', in the sense of 'union'; an ancient Indian system of physical and mental discipline in which the practitioner aims to achieve enlightenment through union with the ultimate reality.

Zazen Formal seated Zen meditation.

Zen (Sanskrit : *Dhyana*, Chinese: *Chan*) 'Meditation' in the broadest possible sense, a meditation that is manifest in both mind and body; unity between the spiritual and the physical.

Zenga Term used to describe Zen inspired calligraphy and painting of the modern period (from 1600 onwards).

FURTHER READING

FOR GENERAL INFORMATION ON ZEN

Einarsen, John. *Zen and Kyoto,* Uniplan Co, Kyoto 2004 – a well-written, well-illustrated guide to the Zen experience in Japanese culture

Foster, Nelson (ed). *The roaring stream: a new Zen reader,* Harper Perennial, New York 1997

Hoover, Thomas. *Zen culture,* Random House, New York, 1978

Kohn, Michael H. *The Shambhala dictionary of Buddhism and Zen,* Shambhala Publications, Boston 1991

Leggett, Trevor. *Zen and the Ways,* Tuttle Publishing, Tokyo 1987 – Zen as expressed in various disciplines, with illustrations.

Wilson Ross, Nancy. *The world of Zen,* Vintage Books, New York 1960, 350 pages with many illustrations and articles on different aspects of Zen

Also informative are:

Bancroft, Anne. *Zen: direct pointing to reality,* Thames & Hudson, London 1987

Reps, Paul. *Zen flesh, Zen bones,* Shambhala Publications, Boston 2004

Sato, Giei. *Unsui: a diary of Zen monastic life,* University of Hawai'i Press, Honolulu 1973

Sekida, Katsuki. *Two Zen classics: The gateless gate & The blue cliff records,* Shambhala Editions, Boston 2005 – useful translations of the two main collections of Zen riddles (*koan*)

Suzuki, D T. *Manual of Zen Buddhism,* Grove Press, New York 1960

Suzuki, D T. *The training of the Zen Buddhist monk,* Cosimo Publishing, New York 2004

Suzuki, Shunryu. *Zen mind, beginners mind,* Weatherhill, Tokyo 1973 – considered the best introduction to Zen practice

Zen Art

Addiss, Stephen. *The art of Zen: paintings and calligraphy by Zen monks, 1600–1925,* Henry A Abrams, New York 1989

Addiss, Stephen. *Obaku: Zen painting and calligraphy,* Spencer Museum of Art, Lawrence, Kansas 1978

Addiss, Stephen. *Zenga and Nanga,* New Orleans Museum of Art, New Orleans 1976

Addiss, Stephen (ed). *A myriad of autumn leaves,* New Orleans Museum of Art, New Orleans 1983

Awakawa, Yasuichi. *Zen painting,* Kodansha International, Tokyo 1970

Barnet, Sylvan & Burto, William. *Zen ink paintings,* Kodansha International, Tokyo 1982

Barnet, Sylvan & Burto, William. *The written image: Japanese calligraphy and painting from the Sylvan Barnet and William Burto collection,* The Metropolitan Museum of Art, New York 2002

Brinker, Hans & Kanazawa, Hiroshi. *Zen masters of meditation in images and writings,* Artibus Asiae Publishers, Zurich 1996

Capon, Edmund. *Sengai the Zen master: paintings from the Idemitsu Museum of Fine Arts,* Art Gallery of New South Wales, Sydney 1985

Covell, Jon & Yamada, Sobin. *Zen at Daitokuji,* Kodansha International, Tokyo 1974

Fontein, Jan & Hickman, Money. *Zen painting and calligraphy,* Museum of Fine Arts, Boston 1970

Furuta, Shokin. *Sengai: master Zen painter,* Kodansha International, Tokyo 2000

Hisamatsu, Shinichi. *Zen and the fine arts,* Kodansha International, Tokyo 1971

Kanazawa, Hiroshi. *Japanese Zen ink paintings: early Zen masterpieces,* Kodansha International, Tokyo 1979

Omori, Sogen & Terayama, Katsujo. *Zen in the art of calligraphy,* trans John Stevens, Routledge & Kegan Paul, London 1983

Rosenfield, John. *Songs of the brush: paintings from the Sanso Collection*, Seattle Art Museum, Seattle 1979

Seo, Audrey Yoshiko & Addiss, Stephen. *The art of twentieth century Zen*, Shambhala Publications, Boston 2000

Shore, Jeff. *Hakuin: Zen painting and calligraphy from the Ryuunji collection*, exhibition catalogue, Hanazono University, Kyoto 2004

Stevens, John. *Sacred calligraphy of the East*, 3rd edn, Shambhala Publications, Boston 1995

Stevens, John. *The sword of No-sword: the life of the master warrior Tesshu*, Shambhala Publications, Boston 1989

Stevens, John. *Three Zen masters: Ikkyu, Hakuin, Ryokan*, Kodansha International, Tokyo 1993

Stevens, John. *Lotus moon: the poetry of Rengetsu*, White Pine Press, Buffalo, New York 2005

Stevens, John & Yelen, Alice Rae. *Zenga: brushstrokes of enlightenment*, New Orleans Museum of Art, New Orleans 1990

Suzuki, D T. *Sengai, the Zen master*, Shambhala Publications, Boston 1999

Suzuki, D T. *Zen and Japanese culture*, Princeton University Press, Princeton 1959

Tanahashi, Kazuaki. *Penetrating laughter: the art of Hakuin*, Overlook Press, Woodstock, New York 1984

Terayama, Tanchu. *Zen brushwork: focusing the mind with calligraphy and painting*, trans John Stevens Kodansha International, Tokyo 2003

Woodson, Yoko with Chong, Doryun. *Zen painting and calligraphy 17th–20th centuries*, Asian Art Museum, San Francisco 2001

Yamashita, Yuji (ed). *Zenga: the return from America: Zenga from the Gitter-Yelen collection*, Asano Laboratories, Tokyo 2000

INDEX

Zen mind, Zen brush
Japanese ink paintings from the
Gitter-Yelen collection

Art Gallery of New South Wales
17 June – 13 August 2006
Museum of Fine Arts, Boston
Summer 2008

Published by the Art Gallery of
New South Wales
Art Gallery Road, The Domain,
Sydney, Australia
www.artgallery.nsw.gov.au

Cataloguing-in-publication data:
Zen mind Zen brush: Japanese paintings from the Gitter-Yelen collection = Zenshin, zensho.

Essays by Clare Pollard and John Stevens.

Catalogue of an exhibition held at the Art Gallery of New South Wales, Sydney, 17 June – 13 August 2006 and the Museum of Fine Arts, Boston, Summer 2008.

Includes bibliography and index
0-7347-6391-3
978-0-7347-6391-4

1. Gitter, Kurt A.,1937 – Art collections – Exhibitions. 2. Yelen, Alice Rae – Art collections – Exhibitions.

3. Gitter-Yelen Art Study Center. 4. Ink painting, Japanese – Zen influences – Exhibitions. 5. Calligraphy, Zen – Japan – Exhibitions. 6. Ink painting – Private collections – Louisiana – New Orleans – Exhibitions. 7. Calligraphy – Private collections – Louisiana – New Orleans – Exhibitions. I. Pollard, Clare. II. Stevens, John,1947 – III. Art Gallery of New South Wales. IV. Museum of Fine Arts, Boston. V. Zenshin, zensho

Book design Vivien Sung
Editing Julie Crawford/Jennifer Blunden
Production Cara Hickman
Index Jo Rudd
Pre-press Spitting Image Pty Ltd, Sydney
Printing Samhwa Printing

Cover image: Nakahara NANTENBO, *Procession of monks* (detail no 64)

Images are reproduced courtesy of the Gitter-Yelen collection

Details
p 1 detail no 69
p 2–3 detail no 58
p 4 detail no 40
p 10 detail no 10
p 18 detail no 35
p 126 detail no 78
p 144 detail no 8

Principal sponsor

Optimal
FUND MANAGEMENT

Celebrating Asian Art and Culture

VisAsia

The Art Gallery of New South Wales is a statutory body of the NSW state government

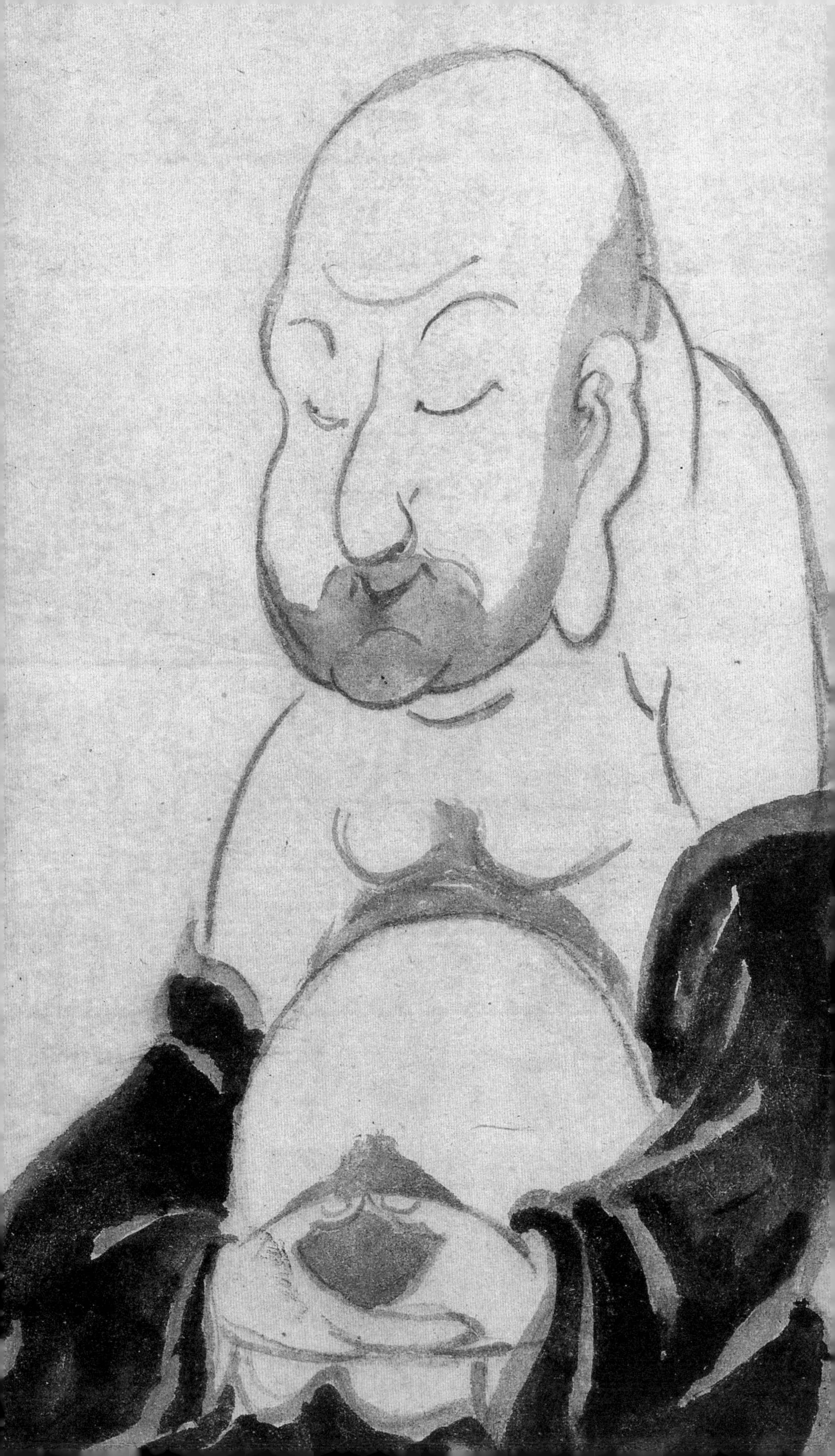